A History of Manufacturing in Baldwinsville and the Towns of Lysander and Van Buren

by Robert W. Bitz

Copyright ©2011 Robert W. Bitz
Published by Ward Bitz Publishing

All rights reserved. Printed in the United States of America. This book may not be duplicated in any way without the expressed written consent of the publisher, except in the form of brief excerpts or quotations for the purposes of review. The information contained herein may not be duplicated in other books, databases or any other medium without the written consent of the publisher or author. Making copies of this book or any portion for any purpose other than your own, is a violation of United States copyright laws.

LCCN: 2011913577
ISBN-13: 9780615520711
First edition, published 2011.

Ward Bitz Publishing
Baldwinsville, NY

The author may be contacted at:
P.O. Box 302
Plainville, NY 13137

PREFACE

Manufacturing dates back many thousands of years, originating in the home. At some point man realized that better results in solving a task could be obtained by making slight changes to a stick or a stone. It could have been a stick designed for self-defense, a specially shaped stone for cracking a nut or simply removing unneeded portions of an animal's skin prior to its use as a garment. Through trial and error and observation, over a period of many years, those simple tools evolved into the sophisticated tools we take for granted today.

Humans, as social creatures, are adept at learning from the action of others. They may imitate the actions of others, perhaps even improve on those actions, and then pass the knowledge on to others. In this way, man learned to manufacture and improve items to meet his basic survival needs.

About 10,000 years ago, the majority of man's time was spent hunting and gathering in an effort to secure enough food for survival. When man learned to plant crops and care for them, production of food increased. He began to store a portion for later use and save some as seed for the next season's crop. Once there was an abundance of food, not everyone was required to produce food, and communities began to evolve. A person with a special talent found that by producing a product others wanted, it could be bartered for food and other needed items. In this manner, industrial manufacturing evolved. As the proportion of the population producing food decreased, both the number of people manufacturing products and the variety of manufactured items increased.

For thousands of years, these manufacturing businesses were small, seldom employing more than a few people. It wasn't until England's Industrial Revolution in the 17th and 18th centuries, that large-scale manufacturing began. England, with a huge fleet of ships and colonies scattered around the globe, had a large market for its manufactured goods.

The efficiency obtained through industrial manufacturing gradually increased man's standard of living. This is an ongoing process that still continues today. The level of a society's standard of living varies with time, location and a multitude of other factors. The specialization and the efficiency of industrial manufacturing, however, is the driving force behind the lifestyle Americans enjoy today.

In Colonial America the population was small and scattered in small hamlets. Transportation was difficult so small industrial establishments making products to meet settlers basic needs could be found every few miles, including in the towns of Lysander and Van Buren. This book recounts the history of manufacturing outside of the home in these two Onondaga County, New York towns from the early 1800s to today. This story, except for specific business names and products, could also be the history of manufacturing in a multitude of other communities scattered throughout the United States.

Along the shores of the Eastern United States, manufacturing industries started a century or two earlier than in these two towns. As settlers moved inland to the Ohio Valley and further points west the development of manufacturing industries followed. During those years, new innovations in manufacturing moved slowly, and a business might exist for a generation or even two simply because competition from other areas came slowly. Today, because of the transmission of technology through almost instant communication and rapid low-cost transportation, new technology becomes rapidly available in almost all corners of the world. To survive today, a manufacturing business must be the lowest cost producer, produce a superior product or provide exceptional service.

The chapters that follow will share with the reader why and how the towns of Lysander and Van Buren developed. They will also provide descriptions of several of the early manufacturing industries and provide pictures to help the reader understand the tremendous changes that have occurred in manufacturing industries during the past 200 years. We can't relive those years and most of us would not want to, but a close look at the past as it relates to the present can offer us a glimpse, foggy though it may be, of what awaits us in the future.

ACKNOWLEDGMENTS

When writing history a person is totally dependent upon others who have taken the time to record activities and events occurring during their lifetimes. Often events and daily activities seem mundane to the recorder but a century later, for a historian, they can be meaningful windows into the past. In searching for facts concerning the history of manufacturing in the towns of Lysander and Van Buren I owe a deep debt of gratitude to dozens of people who over the past two centuries have recorded most of what I have been able to write in this book.

This book's bibliography names books and authors who have been sources for the material presented in this book. Some of these books were in the author's collection but the Onondaga County Library, Baldwinsville Public Library, Towns of Lysander and Van Buren, Cornell University Library and the Onondaga Historical Society supplied others. A special thanks goes to the Baker Library at Harvard University for the information from the 19th century reports of Dun & Co. In addition to these sources there are many others from whom a person absorbs pieces of information and knowledge on a daily basis that becomes part of one's knowledge base without being able to specifically name the source. Some of these sources are museums, lectures by historians, a lifetime of reading, practical experience and conversations with innumerable friends and acquaintances.

The author has been fortunate to have as friends some of the writers of local history of this area who are now deceased. A.J. Christopher (Tony to me) wrote many articles for a number of years titled *Sketches of Yesterday*, published in the *Baldwinsville Messenger*. Many of the chapters in this book draw upon information that Tony had written. L. Pearl Palmer, a beloved teacher and historian, wrote many articles published in the *Baldwinsville Messenger* that were combined to form her book, *Historical Review of the Town of Lysander*. Ruth Connell and Robert Nostrant, both historians, were also friends whose publications were sources of helpful information.

Two historians of today that have been of immeasurable help in putting this book together are Bonnie Kisselstein and Sue Ellen McManus. Bonnie has a lifetime interest in history and currently is Lysander Town Historian and local history librarian at the Baldwinsville Public Library. She has provided me with information, advice and a variety of pictures from the historical collection of the Baldwinsville Public Library. Sue is a huge bundle of local historical energy deeply involved in McHarrie's Legacy and the Museum at the Shacksboro Schoolhouse. She has provided me with counsel and information helpful in preparing this book as well as pictures from the collection at the Shacksboro Schoolhouse Museum. Both Bonnie and Sue read my draft of this book to help limit the number of my historical errors.

My thanks also go to Debbie Stack who read my draft, correcting some of my grammatical errors and making comments to help improve the clarity of the book for the reader and Malcolm MacPherson, a master mechanic descended from a long line of blacksmiths, who was a valuable source of practical information regarding a variety of early industries. Also, thanks go to my wife Janice for contending with my hundreds of hours of research and writing involved with this book. Preparing and publishing a book of history takes a small army, some who have recorded information from long ago and others who provide help today. My thanks to everyone!

ABOUT THE AUTHOR

Robert Bitz has lived on the farm in the Town of Lysander, settled by his ancestors in 1835, since he was born. He spent eight years at the two-room country school in Plainville and then rode on a school bus to attend Baldwinsville Academy for four years.

After graduating from Cornell University he came back to the family farm and developed the farm into a large, widely known business that manufactured and marketed a variety of turkey products throughout the United States. Working with his son Mark Bitz, he also developed a feed-mill, in the adjacent Town of Elbridge, that manufactured feed for their turkeys and also feed for numerous herds of dairy cattle in the Central New York area. They also owned and operated a cooking plant for their turkey products in the nearby Town of Salina

In addition to a half century of manufacturing and farming, Bob has always had a deep interest in history. For a number of years he had a museum on his farm called "The Pioneer Experience". During his retirement he has written three books relating to the history of agriculture, the last one titled *Four Hundred Years of Agricultural Change in the Empire State*. He has also recently completed a book entitled *Tales of a Turkey Farmer.*

TABLE OF CONTENTS

Preface iii

Acknowledgments v

About the Author. vii

Chapters
    1   The Settlement of Lysander and Van Buren 1
    2   Baldwinsville and the Dam 5
    3   Settlements in Lysander and Van Buren 15
    4   Asheries. 31
    5   Blacksmiths. 33
    6   Sawmills. 39
    7   Gristmills. 45
    8   Coopers. 55
    9   Distilleries. 59
    10   Tanneries, Shoemakers, Harness Makers & Rawhide Gears 61
    11   Local Industries Utilizing Minerals from the Earth. 67
    12   Foundries 75
    13   Textile Industries 83
    14   Cigars 89
    15   Dairy Products 95
    16   Wagons and Carriages 101
    17   Pumps. 107
    18   Paper Mills 117
    19   Electricity and Gas 121
    20   Millinery and Beyond. 125
    21   Other 19th and Early 20th Century Industries 129
    22   The Ordnance Works. 141
    23   Manufacturing in Radisson 145
    24   World War II to 2011 Manufacturing 153
    25   The Changing Face of Manufacturing 161

Appendix
    Census and Directory Informaton 165
    Partial Guide to Manufacturing Locations in Baldwinsville
        during the 19th and 20th Centuries. 172
    Dun Reports 174

Bibliography. 181

Index 183

A History of Manufacturing in Baldwinsville and the Towns of Lysander and Van Buren

1

The Settlement of Lysander and VanBuren

Until about 1800, the area encompassing Lysander and Van Buren was an insignificant and unknown part of the great forest that, for thousands of years, covered what is now the Eastern United States and Canada. Only Native Americans inhabited this area until a few white fur traders, explorers and Jesuit priests began to appear in the 16th and 17th centuries.

White settlers did not arrive here until around 1790. Even though Albany, which is only 150 miles east, was settled in the early 1600's, it took about another 150 years for settlers to reach west beyond Fort Stanwix at Rome. Due to qualms about the Native Americans, England had decreed that there were to be no settlements in the colonies west of the Appalachians. The French, longtime enemies of England, encouraged the Iroquois to prey on settlers. This, coupled with the power of the great Iroquois Confederacy in what is now Upstate New York, deterred all but the foolhardy from settling in this area.

In 1779, General George Washington sent an army of several thousand men, commanded by General Sullivan, to destroy the Iroquois in Central and Western New York. Orchards, crops and villages were decimated, with the once powerful Iroquois driven from the area. New York, too, had been devastated by the long war for independence. With a new nation finding its way, change came rather slowly. It took a decade, after the war, for settlement to begin and another decade before people began coming to the area in significant numbers.

The new New York State government made treaties with the Native Americans to acquire much of their land in Central New York. The State awarded 500 acres to certain Revolutionary veterans as payment for their services during the War, 600 acres if the veteran had not received 100 acres in Ohio from the federal government. All of Onondaga County, which included Lysander and VanBuren, along with land in several other counties, was part of what was called the Military Tract. It wasn't until 1789 that the State Surveyor General laid out township tracts of land, each of about 60,000 acres. This provided 100 lots of 600 acres in each designated township. Later, township lines were changed with land being taken from Lysander, leaving it with today's approximately 37,000 acres. Van Buren, originally part of the Town of Camillus, now has about 21,000 acres.

In 1790, balloting for the military lots began with eligible veterans' names put into one box and land grant locations into another box. A slip was drawn from each box to determine the veteran's grant location. By the time the grant locations were determined, the war had been over for seven years. Few veterans decided to settle upon their grant as by now most had families and were comfortably settled in their home communities. It was an unusual family that was willing to head into the wilderness to settle upon an unknown piece of land with relatively little value. The land grants had placed 1¾ million acres on the market creating a glut of land on the market and, therefore, reducing its value. Only one land grant recipient in each of these two towns settled on his grant: Jonathan Palmer on Lot

36 in Lysander and John Cunningham on Lot 38 in Van Buren. Most of the veterans sold or traded their land to speculators in return for very little remuneration. The land speculators would then break the grants down into smaller parcels, which were gradually sold to settlers.

During the 20-year period after the end of the war, an unseen market was slowly building for land on which to settle. There were several factors causing this. Good land in New England was becoming scarce as the population grew due to the increase of large families and also because of the depletion in soil fertility. Some of the loyalists, who had fled to Canada to escape persecution, were now returning as animosities fueled by the war gradually dissipated. In 1779, some of the soldiers in Sullivan's army had admired the fine land in Central New York and decided to settle there. In addition, people with a vision of opportunity were gradually coming from Northern Europe to settle in the United States. Some of these settlers were Hessian soldiers who had been hired by the British to fight against the revolutionists in the colonies and, therefore, were familiar with the area. As favorable reports regarding the fine lands filtered east, all of these factors combined to bring more and more settlers. Forestland began to be cleared for farms and small communities began to develop.

The first highways through the areas were waterways. Early settlers often came up the Mohawk River, portaged up to Wood Creek, came across Oneida Lake to Three Rivers and then traveled on the Seneca River to the area that is now Lysander and Van Buren. Travel over land was on Native American trails through the forests. It is likely that Jonathan Palmer traveled this route when he came in 1792, and then found his way through the forest to his grant, several miles from the river. By the time John Cunningham arrived in 1808, he probably traveled most of the way on primitive roads. It was in 1803 that the state granted a charter for a road from Utica to Canandaigua, called the Seneca Turnpike but commonly called the Genesee Trail. A state road from Onondaga to Oswego was laid out in 1806-7 through McHarrie's Rifts prior to the construction of a bridge across the Seneca River. In 1811, the state ordered that this road be improved from the Seneca River to Oswego. It wasn't until about 1813 that a state road was formed that passed through Van Buren to Sodus near Lake Ontario.

Until improvements were made, referring to these trails as roads would be like calling dirt roads super highways. The roads were simply paths cut through the forest, uneven, winding, full of holes and ruts, and difficult for both man and beast.

There is no question that Baldwinsville

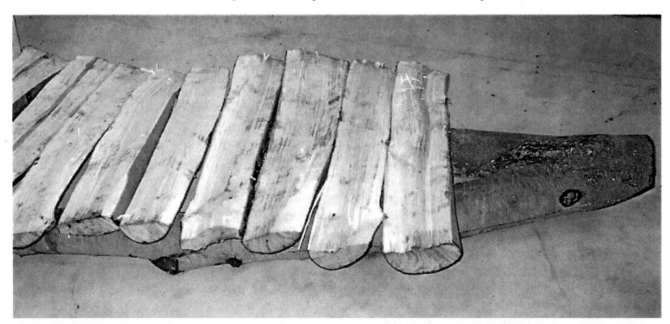

A simple sled, made by the author, similar to what could have been made by an early settler to transport his possessions a few miles or many miles. It would have been pulled by an ox and have been maneuverable through the forest. It consists of a tree crotch topped with some split log crosspieces.

developed because of the rifts in the Seneca River. Shallow water passed over rocks causing the water to race toward lower water below. The construction of a dam at this location captured a large amount of potential waterpower. Once the dam was in place, manufacturing plants, with water wheels, appeared on both sides of the river to make use of this power. Water, in 1800, was the primary source of power beyond that of man and beast. A dam with a seven-foot drop, on a river the size of the Seneca, provided the means of powering many industries needed by people in the area.

The first settlers to arrive in Lysander and Van Buren, after explorers and fur traders, were farmers. They arrived on foot or behind oxen, except for a few wealthier families who may have had a horse. Each farm family purchased land that was appropriate for its needs and what it could afford, usually averaging a little less than 100 acres. An area fully settled, in this pattern of development, comprised about 60 families in each three-mile square area. This was sufficient population to support desired services such as church, school, general store and blacksmith. Services that needed a larger population base to survive, such as a gristmill or sawmill, were often located further apart. In addition, the gristmill and sawmill both needed water power to function effectively so they had to be located near a stream providing enough water with sufficient fall to permit the construction of a dam to provide waterpower. The greater the waterpower available, the more people were attracted to a settlement. As a result, Baldwinsville, on the Seneca River, became the fastest growing settlement in the towns.

Baldwinsville, on the South side of the river, was called a variety of names over the years, first McHarrie's Rifts, then Macksville and finally Baldwinsville. On the north side first it was McHarrie's Rifts as the rifts stretched across the entire river and John McHarrie was the predominating resident, then Columbia, then Baldwin's Bridge and finally Baldwinsville.

The needs of the growing population in both towns were served by numerous settlements. In Lysander there were the settlements of Wilson's Corners (Plainville), Betts Corners (Lysander), Baird's Corners (1½ miles north of Lysander), Palmertown (later Polkville and still later Jacksonville), Little Utica (previously Paynesville), Lamson, West Phoenix, Belgium and Jack's Reef.

In Van Buren the settlements were Van Buren Center (sometimes referred to as Hardscrabble), Memphis (first known as Canton, then Canal prior to Memphis), Ionia, Bangall (previously Slab City and later Sand Springs), Whiskey Hollow, Warners and Jack's Reef. (Similar to Baldwinsville, the Seneca River separated the very small hamlet of Jack's Reef into two townships.)

The majority of the settlements in both towns were located adjacent to waterpower sources. Others like Plainville, Warners, Van Buren Center and Ionia were at crossroads, far enough from other settlements to allow small service centers to develop. Memphis didn't show growth until the Erie Canal passed through that area in 1821.

In the early development of the towns, minor manufacturing facilities came into existence to service local needs. Other than in Baldwinsville, seldom were locally manufactured products moved more than a few miles before finding a user. Often the purchaser went directly to the manufacturer to have an item made for his specific use. Items produced by the blacksmith, the shoemaker and the sawmill fit this category. In other instances, the buyer purchased a standard product directly from the manufacturer, examples of which were the distillery and the gristmill. The tannery sold its product to the shoemaker and the ashery sold its product to manufacturers of soap and glass or for export. Our early manufacturers made and sold their products for the direct benefit of the local residents by either furnishing them with a product they needed or providing a marketing need. Examples of marketing needs were the sale of the farmers' unwanted trees for the production of lumber, bark and potash, and the purchase by tanneries of hides from animals that had provided meat for the farm family.

In the following chapters we will explore the function and importance of these early manufacturing facilities and provide the names and the locations of them.

2

Baldwinsville and the Dam

Unquestionably, the dam and the canal changed Baldwinsville from what was, and would have continued to be, a sleepy little village into a bustling and thriving community! The rough and shallow water of the rifts, at the foot of what is now North Street, was just the catalyst needed to spark the idea of a dam, slightly below the rifts. The dam captured the power of the Seneca River and turned that power into pumps, paper, flour and a multitude of other products serving the needs of people in Baldwinsville and throughout the world.

The Seneca River splits Baldwinsville right down its middle. The part of Baldwinsville on the south side of the river is in the Town of Van Buren and the part on the north side of the river is in the Town of Lysander. Any mention of Baldwinsville automatically includes one of the two towns or both. Without the bridge over the Seneca River there would be two separate and smaller villages.

Local residents saw opportunity and achieved success by convincing Dr. Jonas Baldwin to use his resources to tame the river and turn it into a worthwhile tool for the residents of the little settlement that became Baldwinsville. It was in 1797 that the Baldwin family left their comfortable home of Little Falls in Herkimer County and traveled by waterway past McHarrie's Rifts to settle on a military lot Dr. Baldwin owned at Ovid, forty miles further west. Mrs. Baldwin had left Little Falls with regret but was placated when her husband told her that he would purchase the first place on their trip westward that she might select. On a bright autumn day they rounded the bend in the Seneca at McHarrie's Rifts and Mrs. Baldwin was so charmed with the beauty of the land on the north side of the river that she remarked to her husband that if he were to purchase this property she would be content to dwell there for life. As the Baldwins explored the general area while workmen were getting their boats past the rapids, they became even more pleased with the location. They traveled on to Ovid, and during the next year Dr. Baldwin went to Philadelphia and purchased the property at McHarrie's Rifts.

After spending about four years in Ovid, the Baldwins moved to Onondaga Hill, just a few miles south of what is now the city of Syracuse, staying there until 1807. That year Dr. Baldwin received a request, signed by many of the residents of McHarrie's Rifts and vicinity, to improve his valuable land resource with mills. At that time the nearest gristmill was in what is now Camillus and it was very difficult for residents to transport their grain six to eight miles without roads on which to travel. Although Dr. Baldwin had intended to build mills at some point in the future, he honored their request and promptly began work. He first built log cabins for the workmen. He anticipated obtaining power for a mill with water from what we now call Tannery Creek, supplemented with river water, by placing a wing dam partially across the river. Sickness (malaria) hit the workmen in August with many dying and work was discontinued until the

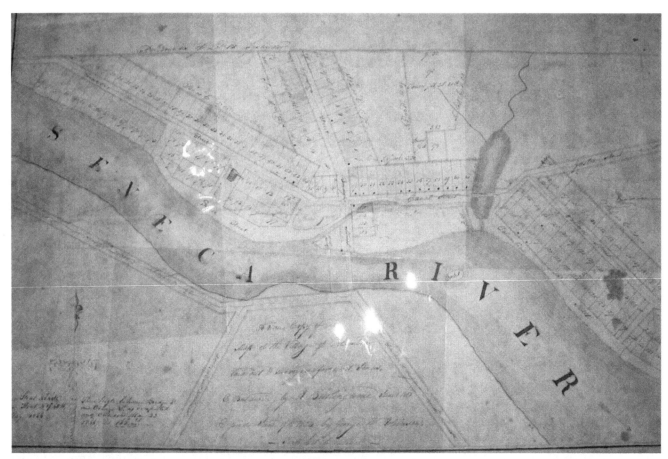

An 1810 map of the village of Columbia laid out and surveyed for Dr. Jonas Baldwin by A. Burlingame. Note the Baldwin Canal as it leaves the Seneca River to the north of the dam and re-enters the river slightly west of what we now know as Tannery Creek. The water flow from the river supplemented with water from Tannery Creek formed a millpond that furnished waterpower for Dr. Baldwin's sawmill. Some years later the Baldwin Canal was extended further east and the millpond was filled in.

following year.[1]

Work continued on the mill and wing dam the next year (1808) before the malaria struck again. Also, because of a miscalculation in the water levels of the creek and the river, the water from the wing dam would not flow into the raceway, leaving only the water from the creek to power the mill. Dr. Baldwin proceeded to extend the dam across the entire river but work was again interrupted by sickness and the dam was not completed until fall. Upon completion of the dam, the mill was able to operate at full capacity.[2]

The river was considered a public highway and since the dam interrupted navigation on the river, Dr. Baldwin applied to the state legislature for the right to build a canal and locks around the dam. Rights to develop such projects had already been granted by the legislature to the Inland Lock Navigation Co. The company was not actively developing such projects at the time and Dr. Baldwin was able to purchase rights extending from Cayuga Lake to the Oneida River. In 1809, the state granted Dr. Baldwin the right to build a canal and locks on the north side of the river. He was given the right to collect tolls from all boats passing through the canal, aptly named the Baldwin Canal, for 20 years, but the state later abrogated his right when it took control. Challenges for Dr. Baldwin continued when in 1809 a heavy water flow in the river washed out the dam, which he replaced the next year. It was not long before Dr. Baldwin had six sawmills operating under one roof. In 1809, Dr. Baldwin constructed a toll bridge across the river near where the current bridge stands. At the north

---

1 Bruce, Dwight H. *Onondaga's Centennial* p.742
2 Ibid p. 743

end of the bridge he built a flourmill, which later became a woolen mill that burned on November 11, 1841.[3]

The original Baldwin Canal touched Canal St. (E. Genesee St.). Improvements were made to the canal at various times during its lifetime. One improvement was moving the canal slightly to the south to allow room for buildings between Canal St. and the towpath of the canal. There were several swing bridges across the canal to provide access to businesses south of the canal. The original lift lock was located midway between Margaret and Tabor Streets but was later moved further east.[4]

The Baldwin Canal preceded the Erie Canal that crossed the State a few miles south of Baldwinsville in the southern edge of Van Buren by more than a decade. Until the Erie Canal was completed the Seneca River with its Baldwin Canal was the key waterway, both east and west from Oneida Lake to Cayuga Lake and points west.

Thanks to the bridge, the communities of Macksville, formerly called McHarrie's Rifts, on the south side of the river and Columbia on the north side gradually became one: Baldwinsville. Without the bridge the growth and prosperity of the village would have been hampered. The original plans called for another canal on the south side of the river but for unknown reasons it was never built; however, a canal did arrive on the south side in the 20th century. Barge Canal construction in Baldwinsville began in 1908, necessitating demolition of businesses on the north side of Water St. Although much anticipated, the Barge Canal did not prove to be an economic engine for Baldwinsville.

The power of water from behind the dam

A float bridge west of the current railroad bridge. It was constructed in approximately 1845 on the north side of the Seneca River to serve as part of the towpath from the Oswego Canal to the Baldwin Canal. Originally there was no rail on the side toward the Seneca River. When the bridge was wet it was dangerous for both the tow horses and drivers because it was slippery. The float bridge was 19 feet wide and 367 feet long, and cut across what was known as Frawley's Pond. Photo courtesy of OHA Museum & Research Center

attracted manufacturers to both sides of the Seneca River. The dam, by harnessing the river, forced the construction of the Baldwin Canal and provided the highway for manufacturers to bring raw materials to their plants and to market their finished products. The Seneca River with its rifts at Baldwinsville provided the opportunity for a thriving village with a strong manufacturing base. Dr. Baldwin and his dam brought it to fruition!

---
3   Hall, Edith *The History of Baldwinsville* p. 9-10
4   Christopher, A. J. *1851 Map Reveals Canal Changes* (August 6, 2007 is the only date listed on the article but it is likely the date it was copied from the *Baldwinsville Messenger* article of some years earlier.)

The E. W. Tucker canal boat made daily trips from Baldwinsville's Baldwin Canal to Syracuse. It is pictured here between the Morris Machine water wheel house on the left and the Morris Machine Works factory on the right. An overhead steel rope drive carried the power from the water wheel across the Baldwin Canal and E. Genesee Street to a receiving station on the roof of the machine shop where it was transferred to a line shaft with large pulleys that powered the Morris machines. Photo courtesy of OHA Museum & Research Center

The Baldwin Canal lock at the canal's end by Lock St. When the canal was constructed in 1808 it did not extend beyond Tannery Creek making this lock one of the later improvements to the canal. The canal was in active use until the completion of the Barge Canal in 1918. It was used to a lesser extent from 1918 to the early 1930s when it was mostly abandoned. Over a period of years, the village purchased all remaining rights to the canal, and the Baldwin Canal was finally filled in 1966.

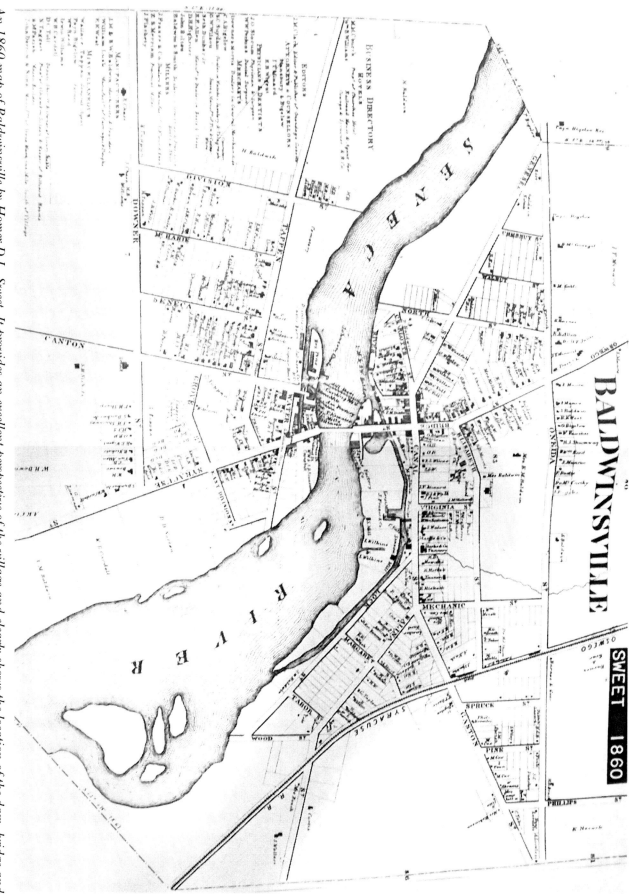

An 1860 map of Baldwinsville by Homer D.L. Sweet. It provides an excellent perspective of the village and clearly shows the location of the dam, bridge and Baldwin Canal in relation to the Seneca River.

A History of Manufacturing in Baldwinsville and the Towns of Lysander and Van Buren

This is an 1857 map of the southern portion of Baldwinsville by French. A number of manufacturing firms are marked on the map.

Baldwinsville and the Dam

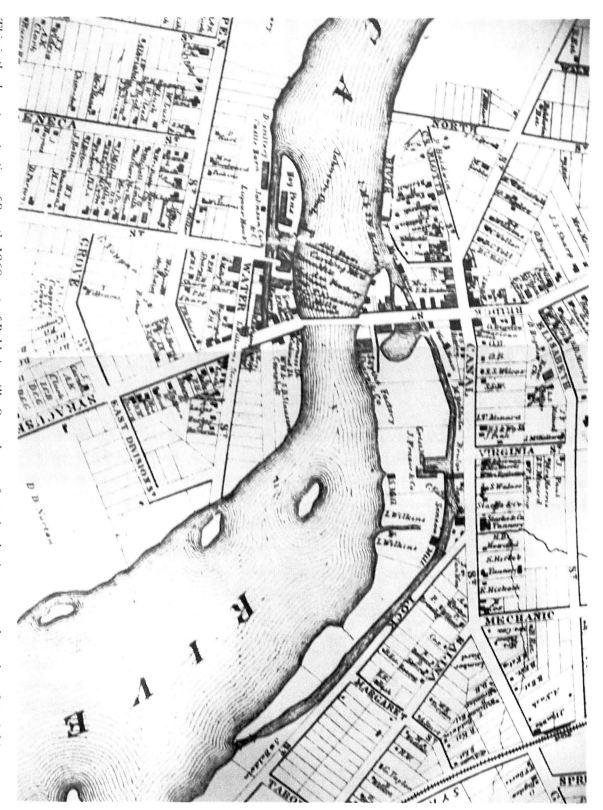

This is the downtown portion of Sweet's 1860 map of Baldwinsville. Several manufacturing businesses are shown but of special interest are the businesses of Johnson, Cook & Co. located on and adjacent to Papermill Island in the middle left, south of the Seneca River. It is an early example of vertical integration. Their flourmill ground grain for their distillery and the waste mash from the distillery provided feed for the hogs and cattle. They also used manure from the livestock as fertilizer for growing tobacco.

The swing bridge over the Clark & Mercer flourmill (later Mercer Milling Co.) millrace in the early 1900s, prior to the construction of the Barge Canal. A spur came from the D. L & W mainline to service the industries south of the Seneca River and this bridge provided access to the railroad from the mills. Photo courtesy of OHA Museum & Research Center

Tannery Creek, which enters the river past the end of Albert Palmer Lane at about 30 E. Genesee St., was the location of Dr. Baldwin's first sawmill. This picture was taken just before the creek goes underground at Elizabeth St. Dr. Baldwin intended to use a wing dam across part of the Seneca River to supplement the water flow of Tannery Creek but it was unsuccessful. Later, a full dam across the river solved the problem. Tannery Creek receives its name from the tanneries that operated along its banks.

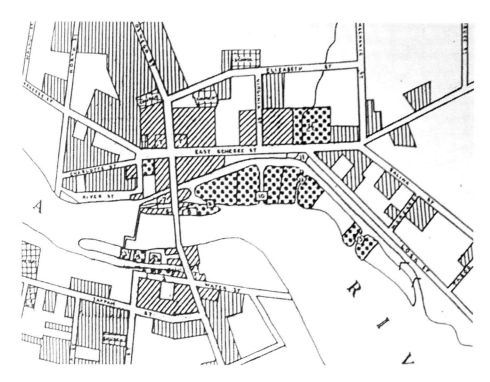

Downtown portion of Baldwinsville from Sweet's 1874 map of Baldwinsville. It clearly shows the Baldwin Canal beginning at the east end of River St., its course through Baldwinsville and it entering the Seneca River along Lock St. The sections with the dark round dots are where there are manufacturing businesses. Notice "paper mill point" and the short waterway from the river to Syracuse St.

A view from the south side of the Seneca River looking northeast. Left to right are the Amos flourmill, Morris Machine Works, the original Baldwinsville & Syracuse railroad yard and the James Frazee Milling Co. The Baldwin Canal is hidden by the buildings and is between the railroad yards and E. Genesee St.

3

Settlements in Lysander and Van Buren

At one time there was a name for almost every settlement located at a crossroad with a few homes and perhaps one or two commercial enterprises. Many of these names changed with time or disappeared and are lost to us today. This chapter mentions only the settlements where there is a record of some type of manufacturing business during the 19th and the first half of the 20th centuries. The settlements are listed by their current name or last known name with earlier names attached. Sources of information are shown in the footnotes of the chapters of this book that deal with specific types of manufacturing.

This chapter is written to show the variety of manufacturing businesses in the various settlements. Each settlement had a need for basic services, so there is a great deal of duplication from place to place. The larger settlements of Memphis and Lysander offered a greater variety of manufacturing businesses. Few of the manufacturers had great success or persisted for more than a generation or two but they filled important needs for local residents.

Town of Lysander[1]

Plainville *(Wilson's Corners)*
Although the first settler arrived in 1806, the first date mentioned for a manufacturing business was 1833, and that was a blacksmith and a wagon shop.

By 1860 there was a tannery south of the village, three different boot and shoemakers, a carriage maker and a blacksmith. By 1876 there were two more blacksmiths, two basket makers and a cheese factory. A planing and molding business appeared around the 1880s. The cheese factory burned and was later replaced by a creamery. A sawmill had been constructed prior to 1874, on what is now Gates Road, and continued operating into the 20th century.

Cigar manufacturing, along with tobacco production, became an important business in the community around the time of the Civil War. There were at least two tobacco warehouses in the community and three cigar manufacturers. The cigar manufacturers disappeared by the early part of the 20th century along with all of the other manufacturing businesses, except for a blacksmith shop, which closed about 1950.

Plainville Turkey Farm began growing and processing turkeys in 1923 but did not become a manufacturing facility until the late 1950s. It became, by far, Plainville's largest business and will be mentioned in a later chapter.

Lysander (village)
(Betts Corners) (Baird's Corners, a mile north of Lysander is included with Lysander because some sources did not separate them)
Lysander (the village) had a long and diverse variety of manufacturing for a community of its size. The first settler arrived around 1804, followed by a number of other settlers. In 1817, the Chauncey

---
[1] The information regarding the settlements in the Town of Lysander came from a variety of sources that along with others are listed in the bibliography.

A History of Manufacturing in Baldwinsville and the Towns of Lysander and Van Buren

An 1874 map of the Town of Lysander by Homer D. L. Sweet. The several hamlets in the town can be located on this map. The town consists of approximately 37,000 acres.

Betts family arrived, the source of Lysander's first name. Mr. Betts built an ashery and distillery soon after his arrival. At various times the village also had blacksmiths, coopers, a rake manufacturer, a bedspring manufacturer, a manufacturer of agricultural implements, a pump manufacturer, wagon shops, a carriage shop, a tannery, a sawmill, a gristmill, shoemakers, harness makers, a churn factory, a cheese factory, a creamery, a lime manufacturer and a foundry.

The list of manufacturers in Lysander is truly amazing, especially because there was both a lime manufacturer and a foundry, neither located near waterpower sources. Foundries and lime manufacturers were normally found only in larger communities with a good supply of waterpower. In about 1854, J. Ballard & Co. tannery was the first business in northern Lysander to utilize steam power. In 1855, the foundry used steam power to make plows, cultivators and castings. A foundry was still listed in *Boyd's Business Directory* in 1881. Ox Creek did furnish waterpower for a gristmill and a sawmill near Baird's Corners. Manufacturing businesses in the village slowly disappeared with none remaining by the middle of the 20th century.

Jacksonville *(first Palmertown and then Polkville)*

The first settlers in the area of what became known as Palmertown were the members of the Jonathan Palmer family who arrived in 1792. They had no neighbors until after 1800 but some decades later, probably around the 1830s, there was a blacksmith, tanner, shoemaker, wagon maker, harness maker, sawmill, grist mill, cigar maker and a cider and jelly mill. It became a thriving little community until, like the other communities, manufacturing moved to larger villages and cities in the late 19th and early 20th centuries.

Little Utica *(Paynesville)*

Picketville (about a half mile southwest of Little Utica and located on the Beaver Lake outlet is included as part of Little Utica)

The outlet of Beaver Lake, although a relatively small stream, provided the power for a number of small manufacturing businesses along its approximately three-mile length in northern Lysander. Sawmills, at various times, were scattered along the stream from south of Ellison Road through Picketville, past Little Utica to the county line. There was also a cider mill on the creek and a cheese factory,

This view is looking west across the Oswego River to West Phoenix. There is considerable fall in the Oswego River between Three Rivers and Oswego, which spawned many substantial manufacturing businesses. West Phoenix first had a sawmill and later furniture manufacturers followed by several paper manufacturing businesses. This photo was circa 1900. Photo courtesy of OHA Museum & Research Center.

⊸ Maps of the Town Settlements ⊸

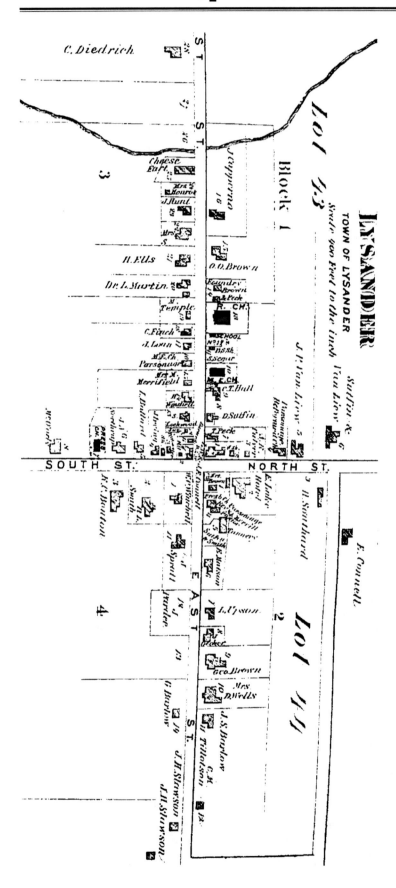

An 1874 Sweet map of Lysander, formerly called Betts Corners. Brown & Peck Foundry is located on the north side of West St. (Lamson Rd.) and a cheese factory is shown on the south side of West St. The Sutfin & Smith tannery is on the north side of East St. (Lamson Rd.).

Maps of the Town Settlements

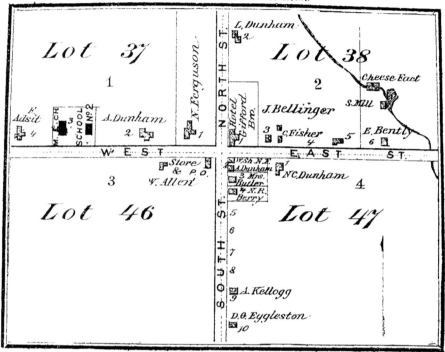

An 1874 Sweet map of Little Utica, formerly called Paynesville. A cheese factory and a sawmill are shown north of East St. (Lamson Rd.) close to a millpond and the outlet from Beaver Lake, which is about two miles southwest.

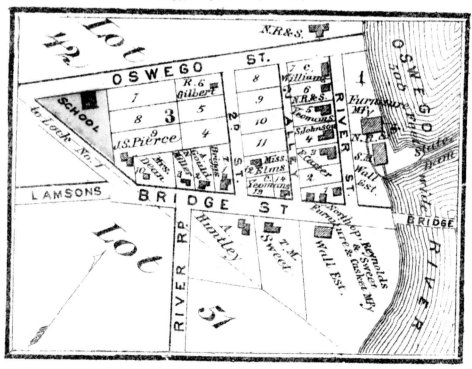

An 1874 Sweet map of West Phoenix. A furniture factory and a sawmill are located on River St. The Northup, Reynolds & Sweet Furniture & Casket Co. is located on Bridge St.

Maps of the Town Settlements

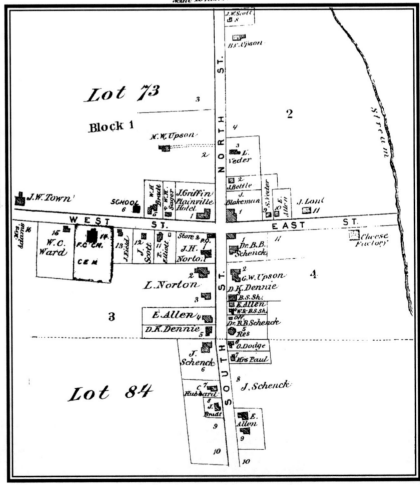

An 1874 Sweet map of Jacksonville, formerly named Palmertown and later Polkville. A steam powered cider mill is shown on the west side of South St. and on the east side is Fancher & Son wagon shop.

An 1874 Sweet map of Plainville. A cheese factory is shown on the south side of East St. (Route 370). E. Allen's wagon & carriage shop is located on the east side of South St. (Plainville Rd.).

which was located slightly northeast of Little Utica. During the 19th century there were also shoemakers, blacksmiths, wagon makers, harness makers, a cigar factory, a tanner and a miller. The businesses slowly disappeared with the advent of the automobile, better roads and increased competition.

Lamson

Lamson, less than two miles east of Little Utica and three miles west of West Phoenix, had a limited number of manufacturing businesses. The author has only found a blacksmith and a shoemaker listed. Lamson and the area around it for several miles received a boost in 1848 when the Syracuse and Oswego Railroad passed through the community providing a more convenient and rapid access of farmers' crops to markets.

West Phoenix

There were a number of manufacturing businesses in West Phoenix that have been overlooked by some Lysander historians because of West Phoenix's proximity to the much larger incorporated village of Phoenix, directly across the Oswego River in Oswego county. Additionally, West Phoenix is removed from most of the Lysander population and is in a different school district. A dam across the Oswego River at Phoenix furnished significant waterpower, which sparked the growth of numerous manufacturing firms. The first manufacturing business was a sawmill constructed in 1829. *Sweet's Maps of 1874* show a large furniture manufacturing firm as well as a separate furniture and casket manufacturing business, both operated by Northup, Reynolds & Sweet. In the latter part of the 19th century and into the 1930s there were three paper mills utilizing the waterpower of the Oswego River. At least two small tool and die shops developed in the area largely to furnish and repair machinery for the paper manufacturers. A hydroelectric plant powered by the Oswego River is still operating at West Phoenix today.

Belgium *(Belgium then West Cicero, Clay Post Office, New Bridge, and finally Belgium again)*

About 1824, a wooden bridge was erected across the Seneca River by James L. Voorhees of Plainville and was operated as a toll bridge for 10 years. The settlement expanded when the Oswego Canal, which connected with the Erie Canal, came through in 1828. At various times there were several blacksmiths, a wagon maker, a brickyard, a sawmill operated by steam, a cheese factory, a boat works and a drug manufacturing business, which at one time employed 30 people.[2]

Town of Van Buren[3]

Herrick's Corners

Herrick's Corners was located at the intersection of the current Van Buren and Maple Roads. There were a number of residents near these corners making barrels, so many in fact that Maple Road was previously called Cooper Street. Two notable manufacturers at Herrick's Corners were O.B. Herrick who operated a wire and sieve factory for many years, and Gayetty & Randall's brick furnace foundry that made a large variety of cast iron products including kettles, plows and stoves.

Hardscrabble *(Van Buren Center)*

Hardscrabble, formerly called Van Buren Center, is located on Van Buren Road, southeast of Route 690, about three miles from Baldwinsville. It developed as a small community in the early 1800s when the first state road to pass through Baldwinsville was laid out in 1806-7. The road connected Onondaga Hill, Onondaga's county seat, with Oswego. Travel on the road brought business to Van Buren Center. There was a blacksmith, a wagon repair shop and a woodworking shop. After the railroad was constructed from Syracuse to Oswego in 1848, travel on the road decreased and the settlement lost much of its activity.

Warners

The members of the Warner family who settled there in 1807 were numerous enough to give this locality its name. A post office with the name of Van Buren Center was established here in 1837 but the mail was so often mixed up with that of Hardscrabble that the post office name was changed to Warners in 1870. The railroad passed nearby in 1851, and the cement factories that came later

---

2 Christopher, A.J., *Belgium Hamlet was Once Known as New Bridge* May 19, 1966

3 Most of the information concerning the settlements of the Town of Van Buren was taken from several different articles by A. J. Christopher in *Sketches of Yesterday* published in the *Baldwinsville Messenger* and from *History of Van Buren* by Louis Dow Scisco.

A History of Manufacturing in Baldwinsville and the Towns of Lysander and Van Buren

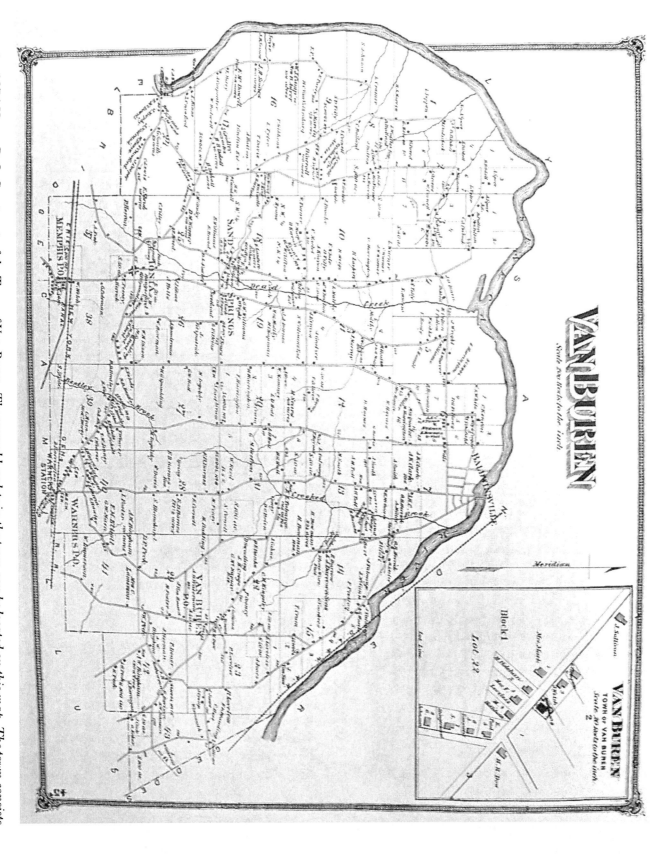

An 1874 Homer D. L. Sweet map of the Town of Van Buren. The several hamlets in the town can be located on this map. The town consists of approximately 21,000 acres.

Maps of the Town Settlements

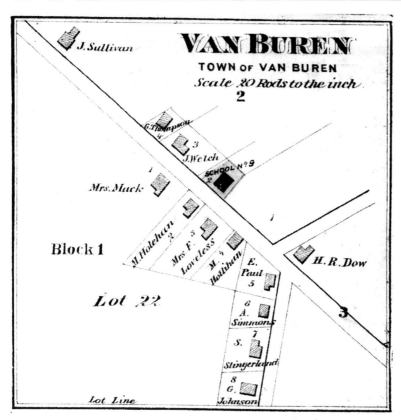

An 1874 Sweet map of the hamlet of Van Buren, formerly called Van Buren Center and sometimes Hardscrabble, located on what is now Van Buren Rd. about three miles southeast of Baldwinsville. It was a busy community in the early 1800s but after the railroad was constructed between Syracuse and Oswego in 1848, activity in the community declined.

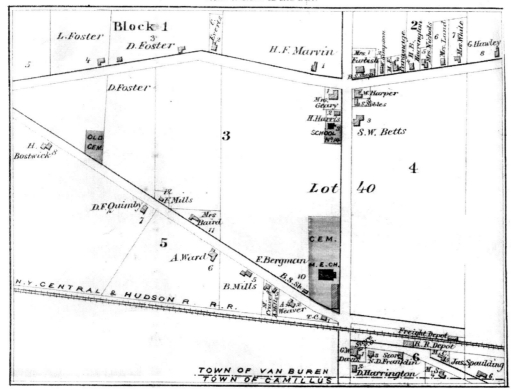

An 1874 Sweet map of Warners. The New York Central & Hudson River Railroad freight and passenger depots are shown on the map

Maps of the Town Settlements

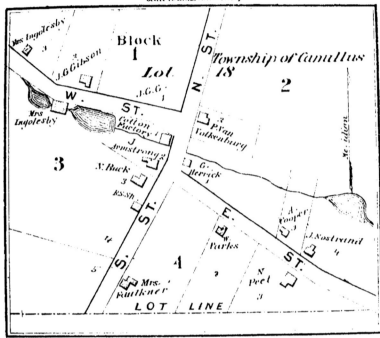

An 1874 Sweet map of Sand Springs, formerly called Slab City and later Bangall. A cotton factory is shown adjacent to a millpond on West St. Note that Sweet has the words "Township of Camillus" in the upper right hand corner of the map. This is an error as the township of Camillus is two miles to the south of the map area. Prior to 1829 Van Buren was part of the Township of Camillus so if not marked erroneously, Sweet must have been referring to the original Township.

An 1874 Sweet map of Ionia. Ionia was the leading community in Van Buren for a short period in the early 1800s. With the opening of the Erie Canal, about a mile south in 1821, businesses left the settlement and went to Memphis. Note that Sweet has the words "Township of Camillus" in the upper right hand corner of the map. This is an error as the Township of Camillus is located a mile to the south of the map area. Prior to 1829 Van Buren was part of the Township of Camillus so if not marked erroneously, Sweet must have been referring to the original Township.

Maps of the Town Settlements

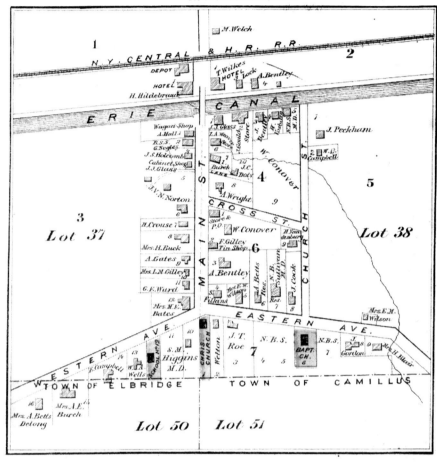

An 1874 Sweet map of Memphis, formerly named Canton and later Canal. A wagon shop and a cabinet shop are both shown on the west side of Main St. south of the Erie Canal. A tin shop is shown on the east side of Main St.

The New York Central Railroad mainline tracks at Warners. The railroad first passed through Warners in 1838 connecting Geddes (Syracuse) and Auburn. The rails were made of wood and horses pulled stagecoaches, with specially designed wheels, on the rails. In this much later image the passenger station is on the right, the freight depot on the left and the brick factory is in the distant left. Photo courtesy of OHA Museum & Research Center

in the century brought increased development to the community. There was a blacksmith early in the community's development, and for many years there was a large brick factory.

Ionia

Ionia was the first community in Van Buren to take on the semblance of a village. This occurred due to the laying out of the state road through Ionia toward Sodus Bay in 1813. The prosperity of the community was short lived as the Erie Canal passed a mile south in 1821, and the taverns, stores and other businesses relocated near the canal to what is now Memphis where there was much greater activity.

Memphis *(Canton and later Canal)*

Memphis was laid out and named Canton in 1821 shortly after the Erie Canal, passing through it, opened between Rome and Montezuma. With the establishment of a post office in 1828 its name became Canal and in 1860 its name was changed to Memphis. The settlement became a rapidly growing community with blacksmiths, coopers, wagon shops, shoemakers, foundry, cigar factory, sawmill, cider mill and harness maker. The New York Central & Hudson River Railroad passed through the village in 1851 bringing even more business. A second railroad, the West Shore, came through the village with tracks parallel to the Central's in 1883, and in 1909 the Syracuse, Rochester & Eastern trolley passed through Memphis providing hourly passenger service. The 20th century was not kind to the village. The Erie Canal was abandoned, the trolley discontinued, a railroad removed and both railroad stations closed.

Bangall *(Sand Springs, Slab City)*

Bangall, located on Lot 18 with waterpower from the nearby Sand Springs, was the location of the first sawmill and the first gristmill in the Town of Van Buren. For a period in its early history, it was known as Slab City because most of its houses were built from rough slabs of lumber from the sawmill.

A distillery also operated here for a number of years.

Jack's Reef

The towns of Van Buren and Elbridge meet on the south side of the Seneca River at Jack's Reef, and the town of Lysander sits to the north of the river adjacent to both towns. Jack's Reef receives its name from the rifts in the river west of the hamlet. However, the waterpower that might have been developed was never used. There was a creamery located at Jack's Reef in the early part of the 20th century.

Additional information concerning the industries in the settlements of Lysander and Van Buren will be provided in the succeeding chapters along with information regarding the manufacturing industries in Baldwinsville. The appendix also provides names of many manufacturers taken from a variety of directories.

A 1915 image of county road construction at Warners. The roadbed was graded and stones, from a stone crusher, were added to form the base of the road before concrete was poured on top of the stones. Farmers drew the stones, with horses and wagon, from stone piles that had accumulated on their farms over many years. The modern improved roads, like this one, and motorized trucks combined to gradually move manufacturing away from the canals and railroads that previously had been necessary for receiving raw materials and shipping manufactured goods. Photo courtesy of OHA Museum & Research Center

Memphis, looking north to the bridge that passed over the Erie Canal. The canal, for almost a century, turned Memphis into a busy little village with several small manufacturing businesses. Photo courtesy of OHA Museum & Research Center

Railroad work crew at Memphis railroad station. The author remembers a main line New York Central passenger train stopping to let off a single passenger at this small Memphis station during the 1930s. Photo courtesy of OHA Museum & Research Center

Settlements in Lysander and Van Buren

The L. & G. Crouse coal elevator at Memphis, looking east along the Erie Canal. Note the elevator that reaches down in the canal boat to elevate the coal to the overhead storage. Piles of lumber and clay tile for sale are on the right. Photo courtesy of OHA Museum & Research Center

Looking east along the Erie Canal at Memphis in the 1890s. The L. & G. Crouse coal and lumber business is on the right and the Warners Portland Cement Works is visible in the distance on the left. On the left a team of horses is pulling the canal boat. Photo courtesy of OHA Museum & Research Center

29

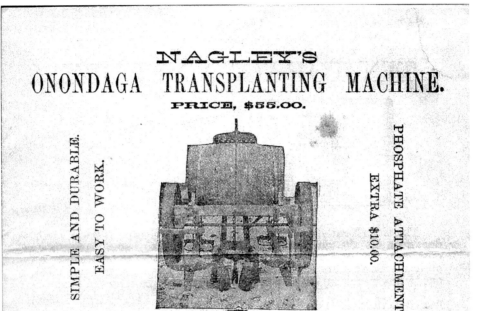

This is an 1893 advertisement by C.C. Nagley & Son in Memphis of a transplanter for setting tobacco and other started plants in the ground. The Nagleys operated a blacksmith shop for a number of years and then expanded it into the manufacture of several different pieces of equipment used in the production of tobacco. Advertisement from the author's collection

4

Asheries

It was an environmental tragedy! Little did they realize what they were doing! Thousands and thousands of acres of virgin forest destroyed, forests that had been thriving for centuries, decimated into ashes. Throughout the northeastern United States the sound of the axe, cutting away the lives of gorgeous old trees, was ringing through the countryside.

The English colonies in America had fought a long war and won independence. The Native Americans were no longer a serious threat to New York settlers. Several generations of large colonial families and an influx of thousands of oppressed from Europe, who came searching for opportunity in America, caused the population to boom. As a result in the early 1800s a vast river of people flowed up the Hudson River continuing up the Mohawk Valley to settle in upstate New York and the vast lands beyond.

All of these people were searching for opportunity. There were craftsmen, preachers, lawyers, businessmen and doctors. Others were speculators looking for the opportunity to make a quick dollar. The vast majority, however, were farmers or those looking for a piece of land on which to settle, raise their families, enjoy freedom and, hopefully, prosperity.

There was a huge obstacle confronting these settlers. The entire countryside, except for a few areas previously farmed by the Native Americans, was covered with large trees. The settlers needed food and they needed a source of income. Their answer was to cut the trees and plant crops. A few trees were needed to provide a log cabin home. Initially, most communities did not even have a sawmill. When sawmills were constructed, the number of trees that could be sawed into lumber and sold was only a small portion of the trees the settlers wanted removed.

The solution to the problem, of too many acres of trees where the farmer wanted to grow crops, was to burn the trees and utilize the remaining hardwood ashes for potash. In Albany there was a good market for pearl ash, the refined product from the hardwood ashes. A settler was able to receive about six cents a bushel for his ashes when delivered to the local ashery.

The hardwood species of beech, maple, chestnut, oak and elm, were felled so the tops would fall onto each other in the center of a large circle. Then, after they had dried, the trees were set on fire with most of the tops consumed in the flames. Later the remaining trunks of the trees would be cut into manageable lengths and oxen would be used to pull them together into piles for burning. After the trees were burned, the ashes were gathered and carted to the local ashery or, in remote areas without asheries, used as a crop fertilizer.

At the ashery the ashes were put in a container and water was slowly added permitting it to seep through the ashes. The liquid leaching through the ashes became caustic lye. (This is the same method, but on a much smaller scale, used by numerous early American households to produce lye for making soap.) The liquid lye was put into a large iron kettle and boiled down into "black salts"

This is an iron kettle for making potash. Thousands of acres of hardwood forests were burned to obtain ashes. The hardwood ashes were first leached with water to form lye and then the lye was boiled in an iron kettle to form "black salts" called potash. The "black salts" needed further refining in a kiln to remove the carbon and leave the remaining valuable product called pearl ash. The pearl ash was shipped east to Albany, New York City and Europe to be used in the manufacture of glass, soap and many other products.

or potash. Sometimes the landowner did his own leaching and boiling and then sold his black salts to the ashery for about $3.00 per hundred pounds. This was rare due to the cost of the large and expensive iron kettles and lack of skill on the part of the landowner. Black salts were heated to a high temperature in a brick kiln to produce the valuable "pearl ash". The heat in the brick kiln removed the carbon and impurities leaving a fused bluish-white, much purer product.[1] Pearl ash was used in the manufacture of glass, soap, leather goods, gunpowder, paper, and cotton and wool processing. Much of the pearl ash was shipped to England and other European countries.

Forests were gradually fading away as this process continued in many locations throughout the area. By 1845 there were almost 40,000 acres of farmland in Lysander and Van Buren that had been forests a half century earlier. A good portion of these 40,000 acres of trees had been turned into ashes. The *1835 New York Census* listed four asheries in Lysander and two in Van Buren, but by 1845 asheries ceased to exist in both towns.

As the 19th century moved forward, production of pearl ash was discontinued in Lysander and Van Buren. During the next 30 years another 10,000 acres of forests were leveled in the two towns with the timber from these acres used mostly for lumber and fuel. After 1845 forests were still being burned for their ashes in more remote areas of the country, but with the discovery of mineral ash in Germany in 1861, and later in Canada and England, the age of the commercial wood ashery came to an end.[2]

Chauncey Betts and his brother-in-law, Skinner, had a potash factory (ashery) in the village of Lysander. Cornelius Hubbard had a potash factory in Baird's Corners about 1820.[3] There were several asheries in Van Buren. Luthur Seaver had one on Lot 27 in 1813 and Abijah Hudson had one near Warners as early as 1825. Isaac Hill had one in Canton about the same time and there was also one in the northwest part of Van Buren.[4] There was also an ashery near the west line of Baldwinsville on the South side of the river.[5] In 1827, there was an ashery near where Van Wie Chevrolet is located.[6] (Approximately at 10 E. Genesee St.)

Ashes from Lysander and Van Buren's hardwood trees were a source of income for many of the early settlers and was, perhaps the towns' first manufacturing industry. It was an industry that had a short life, but one that had a tremendous effect upon the towns' landscapes. The forests would have been cleared, but it is sad to think of the thousands of magnificent trees being turned into ashes.

---

1 Van Wagenen, Jared Jr. *The Golden Age of Homespun* p. 166-167
2 Historic Kirkland, Ohio ashery web page
3 Bruce, Dwight H. *Onondaga's Centennial* p. 749
4 Ibid p. 730
5 Hall, Edith *History of Baldwinsville* p. 16
6 Palmer, Pearl *Historical Review of the Town of Lysander* Part 81

5

Blacksmiths

Today few people would consider a blacksmith to be a manufacturer, but from the first settlements in Central New York and well into the 20th century, the blacksmith was very much a manufacturer. Blacksmithing was one of the first businesses formed. For example, when the village of Baldwinsville's first settlers arrived, there were no blacksmiths. As the number of residents in the area increased, one soon appeared. As the village grew, other blacksmiths arrived to fill the needs of a growing population.

The word "smith" is derived from the word "smite", which means one who strikes. The smith strikes with a hammer. A blacksmith works with iron and the metal is always heated to a reddish color for shaping. At this temperature a black oxide is formed on the exterior of the iron and, therefore, we have the name, blacksmith.

Iron is the most common of the metals used by man and had many applications in the early 1800s. The blacksmith made fasteners, hinges, latches, knives and a variety of tools. Because of his ability to weld wrought iron, he could fabricate relatively intricate objects from iron. Sawmills and gristmills are often thought of as communities' first industries but neither of them could come into being without the aid of the blacksmith to manufacture the necessary components. The blacksmith also made many items using wood, such as wagons, coaches and sleighs, because of their numerous iron components. The author remembers the local Plainville blacksmith, Fred Pickard, making the author's father a variety of items including wooden wagon racks. When the early settlers arrived in this area, they brought a few necessities made from iron, but if anything of iron needed repairing or replacing a blacksmith was needed.

Often a blacksmith had what was called a wheel-stone outside his shop, which was used when fitting the iron tire to the wooden rim of the wheel. The wheel-stone had a greater diameter than a millstone and had a larger hole in the center to accommodate the wheel's hub. During the last half of the 19th century and into the early part of the 20th century, shoeing horses gradually became a major portion of the blacksmith's work. This was timely as many of the items such as nails, bolts and axes, previously made by the blacksmith, were beginning to come from larger manufacturing facilities often more than 100 miles away. As draft horses became more common on area farms (oxen were the predominant source of power on a farm prior to 1830), the blacksmith was the person that made and applied the iron horseshoes to the animals' feet. In the first half of the 19th century the blacksmith actually forged the shoe from a bar of iron. In 1835, a manufacturer in Troy, New York patented a machine that could make 20 shoes a minute. Gradually these pre-manufactured shoes made their way to area blacksmith shops. In 1825, there were only 326 horses in the Town of Lysander, many of which were used for driving and riding, but by 1875 the number had increased to 1627. The number of horses remained relatively high until the 1930s.

A. J. Christopher, in several of his, *Sketches of Yesterday* column, published in the *Baldwinsville*

This image is the Martin J. Maroney blacksmith shop along Meadow St. circa 1900. The Barge Canal displaced the blacksmith shop in 1908. The blacksmith shod horses, repaired wagon wheels and performed many other tasks associated with iron. Note the heavy leather aprons the three blacksmiths are wearing and the iron wagon tires, on the left, leaning against the building. Photo courtesy of OHA Museum & Research Center

Messenger, mentions a number of area blacksmiths:

- He tells of Joseph M. Fugette (a former slave), a 20 year-old "dusky" lad brought back from the south by Dr. Kendall, a Baldwinsville surgeon who served in the Civil War. Joseph apprenticed successfully to Henry Russell, a Belgium blacksmith, and in 1877, was a partner in the blacksmith shop of Fugette & Burgess. His business became Union Carriage Works, located at the southeast corner of Water and Syracuse Sts. He operated until 1906 when he sold his business.[1]

- He mentions C.J. Hay who ran a blacksmith shop approximately at 18 E. Genesee St. He stated that there were three separate shops across the street from Hay's. No name is mentioned for one, but the other two were owned by a Mr. Fink and Lewis Eggleston. There were at least two more between the Baldwin Canal and the Seneca River and at least six more on the south side of the river. Construction of the Barge Canal removed at least three of these shops. Between Baldwinsville and Warners there were about five blacksmith shops.[2]

- He mentions Holihan's and Elmer Post's, Weaver, Parley Hand, Maroney and Michael Neupert. He tells that Neupert had shod horses for the army during the Civil War and opened a shop in Baldwinsville. Neupert removed, sharpened and replaced 40 shoes on horses by himself in 6 ¾ hours on January 19, 1882. In 1891, Neupert built a blacksmith shop at the back of his home at 63 Syracuse Street.[3]

Few blacksmiths are listed in historical references prior to the Onondaga County Directories of

---

1 Christopher, A.J. *From Bondage to Blacksmith* June 16, 1966

2 Ibid *Blacksmith Shops Many in Village* October 31, 1968

3 Ibid *Michael Neupert – Blacksmith, Horseshoer* July, 1971

the 1860s. By and large the first blacksmiths were part-time, with another additional part-time occupation. A forge and bellows, to force air into the flame, were necessary to obtain sufficient temperature to shape and weld iron. A heavy hammer, iron tongs and an anvil completed the most essential tools. As his business prospered, the blacksmith added additional tools to increase his breadth of operation and efficiency. These tools were heavy and would have come to the area by boat or on a sled. Wagons were very uncommon before the 1820s.

Coal for the blacksmith's forge was not readily available in a developing community so charcoal was used to obtain sufficient heat. To forge iron means to shape it. The heat that was developed in the forge by the bellows blowing air on the burning charcoal made the forging or shaping of the iron possible. A blacksmith could tell when the iron was ready to be shaped, welded or tempered by its color. As the heat increased, the iron's color changed from red to orange to yellow, finally white, and then to its melting point. It was necessary for the blacksmith to have indirect light to clearly see the glowing color of the metal and remove it from the forge at the correct temperature.

The blacksmith worked with wrought iron, which was low in carbon and malleable when heated. If the blacksmith wanted to produce a product that required a high wear surface, he usually hardened it by immersing the iron part in a carbon rich material while it was red hot. Repeated applications of the carbon would allow the iron to absorb a thin layer of carbon on its outside surface. When the iron was quenched in water its exterior molecular structure was changed making an item with a strong internal structure and a very hard exterior surface.

A working blacksmith shop depicting the year 1840 at Old Sturbridge Village in MA. Notice the multitude of tools that the blacksmith used in his work. The blacksmith's hand is working the bellows near the ceiling to blow air into the forge to increase its temperature.

Fred Pickard is standing by his blacksmith shop in Plainville circa 1920. The era of the local blacksmith was ending at this time and you will note the signs on his shop for woodwork and International Harvester Farm Machines. He was branching out in associated fields and was able to continue his business until his retirement in the early 1950s. Photo courtesy of Kaye Forsythe

Striking the heated iron repeated times with a hammer gives it the desired shape. A heavy sledgehammer was used for larger pieces. The large pieces required a helper to swing the sledgehammer, while the blacksmith held the hot iron positioned on the anvil with tongs. This is hard work when done over long periods, and a reciprocating power hammer called a trip hammer was developed to ease this task. A water wheel provided the power for a trip hammer. Only the larger establishments used trip hammers because small blacksmith shops did not have the necessary waterpower. The Morris Axe Factory, west of Oswego St. between the river and Baldwin Canal, had six trip hammers, which provided a loud medley of iron hitting iron in the area around the factory. One can imagine the neighbors' joy when the banging of the trip hammers ceased at the end of the day.

Following are some early blacksmiths mentioned by local historians. In 1834, Behm Palmer opened a blacksmith shop about three miles north of Baldwinsville on what is now Route 48.[4] A blacksmith and wagon shop started in Plainville in 1833.[5] Andrew W. Baird moved at an early date to what became known as Baird's Corners, about 1½ miles north of Lysander, and put up a blacksmith shop.[6] Abner Hitchcock, a blacksmith, settled on Lot 40 near Warners prior to 1820.[7] Adam Lipe had a blacksmith shop in Memphis.[8] Stephen Prouty had a blacksmith shop in Van Buren Settlement in 1829.[9]

4   Palmer, Pearl *Historical Review of the Town of Lysander* Part 94
5   Clayton, W.W. *History of Onondaga County* p. 326
6   Bruce, Dwight W. *Onondaga's Centennial* p. 750
7   Scisco, Louis Dow *Early History of the Town of Van Buren* p. 22
8   Ibid p. 21
9   Ibid p. 23

Beginning with the October 20, 1846 *Onondaga Gazette's Business Directory* the blacksmith shops of Jeremiah Fink and Carrington & Magee, both on Canal St. (now E. Genesee St.), are named. From the August 8, 1850 *Onondaga Gazette's Business Directory* are listed the Empire Blacksmith Shop (Perry & Kasso) on the south side of the river near the bridge and Cronkite & Reese on Syracuse St.[10]

The hand written reports of *R. J. Dun & Co.*, predecessor to the financial rating firm Dun & Bradstreet, are housed in the historical collections of the Baker Library at the Harvard Business School. They list 35 blacksmiths in Lysander and Van Buren, on which they provided financial ratings during the period 1861 to 1883. These listings provide a vivid insight into the importance of blacksmithing in the 19th century. The ledgers are hand written so it is likely this author made errors in interpreting the spelling. The location is followed by the names of the blacksmiths and then the year or years of the analysis by the *Dun Co.* The years listed provide no indication of when the businesses started or when they ceased to exist. The list, which is by no means a complete list of blacksmiths in the two towns, is as follows.

Baldwinsville: Joseph Russell, 78 & 80; John Bollow, 62; Jeremiah Fink, 61; Hilton & Eggleston, 69 to 83; B.Y. Veeder, 78; Joseph Fugett, 79; Joseph Larmer, 75; James M. Fugett, 83; James Russell, 81; Michael Neupert, 82; Beeder & Hoolihan, 77 & 78.

Jacks Reef: Thomas Cavenor, 74.

Little Utica: George Fisher, 71; Alanson Dunham, 69.

Lysander: Thomas Hammond, 69; John Irvine, 69; David G. Lown, 69; Andrew W. Baird, 69, Seager & Vinal, 70; Sylvester Seager, 82.

Memphis: R.P. Newport, 76; Charles Nagley, 73; Mrs. Charles Nagley, 75.

Plainville: David Dennie, 71; Jacob Lamb, 76; James Schenck, 76; John Bratt, 79 Charles Bratt, 82; John Bratt & Son, 83; John Scott, 77 to 82; Edward Fay, 79.

Polkville: Joseph Virginia, 72; F. Whitbeck, 82.

Warners: Wellington Bros., 74; William Wellington, 81 (both of these were listed as blacksmiths and wagon makers)

On the southeast corner of the Plainville four-corners, Fred Pickard operated a blacksmith shop from about 1920 to the 1950s. He had a forge that burned coke and a hand cranked centrifugal blower to force air into his forge. He repaired almost anything made from iron and made replacement parts for the tools of many local farmers. He sold farm machinery in the 1920s and also did horseshoeing. Possibly there were other blacksmiths still operating in the Baldwinsville area at that time but Mr. Pickard is the only one the author remembers.

Without question there were numerous other blacksmiths located in the two towns in the years prior to World War II. Blacksmiths, although very important, in common with school teachers and farmers, were not often named in historical writings. Refer to the appendix for additional listings of blacksmiths.

---

10 Palmer, Pearl *Historical Review of the Town of Lysander* Parts 118 and 119

6

Sawmills

A sawmill was one of the first businesses in the Baldwinsville area. Until the sawmill appeared, area buildings were made of either logs or poles covered with bark, not especially desirable during the cold winters of Central New York.

For centuries, a pit saw powered by two men was the accepted method of sawing lumber. A pit saw was similar to a cross cut saw except it was longer and had different handles. The log being sawed was placed over a pit with one sawyer (called a pitman) standing below the log and the other sawyer (called the tiller) standing above, directly on the log. The log was cut on the down stroke as the pitman pulled the saw down, and then the tiller pulled the blade back up into position for another stroke. It was a long, slow process, sawing one board at a time. This method was not commonly used in 19th America except where waterpower was unavailable.

The Baldwinsville area had numerous sources of waterpower. Sawmills were constructed, using a similar "up and down" method to the pit saw, but were powered by water. The common name for the sawmills using this type of saw was sash mill. These mills were quite inefficient as 50% of the stroke was waste motion since they cut only on the down stroke. Some mills were constructed with "gang saws", which could cut several boards at once but these were only used where there was a large source of waterpower. Circular saws were invented in the 1830s and by about 1845 they came into common use. They were faster and more efficient as they provided continuous cutting with less friction.

Water dropping in elevation powered a water wheel and the circular motion of the water wheel was converted to the up and down motion of the saw blade by a connecting rod known as a pitman arm. The waterpower made sawing much faster and provided greater accuracy. The first sawmills were simple structures covered with a roof and sides partially covered with slab wood. Before the movable carriage, also water-powered, was invented, the logs had to be moved forward into the saw by hand. The sawmill operator needed to be well versed in filing and setting the saw to maintain a keen edge and appropriate width of cut to permit the saw to easily move through the wood.

White pine was a favored tree species for much of the finish carpentry in buildings. There were hundreds of acres of magnificent white pine trees west of Baldwinsville on the sandy and gravelly soils in the Beaver Lake area. James L. Voorhees, referred to as "the tall pine of Plainville" was extremely successful buying land, harvesting timber and turning the timber into structures. Other species of trees utilized by the sawmills were chestnut, oak, maple, cherry, sycamore, beech and hemlock. The fertile soils in the area, coupled with adequate rainfall, permitted nature to provide thousands of acres of virgin forests for the logger, sawmill and the builders of Central New York.

The sawmill supplied lumber for houses, commercial buildings, public buildings, bridges, furniture, tools, pipe, caskets, wagons, sleighs, barrels, roads and a multitude of other uses. The number of people employed using lumber to

A sawmill at Old Sturbridge similar to the sawmills in and around Baldwinsville in the middle of the 19th century. Logs are waiting to be sawn on the right of the picture and the water wheel and millpond are out of sight in the rear.

manufacture all of these items was far greater than the number of people cutting the trees and sawing them into lumber. The economy of the area was fed by the lumbering industry for over half a century.

The Seneca River served not only as a source of power, but also as a means of transporting the logs from forest to sawmill. Logs were floated down the river in log rafts with the logs held together by chains, wooden pegs and saplings. A marking axe, sometimes referred to as a branding iron, was used to mark the ends of the logs to show ownership.

In areas where the Seneca River was not available for floating logs to a mill, it was easier to bring the sawmill to the logs rather than to haul the logs to the sawmill. This is why several sawmills appeared at various points along the outlet to Beaver Lake.

The Seneca River, Baldwin Canal, Oswego Canal and the Erie Canal served the Baldwinsville area as an outstanding conduit for the marketing of the sawed lumber. The lumber could be transported to distant markets quite economically on this water system. Locally sawed lumber was used in most of the older structures of area communities and by wood based industries in Baldwinsville, but this amounted to a very small percentage of the total lumber sawed.

The *1824 Gazetteer of the State of New York* indicates that there were six sawmills in the town of Lysander. None are listed for Van Buren since it was formed in 1829 from part of the town of Camillus. We do know, at that time, there were at least two sawmills in what is now Van Buren for they are noted in Scisco's *Early History of the Town of Van Buren* as having been built prior to 1824. The sawmill was an important industry in the area as evidenced by the *1835 New York Census* showing 17 sawmills in Lysander and six in Van Buren. The number of sawmills decreased in Lysander to 13 in 1845, and to nine in 1855. In Van Buren the number of sawmills stayed the same in 1845 but dropped to two in 1855. As the forests gradually disappeared the sawmill industry faded away.

In 1807, Dr. Jonas Baldwin constructed the first sawmill in Baldwinsville, near the mouth of Tannery Creek. To provide a sufficient supply of water to the sawmill, Dr. Baldwin had constructed a wing dam partway across the river. An error had been made in determining elevations and there was insufficient waterpower to operate the mill. The next year he constructed a dam across the entire Seneca River and was able, in the fall of 1808, to put the sawmill into operation.[1] In 1819-20 a second sawmill was erected on the riverbank west of Oswego Street. Start & Mott built a sawmill, which had two saws in 1824. This mill burned in 1834 and later was rebuilt

---

1 Clayton, W.W. *History of Onondaga County* p. 316

by Richard M. Beach. In 1826, James Johnson had a mill with four saws and the same year Stephen & Harvey Baldwin erected a mill on the south side of the river. This mill had a "gang" of 15 saws so that an entire log was sawed into boards in one operation. In 1839, Thomas P. Campbell had a mill with four saws and carriages. In 1848, Howard and Cool erected a mill with two saws.[2]

A significant amount of waterpower was necessary to operate all of these saws. The sawmills of Baldwinsville were turning out thousands of feet of lumber daily.

Following is a comprehensive summation of the Baldwinsville sawmill industry provided by A. J. Christopher in his column, *Sketches of Yesterday* published in the *Baldwinsville Messenger* on January 25, 1968.

> "From 1807 to the fifties, at least a dozen sawmills were built within the village, some containing as many as six saws to completely rip a log in one operation. All these old mills operated on power created by the force from the Seneca River, and they were pretty well scattered about. They ran and developed a prosperous industry until the supply of nearby timber became depleted.
>
> There was a sawmill at both ends of the dam. At least one stood on either side of Bridge Street* on the 'island'. South of the river, where later the paper mill* and the stone flourmill* rose in place, James Johnson and the Baldwin Brothers had three sawmills running as early as 1825. Down the old Baldwin* or Power Canal, three more sawmills once turned virgin timber into building material.
>
> The last village sawmills – for the many dwindled as the forests became extinct – remained on the long neck of land called 'the Island'. Frazee & Decker's Mill* stood on the lot of the flourmill that also carried the Frazee name. Lumber was sawed here as late as the early nineties.

---
2   Hall, Edith *The History of Baldwinsville* p. 15

This is the flume bringing water from the millpond to the water wheel, which powers the saw. It was common practice to lay up stones for the flume to withstand the continual passage of water flowing to the water wheel. Photo at Old Sturbridge Village by the author

Probably the final one in operation may have been the Fairbanks and Taggart Mill at the end of Lock Street, but on the heel path of the old canal. Built about 1839, it continued to turn out lumber for over half a century. The power of running the different machines used here was furnished by three Camden water wheels, two of 60 horsepower and one of 40. In the early years all the saws were of the up-and-down variety but the circular type gradually came into use after 1840.

- *Bridge Street – ran from the intersection of Elizabeth and Oswego Street to the Baldwin Canal Bridge.*
- *Paper Mill – located on Paper Mill Island.*
- *Stone Flour Mill – was on the south bank of the river behind 4 Syracuse Street.*
- *Baldwin Canal – ran from River St. along Genesee (Canal St.) to Lock and turned south to reenter the river at the end of Lock.*
- *Frazee & Decker Sawmill – 24 East Genesee Street."*

Boyd's *1881 Directory of Onondaga County* lists only the W.L. Frazee sawmill in Baldwinsville. The *1892-3 Boyd's Directory of Onondaga County* lists a Fairbanks & Taggert sawmill on Canal Street. These two mills represented the end of the great sawmill industry in Baldwinsville.

Other sawmills were being established in Lysander & Van Buren in settlements outside of Baldwinsville. In 1825, Dunham & Baker built a sawmill at the outlet of Beaver Lake near Little Utica, which was still operating in 1878.[3]

In *Boyd's 1876 Onondaga County Directory* a sawmill is listed as being operated by N.C. Dunham, and in *Boyd's 1881 Directory of Onondaga County* a sawmill is listed owned by Dunham & Bellinger. Both of these Little Utica listings may have been the same mill.

In 1829, John Wall built a sawmill on the west bank of the Oswego River at Phoenix.[4] A sawmill is shown on *Sweet's Map of 1874*, which is likely to have been the same sawmill.[5]

There was also a sawmill at the bend of Gates Road, near the Seneca River on Pea Hawk Creek, owned by the Voorhees family. A sawmill was sporadically operated on this farm until the 1950s. Originally the sawmill was powered by water from a millpond but in later years was powered by a gasoline engine.

The *Onondaga County Directory of 1886* lists a sawmill in Plainville operated by Bowen & Smith. No sawmill other than the Voorhees sawmill had been listed previously in the Plainville area. Since no other known source of waterpower existed, the Bowen & Smith Sawmill may have been powered by a steam engine.

Louis Dow Scisco in his *Early History of Van Buren* tells of several sawmills in Van Buren.

In 1815, or possibly earlier, Nathan Skeels and Solomon Paddock constructed a sawmill on Lot 18, north of Ionia in Bangall.

In 1822, Reuben, Levi and Daniel Elsworth built a sawmill a little further north in Bangall. Over time, both mills had different owners and operated sporadically.

A little later John McHarrie Jr. and Gabriel Tappen constructed a mill on Lot 7 on Crooked Brook. He noted that the dam broke in 1845 and the mill was abandoned and later rebuilt. (just south of Baldwinsville)

Further up Crooked Brook, Hiram H. and James A. Scoville in 1824 built a sawmill on Lot 13. This mill had several different owners over the years.

Scisco notes that a little later, Joseph Hopkins constructed a sawmill on Lot 21 still further south on Crooked Brook. (near Canton St. Road about halfway to Warners) Interestingly, he remarked that the mill closed in the 1850s when timber ran out.

About 1825 James Johnson had a sawmill near the south end of the dam in Baldwinsville, which was run by different owners until the 1850s. (Later there was a distillery on this site and a succession of paper mills.)

Issac Hill built a sawmill west of Dead Creek on Lot 3 in 1825, which had different owners until 1886.

In 1843, Belding Resseguie, on his own farm and at great expense constructed a sawmill and a millpond. He excavated and tapped springs on his farm as well as neighboring farms running the water to the pond

---

3 Clayton, W.W. *History of Onondaga County* p. 326
4 Palmer, Pearl *Historical Review of the Town of Lysander* part 87
5 Sweet, Homer D. L. *Atlas of Onondaga County* p. 19

This sawmill is using an up and down vertical saw to cut the log. The saw cut only on the down stroke so the process was relatively inefficient. A number of the Baldwinsville sawmills, with sufficient water power from the river, had several saws, side by side, about an inch apart and could cut an entire log into boards with one pass. All sawmills used the up and down saw at the time the Baldwinsville area was settled as the circular saw did not become common until the middle of the 19th century. Photo at Old Sturbridge Village by the author

in hollowed out logs. It was abandoned in 1859.[6]

The *Onondaga County Directory of 1868* lists a sawmill and cider mill operated by Warren Ingoldsby at Memphis. This was the mill on the site of the original Paddock sawmill, which had been rebuilt in about 1832 by Ira Barnes. It was rebuilt again by George Wood and successively run by Wood, Jonathan Warner, Simon Warner and Warren Ingoldsby. It was still in partial operation in 1895.[7]

A.J. Christopher, in his *Sketches of Yesterday* column published May 22, 1969 in the *Baldwinsville Messenger*, describes seven sawmill sites that had been powered by water from the outlet of Beaver Lake. He stated:

"*In a notarized instrument sworn to before Justice of the Peace N.C. Dunham, dated August 24, 1867, Enoch Ferguson leased to James Smyth the (site 1) mill site for 99 years and that Smyth may build a dam across the outlet of Mud Lake and raise the said lake one foot above the low water mark.*" He goes on to say, "*that each of these mills was about 1/3 mile apart except for the seventh, which was known as Cook's Mill located slightly south of the County Line Road.*"

---
6 Scisco, Louis Dow *Early History of the Town of Van Buren* p. 41-42
7 Ibid p. 41

(about four miles north of the lake) "Other operators of the mill in addition to the Cook family were Woodruff, Hudson and Howard Johnson. Site No. 2 was at Picketville located between Ellison Road and Little Utica. This sawmill was listed on Fagan's map of 1854. Site No. 3 was about 1/3 mile further and Site No. 4 was slightly north of Lamson Road. In 1860 and later, this mill was operated by the Dunham Brothers and Bellinger. A cheese factory operated at this site at a later date. On site No. 5 a mill was started just west of East Mud Lake Road but never completed. Site No. 6 was another 1/3 mile further north on the outlet and operated at one time by a Mr. Dickie."

The *New York State Business Directory of 1876* states that there was a sawmill near Lysander operated by Richard Clute and Francis Perine. *Sweet's Map of 1874* shows a sawmill adjacent to Halsted's gristmill near Baird's Corners, which may have been the sawmill listed.

The *Baldwinsville Directories of 1950 and 1957* both list Parks & Aller Sawmill on Van Buren Road. This sawmill was located near where the Van Buren town offices are at this time. Elias Turner told the author that in the 1940s Harry Johnson was still operating a sawmill in Bangall.

The Stachurski Brothers operated a sawmill on Rt. 370 at the north end of Tater Rd, one half-mile west of Plainville, from the 1950s to the 1990s. They sawed many kinds of wood but specialized in hard woods for the furniture industry.

In the last 20 years there have been a number of people in the area who have purchased small portable sawmills. Some saw only at one location while others move their mills to the source of logs for perhaps a day or for several days. These are normally part-time sawmills and use the newer band saws.

Logs are still being harvested from woodlots on farms in Lysander and Van Buren today. A well-managed woodlot is thinned about every 20 years with just the mature trees being removed. Most of the logs from these trees are transported on special logging trucks to sawmills within 100 miles. The wood from these logs can end up in almost any part of the world. On occasion, a piece of the lumber may come back in the form of furniture near the home of the tree from which it was nourished.

7

Gristmills

Baldwinsville was a major wheat-milling village for well over 100 years. Waterpower from the Seneca River, transportation on the Baldwin Canal and the Seneca River, along with the fertile farmland in the area all contributed to its success. In later years the railroad, for both receiving grain and shipping flour, was of great importance.

Soon after a blacksmith arrived and a sawmill was constructed in a community, the gristmill followed. A gristmill was a much more elaborate structure than a sawmill and needed a substantial amount of sawed lumber for its erection. The flume, which carried the water to the water wheel, and the water wheel and the power train were all made from sawed lumber. All of these essential components also needed the skills of a blacksmith to bring a working gristmill into fruition. The building needed to be of substantial height for storage of grain above the millstones and for the processing and storage of the flour below. Barrels were made from sawed lumber to transport the flour. There was no possibility for a gristmill to exist without the sawmill and the blacksmith.

The miller needed considerable financial resources to build a mill and substantial expertise to run it. Setting up a mill required technical knowledge in order to produce a good quality product efficiently. In addition, millstones, which weighed several hundred pounds, had to be purchased and transported from a stone quarry often many miles away. Millstones needed to be hewn from very hard rock, which was often granite or sandstone. Millstones manufactured in France worked very well but were expensive. The stones had to be "dressed" regularly to maintain sharp edges to cut the kernels of grain passing between the stones into fine particles. A special steel hammer called a millpick was used to sharpen the edges of the furrows in the millstones. The millpick required a critical temper to sustain its pounding on the hard stone surface. Skill was required to dress a stone properly and when a number of mills developed a professional traveled from mill to mill sharpening the millstones. A stone with sharp grooves produced a much finer grind than a dull stone, enabling the miller to produce high quality flour.

The first settlers in an area were forced to use a mortar and pestle to grind their grain. This would have been the method used by the John McHarrie, Jonathan Palmer and other early settlers' families in their first years in the Baldwinsville area. Pounding grain in a hollowed out tree stump with a heavy piece of wood to obtain flour was a long slow process.

In 1793, a gristmill was constructed on Butternut Creek about 15 miles from Baldwinsville, but without roads a trip of that distance through the forest with a sack of grain on a person's back was impractical. In 1806, a gristmill was built in Camillus, which was closer, but still a long and difficult trip. It is no wonder that the settlers in the Baldwinsville area looked to Dr. Jonas Baldwin with hope for a solution to their milling difficulties. The construction of the dam across the Seneca River in 1808 and the subsequent gristmill were great steps forward for the new community. There does not

This waterwheel, similar to some in the Baldwinsville area, is of double width and furnished twice the power of a similar narrower width wheel. The weight of the water on the wheel, combined with the distance of the fall, determine the power a waterwheel generates. Photo at Old Sturbridge Village by the author

seem to be a definitive date for the first gristmill but a quote from Dwight Bruce's *Onondaga Centennial* follows: "*Soon after building the new dam (1810) Dr. Baldwin erected a new and larger gristmill.*" It is likely that his first gristmill had been erected at the time the first dam was completed in 1808 or early 1809. (The second gristmill was converted into a woolen mill and later operated by Kellogg & Farr.[1])

The gristmill was an important business in any early 19th century community for several reasons. Flour was an important ingredient in bread, cakes, pies and other common household foods. In addition, farm animals made more effective use of ground grain than of the whole kernels. An often overlooked and important need for the gristmill was to grind grain for the production of whiskey, which was commonly consumed by the early settlers.

The first mills for grinding grain were called gristmills rather than flourmills. Grist is a term used to describe grain for grinding. The grist passed between two grooved millstones, which broke the kernels of grain into numerous particles of varying size. It was common practice for the end user to have several horsehair sieves to sift the grain into fine flour, medium flour, coarse flour and larger particles. The coarser particles were often fed to livestock. The housewife used the fine flour for her finest baked goods often making the bottom crust of a pie with coarser flour and the top crust with the finer flour. This is where the term "top crust" comes from, referring to the best.

---
1 Hall, Edith *History of Baldwinsville*

The farmers brought their grain (grist) to the mill in sacks made from flax. The sacks of grain were dumped into a hopper above the millstones. Wooden gearing transferred power from the water wheel to the top millstone (the runner stone), which turned slowly above the fixed bottom stone (the bed stone) pulverizing the kernels of grain between the two stones. The top stone could be adjusted up or down to affect the size of the grain particles. It was critical that the stones be positioned properly as stones touching each other could ruin the flour and damage each other. The bed stone had to be carefully leveled before use. The runner stone was movable and had to be balanced to prevent it from rubbing heavily against the bed stone. This was accomplished by placing small weights at appropriate locations on top of the runner stone.

Wooden shovels and scoops were the preferred tools as metal tools could cause a spark and start a fire. Dust in a mill was very explosive and mills were always in danger of fire.

Grain ground for livestock was often referred to as custom grinding and was not ground as finely as flour for human consumption. The grist brought to the mill was returned to the farmer for feeding his livestock. Grain used for the manufacture of whiskey also had a coarser grind.

In the early 1800s it was common practice for the miller to be paid by taking a portion of the grain, usually about one-eighth. It was a form of

A millstone at the Mercer Milling Company, 4 Syracuse St., being moved by John Naylor and Gardner Mercer for sharpening in this 1954 picture. The runner stone, which weighed several hundred pounds, had to be removed from the bed stone so both could be sharpened with a mill pick. It was an exacting job that only a well-trained person could do successfully. Dull stones produced less valuable coarse flour. Photo courtesy of OHA Museum & Research Center

This picture shows the wooden housing that encloses the millstones and the hopper where the grain is dumped for grinding. There is a movable slide at the bottom of the hopper to regulate the flow of grain. The eight-sided wooden housing serves both to keep flour from escaping and to exclude any foreign matter from contaminating the flour. Photo at Old Sturbridge Village by the author

barter with no money changing hands. As a means of protecting the customer, laws were often passed limiting the portion of grain that the miller could retain as payment.

With the passage of time, local gristmills began being referred to as flourmills as additional equipment was added. The flour, after passing between the millstones, was conveyed to a bolter that sifted the flour into different grades. The bolter enabled the baker to purchase flour of the desired coarseness to meet his needs. Gradually some of the larger flourmills changed from millstones to steel roller mills, which were faster and more efficient.

Wheat was almost as revered as cash in the early 1800s. Wheat was the farmers' cash crop, which paid for the farm, taxes on the land and many of the items that required money for purchase. Wheat crops flourished in Central New York until about 1845 when a small insect called the midge invaded the local farmers' wheat fields. Although the quantity grown locally decreased after that date, production of wheat still continues on local farms today. Obtaining wheat for the local mills was not a problem even after 1845, as the Erie Canal opened 20 years earlier and thousands of bushels of wheat were being shipped east from western New York, Ohio and the Midwest. Shipments via the Erie Canal to Syracuse and then on the Oswego Canal to the Seneca River were cost effective. Later the railroad brought wheat to the local mills and transported flour to distant points.

In 1872, great quantities of grain came to the

This photograph is looking northeast from the south side of the Seneca River and shows the Amos flourmill, south of E. Genesee St. and east of Oswego St. It was sometimes called the Empire mill and was erected in 1868. This location had previously been the site of the Old Red Mill, which was constructed in 1835 and burned in 1842. A private flume brought water from behind the dam, under the J.C. & J.C. Miller knitting mill located northwest of the bridge, across Oswego St., under a three-story building, to the Amos Mill's water wheels. The Amos Mill, although huge and costing $100,000, was not as large a producer of flour as the Frazee Mill.

Baldwinsville flourmills by horse-drawn boats with barrels and sacks of flour going out in the same manner. Canal receipts indicated that Jacob Amos received 41,000 bushels of corn, barley and wheat in October of that year. In April of the same year, 4,435 barrels and 4,574 sacks of flour were shipped by railroad from Baldwinsville.[2]

As mentioned earlier, flour milling was big business in Baldwinsville. Stephen W. Baldwin and John McHarrie, Jr. erected another famous mill in 1830-31. It was on the south side of the river and was known as the "White Mill", later becoming known as the Farmers' Mill.[3] The mill continued to operate as Mercer's Mill into the 1980s, still grinding grain with the old millstones. The old mill was remodeled into the Red Mill Inn in 2006 and still contains much of the timber from the original 1830 mill.

In 1836-7, Sandford C. Parker built a 60 by 100 foot, four-story gristmill with a basement. It was capable of grinding 200 barrels of flour a day in addition to custom grinding.[4] It was erected with local limestone from the Bigelow quarry near the corner of Route 48 and Church Road.[5]

W.W. Clayton's 1878 book, *History of Onondaga County* lists five mills in Baldwinsville that had a total capacity of over 1,000 barrels of flour a day.

---

2 Christopher, A.J. *Baldwinsville a Century Ago* August 16, 1972
3 Hall, Edith *History of Baldwinsville* p.16
4 Clayton, W.W. *History of Onondaga County* p. 318
5 Hall, Edith *History of Baldwinsville* p. 16

- James Frazee & Co., 50 by 100 foot building of four stories, constructed in 1859- 60. (It was operated as a feed mill until 1957 when it was destroyed by fire. It was located south of the Baldwin Canal, at approximately 34 E. Genesee St., across from the present Baldwinsville Library.)
- Jacob Amos & Sons, on the site of Old Red Mill erected around 1835 and burned in 1842, cost $100,000 when constructed in 1868. (It was located where the Baldwinsville Fire Department site was in the late 20th century, north of the bridge and east of 10 Oswego St.)
- G.H. & A.T. Hotaling in 1870, commenced operations, in the Stone Mill erected by Sanford C. Parker in 1836 and purchased by Johnson, Cook & Co. in 1854. This mill had changed hands several times after the Johnson, Cook purchase, prior to the Hotaling purchase. The Hotalings operated it successfully until it was totally destroyed in a fire in 1898. It had a capacity of 200 barrels of merchant flour a day. (Back of what is now the Red Mill Inn at 4 Syracuse St.)
- D. & G. Morris mill stood on the "second privilege" and was known for a long time as the Farmers' Mill of Van Buren. (Later became Mercer Milling Co., where the Red Mill Inn is now located at 4 Syracuse St..)
- W. L. Wilkins Flour and Feed Mills with four runs of stones was built in 1854.
  (Later this mill was operated by Rumont Kratzer who renamed it Seneca Mills and then by Clarence E. Hart. It was on the site later occupied by the American Knife Works and slightly west of the location of the Lysander Town Hall at 6 Lock St. in the latter part of the 20th century.)

There was an occasional gristmill outside of Baldwinsville in each of the two towns. A gristmill required a good flow of water to provide the

The James Frazee & Co. flourmill was constructed in 1859 and located between the Baldwin Canal and the Seneca River, across East Genesee St. from the present library. The facility had capacity to mill 500 barrels of flour daily and was the largest flourmill producer in Baldwinsville. It operated as a mill and a feed store until 1957 when it was destroyed by fire. Note the canal boat in the slip at the right of the picture. The mill had a cooperage shop in the rear where they made barrels in which to ship the flour. Photo courtesy of OHA Museum & Research Center

The Wilkins or Seneca Mill was erected in 1854. It was the smallest of the major Baldwinsville mills and was founded by William L. Wilkins. The building stood between the river and the old canal, somewhat back of the present Dunkin Donuts on East Genesee Street. Water from the Baldwin Canal turned the waterwheels that powered the mill. Mr. Wilkins ran the mill until 1889 when he sold it to John Bellen. Ownership changed several times with this small mill once called Hart's Mill from the name of one of the owners. Towards the last, Rumont Kratzer operated the mill for a number of years. The Seneca Mill property, after lying idle for some time, was acquired in 1902 by the American Knife Works. It was the site of the Town of Lysander offices from the 1960s to the early 2000s.

necessary power to operate and there were few locations where streams provided a sufficient quantity of water.

James Paddock built a gristmill in about 1817 on Lot 19 a little north of Bangall. It passed through several hands and in 1825 became owned by Calvin and Chauncy Goodrich who built a distillery to run in conjunction with the mill.[6]

In the 1840s, Albion J. Larkin constructed a gristmill on the brook on Lot 18, near the earlier sawmill sites. (East of both Dead Creek and Lot 19) Later, it was turned into a cotton mill.[7]

---

6 Scisco, Louis Dow *Early History of the Town of Van Buren* p. 42
7 Ibid

Dwight Bruce, in his book *Onondaga Centennial*, states there was an early gristmill operated by Thomas Ambler in Baird's Corners. The *1859-60 Onondaga County Directory* listed a gristmill in Lysander owned by George W. Kennedy. The *1868-9 Onondaga County Directory* lists Herman Halsted operating a gristmill near the village of Lysander. It is quite likely that both the 1859 and the 1868 references refer to the same gristmill as the one Bruce refers to. Baird's Corners was only a mile and a half north of Lysander and mail for that hamlet came to Lysander. *Sweet's Map of 1874* shows a gristmill north of Lysander near Coppernoll Road owned by Herman Halsted, which is indicative that all three references are probably for the same mill. Herman

The Stone Mill, constructed by Sanford C. Parker in 1836 from limestone quarried about a mile north of Baldwinsville, was located west of today's Red Mill Inn on the eastern end of Paper Mill Island. The flourmill measured 60 feet by 100 feet and was four stories high. At the time of construction it had 11 run of stone for the milling of grain. The mill was purchased by Johnson, Cook and Co. in 1854 and was partially destroyed by fire in 1861. It changed hands several times and was purchased by G.H. & A.T. Hotaling in 1870 and was totally destroyed in a fire in 1898.

Halsted was still listed as the owner of a gristmill in Lysander in *Boyd's 1881 Business Directory of Onondaga County*. There is an advertisement in the June 14, 1888 *Gazette and Farmers' Journal* by Sullivan & Bogardus of Lysander notifying customers that their mill will run for custom grinding after June 9 only on Wednesdays and Saturdays. The author suspects this is the same mill mentioned earlier and that a short supply of water curtailed the milling operation.

Very often, history is a mystery. For example, an article in the April 4, 1884 *Syracuse Standard* stated that a sawmill and flourmill had burned near Plainville the previous February. The article also stated that the mill was owned by Judge Voorhees and leased by William Ford. In talking with Bonnie Kisselstein, Town of Lysander Historian, she said that she was descended from William Ford and that the mill was on Coppernoll Road. Perhaps Sullivan & Bogardus replaced the burned mill or operated at another location.

The *Onondaga County Directory of 1868* lists Harry Shants as a miller. In all probability this mill was located in the Bangall area. *Boyd's Onondaga County Directory of 1870* lists a miller by the name of A. R. Palmer at Little Utica. This mill would have been located on the Beaver Lake outlet. More than likely both of these mills operated sporadically to grind grain for livestock or for distilling.

As progress in the milling industry continued, the mills in Baldwinsville made improvements to remain competitive. There were times when the

This is a circa 1950 image of the Mercer Milling Co., now the Red Mill Inn, at 4 Syracuse St. The mill was constructed in 1827 by Stephen W. Baldwin and was known as the McHarrie Mill. It was later known as the D. & G. Morris Mill, the Farmer's Mill of Van Buren and the Clark & Mercer Mill.

flow of water in the Seneca was insufficient to power the water wheels. Steam power was first installed in the 1870s to provide power when the water wheels would not operate.

About 1880, Mr. Amos was the first to install roller mills, which crushed the grain and tended to make better flour. Soon after, most of the other Baldwinsville mills also changed from millstones to metal roller mills.

Near the latter part of the 19th century, the flour industry of Baldwinsville was diminishing. The flour milling industry was moving further to the west. Midwestern cities on the Great Lakes became the large production centers because of their proximity to major areas of wheat production and favorable freight rates for direct shipments to the coast. Other factors such as the movement away from barrels holding 196 pounds of flour to sacks and bulk shipments, and the development of larger steam engines and electric motors all played a part. Improved milling machinery was being produced and replacement of older equipment in local mills was not practical in most cases. The *1909 Baldwinsville Directory* lists only two mills: Clark and Mercer at 6 Syracuse Street and the Frazee Milling Co. at 24 East Genesee Street, across from Morris Machine Works.

The Clark & Mercer Mill, later known as Mercer's Mill, continued in business until the 1980s producing specialty flours and servicing the needs of local farms. They continued to operate with waterpower and still used stone millstones to grind their grain. The mill served as a mixing and distribution center for manufactured feed ingredients until 2002 and was sold in 2005. It was then converted into the Red Mill Inn, which offers fine lodging and rooms for special events.

The Frazee Milling Co. started construction of a new "state of the art" flourmill in 1920 at 75 East Genesee Street adjacent to the railroad, and it began operations in 1923. The Frazee interests ran the mill spasmodically into the 1930s when it was sold. It had several different owners until purchased by the International Milling Company in 1943. International produced more than 200 tons of semolina flour daily. (Semolina flour is produced from durum wheat and is primarily used for pasta.)[8] ConAgra purchased the mill as part of a package deal in 1988 and operated it for about three years. The mill was closed in the early 1990s and was sold in 2000. Subsequently the mill was demolished and a new building was constructed, which now holds the North Side Collision Co.

Once the dominant industry of Lysander and Van Buren, gristmills and flourmills have completely disappeared and now are only a piece of history. The flour used by consumers comes from hundreds or thousands of miles away. Farmers that used ground feed for their livestock either grind it on the farm or purchase it from outside the area. The mill stones that helped make the flour mills operate now lie buried under the rubble of old mills, and any that are still visible, like the ones at the Van Buren Town building, are for decorative purposes to remind residents of the community's rich milling history.

---

8 Christopher, A.J., *Our Old Flouring Mills* April 23, 1964

8

Coopers

Coopers are probably one of the least recognized manufacturers in Central New York. In the days prior to steel barrels, plastic containers, cardboard boxes and bulk handling, much of what was manufactured in Central New York was packed and shipped in casks or barrels manufactured by local coopers. Flour, salt, beverages, fruit, meat, potatoes, nails, horseshoes and a multitude of other items all went into barrels made by coopers.

Coopering, the art of making wooden containers out of staves and hoops, is an ancient trade that attained a high degree of perfection centuries ago. Barrels (staved containers with a bulge) were widely used in the Roman Empire. Straight-sided containers, made of staves and hoops, such as pails and tubs were in use at least 3,000 years earlier. By the 12th century, wooden barrels were the standard means of transporting both liquid and dry products. The cooper had become indispensable![1]

The only raw material used by the cooper was wood, and Baldwinsville was surrounded by one gigantic forest. Staves, the sides of all containers made by the cooper, came from the sawmill in the form of boards, which were cut to length and shaped by the cooper. Some sawmills took the sawing a step further and furnished rough staves for assembly into barrels. In 1829, Gardiner Northrup manufactured barrel staves on the west bank of the Oswego River at Phoenix.[2] Many local men with other jobs assembled barrels at home in their spare time. Hoops around the barrel to hold the staves together were made from small saplings that were split lengthwise. In the latter part of the 19th century hoops were made of iron but by this time metal drums and cardboard boxes were rapidly replacing wooden barrels.

Coopers used a number of tools that were common to other types of woodworkers including the shaving horse, froe, drawknife and adz. There were also several special tools designed specifically for the cooper. The cresset was an iron basket in which wood was burned inside an open-ended barrel. The heat and steam produced made the staves pliable enough to be bent. The howel cut a channel about an inch below the chime bevel (the bevel cut on the end of each stave) inside the barrel and the croze cut a narrow groove inside the howel channel into which the barrelhead was forced. Two other tools were the scorper, used to shave the inside of the barrel smooth, and the bung auger, to drill the bung-hole for filling and draining barrels with liquid contents. Pearl Palmer wrote that one of the products produced by R. Rogers of Baldwinsville in 1846 was barrel-bungs. Coopers' tools are commonly available at antique shows and the numbers that have survived is an indication of the large number of coopers in the 1800s.

Although a filled barrel was heavy, it could be moved quite easily by rolling or when standing on end, it could be moved short distances by partially tipping it and turning it on its chime. During colonial days, in the southern states, tobacco was packed

---
1   Arbor, Marilyn *Tools & Trades of America's Past* p. 26
2   Palmer, Pearl *Historical Review of the Town of Lysander* Part 87

A cooper is at work shaping one of the bands, which encompass the barrel to hold the staves tightly together. Wooden bands split from small saplings were used prior to the more recent metal hoops. The barrels in the photo show both kinds of hoops. In the 1800s, many men in the Baldwinsville area were employed as coopers, some full time and others working part-time by the piece. Photo taken by the author at Old Sturbridge Village

in huge hogsheads (large barrels) and rolled onto ships heading to Europe.

There were three kinds of coopers. The wet cooper was highly skilled and made barrels that would hold products like beer, whiskey and cider. The dry cooper made barrels for dry products like apples, potatoes and china that didn't need the staves fitted quite as closely. The third kind of cooper was called the white cooper, and he made all types of straight-sided vessels such as pails, tubs and vats.[3]

Actually, dry coopers are divided into two categories; dry tight and dry slack. Dry tight coopers made many of the barrels produced in the Baldwinsville area to hold flour or salt. These barrels had to be tight enough to keep the fine particles inside and outside moisture from coming into the barrel.

There are a number of historical references regarding the cooperage businesses in the Lysander village area. An unpublished reference by Missy Eileen Shapiro in *Time Past; People, Life and Landscapes in Northern Lysander*, states that coopers were a significant group in both Betts and Baird's Corners. Pearl Palmer writes that Mrs. Spratt Hull, born in 1860, remembered three cooper shops in Lysander from which barrels were drawn to Jordan for shipment on the Erie Canal. *Boyd's 1859 Directory of Onondaga County* names Hastings Merrifield and Norman Merrifield as coopers.

---

3 Arbor, Marilyn *Tools & Trades of America's Past* p. 26

In Baldwinsville, between 1880 and 1900, five flourmills had a capacity of over 1,000 barrels of flour a day. Imagine the lumber and the labor to turn out barrels for all that flour! The Amos and Frazee mills had their own cooperage shops. Frazee's shop, behind the mill, was located across the Baldwin Canal at approximately 34 East Genesee St. Elm hoops were soaked in the Baldwin Canal, and the finished barrels were rolled into the flour mill to be filled. After filling with the standard 196 pounds of flour, the barrels were rolled out the back door onto a boxcar. The Amos Mill's cooper shop was located south of the mill along the river and south of the current village parking lot at approximately 2 Oswego Street. They used the same production line operation as the Frazee Mill.[4]

---
4 Christopher, A.J. *Barrel Industry Flourished Here* March 23, 1967

This is a flour barrel similar to the thousands used to transport flour from the local flourmills to market. This is a dry tight barrel, one that is sufficiently tight to hold flour but not designed to hold liquids. A barrel of flour was required to contain 196 pounds to meet official standards.

There were at least two independent cooper shops in Baldwinsville in the 1880s. The *Dun Co.* mentions visits to Andrew Clary from 1877 to 1883 and also to D. Delane in 1882. Both of these businesses are listed in business directories of 1878 and 1881. There are also two coopers listed in the *1892 Boyd's Syracuse Directory with 40 Villages*: Andrew Clary and Martin Haendle. Listed by occupation in the *Onondaga County Directory of 1868* as Baldwinsville coopers are: Asa Candee, Andrew Clancy, Isaac Hubbard, Delos Kinney, Michael Molumby, Frank Myneer and Isaac Lynn Dettbarn. These gentlemen probably worked in the cooperage shops of various millers, although it is possible that one or more may have operated their own business.

We will never know the number of men in the Baldwinsville area that worked in cooper shops or assembled barrels in their own homes, but it must have been in the hundreds. For example, Robert Nostrant, in his article *The Erie Canal and Cement*, mentions that when the Empire Cement Plant near Warners burned in 1902, 40 men making barrels for that plant were put out of work. The production of that plant, in barrels per day, was less than the total production of the flour milling businesses in Baldwinsville a few years earlier. Maple Road, extending southeast from Baldwinsville, used to be known as Cooper Street because of the number of residents that assembled barrels. The people making barrels in the Baldwinsville area made it possible for other industries to market their products. Coopering is an industry that deserves great recognition for the important part it played in the Baldwinsville area's history.

The last mention of coopers in Baldwinsville was in the *1892 Boyd's Directory*. Coopers rapidly disappeared about a century ago. To observe a cooper at work today we need to visit a museum like Sturbridge Village in MA or travel to a distillery where oak barrels are still being produced to appropriately age and flavor the "spirits" inside.

9

Distilleries

When and where was the first distillery in Lysander and Van Buren? There is probably not an accurate answer to either question. We know distilleries appeared early in newly developing communities. The drinking of liquid spirits was an accepted part of life in the early 1800s. Often water was of poor quality and the consumption of alcohol was standard practice.

Whiskey was the drink of choice in the frontier areas. All one needed was corn, rye or barley, (sometimes a mixture, but usually corn) yeast and some simple equipment to start a small distillery. A gristmill in the area was a real asset as coarse ground grain speeded fermentation and increased the availability of the starch. Water was added to the ground meal and then yeast was added for fermentation in wooden vats for several days. The process changed the starch in the grains to sugar, which changed into alcohol. The alcohol was boiled off and collected for drinking.

There were numerous factors in the process that affected the quality of the whiskey. The kind and quality of the grains, the equipment, the temperatures and the timing of each process, all contributed to the final end product. Traditionally fine whiskey is aged in oak barrels. Often, in early times, there was no aging involved. A reminiscence of Richard Smith, regarding the early Betts Distillery in the hamlet of Lysander, was that the distillery would run off a pail of whiskey during the day, bring it to the store in the evening, and then a tinhorn was blown to notify the customers that the whiskey was on tap.[1]

Whiskey's popularity gradually declined during the 19th century. The two major reasons were a successful temperance campaign and increased prices. There was little effect in Central New York when Congress imposed an excise tax on whiskey to help pay for the War of 1812. This tax ended in 1817 and was not imposed again until 1862 when a 20-cent per gallon tax was placed on whiskey to help pay for the Civil War. The tax reached as high as $2 a gallon during the war and was reduced to 50 cents a gallon in 1868.[2] The distilling of whiskey in the Baldwinsville area ended during this period of high taxation. By this time small distilleries were disappearing and larger distilleries with more modern equipment, greater quality control and strong marketing programs were the survivors.

The *New York Census of Manufacturers in 1810* shows there were two distilleries in Onondaga County that produced a total of 7,232 gallons of whiskey during the previous year. They were likely located further south in the county in communities that had been settled prior to Baldwinsville. The *1820 New York Census of Manufacturers* shows two distilleries in the Town of Lysander. The census report stated the following facts: that Chauncey Betts, in the area of what is now the village of Lysander, during the previous year used 800 bushels of grain, the cost of raw materials was

---
1 Bruce, Dwight H. *Onondaga's Centennial* p. 749
2 Kleber, John E. *The Kentucky Encyclopedia* p. 266

$248, two men were employed, his capital was $350, annual wages were $72, contingent expenses were $75, whiskey manufactured had a value of $600 and that business was fairly good at present.

The *1820 Census of Manufacturers* also shows the distillery of Stonard & Barber located in the town of Lysander used 2,550 bushels of grain costing $970, employed three men, used one steam still, had a capital investment of $500, annual wages of $480, contingent expenses of $30, whiskey manufactured had a value of $1,976 and business was formerly good but at present made bad whiskey and it was not in good demand. (This is a direct statement taken from the original 1820 Census report.)

Pearl Palmer, in Part 81 of *A Historical Review of the Town of Lysander* states there was a distillery west of the village on property owned by Judge Bigelow. Edith Hall in *History of Baldwinsville* refers to a distillery on West Genesee Street west of the village line. These references could have been to the same distillery or two different ones as generally the life of a distillery in those times was relatively short.

A. J. Christopher, in his *Sketches of Yesterday* column of the February 11, 1965 *Baldwinsville Messenger* story, *Old Earthen Dam*, tells of the gristmill on Lot 19 in Van Buren, established by James Paddock in 1817, changing hands and the Goodrich brothers adding a distillery. It was sold numerous times and ran until 1850 as Cook's Distillery. It became unprofitable and closed after running 25 years. Tradition tells of the final barrels of whiskey being buried in Whiskey Hollow to avoid payment of tax. (Possibly giving the area its unusual name.) People of the area later tried to locate the concealed barrels by use of probing sticks.[3] There is no record of any success from their endeavors.

In 1856, Johnson, Cook & Co. purchased Block 36 on Paper Mill Point to use for a distillery along with the adjacent Parker "stone" mill on Block 37. Block 36 had been occupied by a sawmill since 1825. The company later became Wetherby, Cook & Co. The J.H. French Baldwinsville map of 1857 shows that Wetherby, Cook & Co. also owned a large area of vacant land across from Paper Mill Point and a large tract of land south of Downer Street and west of Canton Street, in addition to the previously mentioned two mill sites.

Waste mash from the distillery, sometimes called "still slop" and today referred to as distiller's grains, was used to fatten livestock on the tract of land across from Paper Mill Point. The animal waste from this feedlot was used to fertilize the land south of Downer Street for growing tobacco. This business was an early example of the vertical integration of several operations. Grain was ground at the gristmill next door to the distillery, the waste mash moved next door to feed the livestock and the waste from the livestock moved a bit south to fertilize the tobacco crop. The use of the manure from the livestock to grow tobacco was successful as evidenced in the 1865 New York Census showing Herber Wetherby as producing 25,600 pounds of tobacco on 22 acres of land. This was one of the largest acreages of all time in Onondaga County.[4]

An article in the August 1, 1860 *Onondaga Gazette* noted, "Johnson, Cook & Co. will ship to New York a drove of 1,400 fat hogs with an average weight of 290 pounds." This number of hogs produced a large quantity of manure with an unpleasant odor. Add to this the manure from cattle also being fattened and the stage was set for great quantities of flies in addition to the offensive odors. The strong odors from the livestock fattening pens traveled to various parts of the village, depending upon the direction of the wind. Needless to say, not all of the villagers were unhappy when the distillery ceased operations in about 1866.

Distilleries disappeared from Lysander and Van Buren about 150 years ago. Whiskey, however, is still available in the towns today but comes from large distilleries scattered around the globe. During the last century, beer and wine have replaced whiskey as the alcoholic beverages of choice. The manufacture of beer, in recent years, has become a major industry in Lysander, and is described in the chapter, "Manufacturing in Radisson."

---

3   Christopher, A.J. *Sketches of Yesterday*, Bangall Gristmill Became Distillery

4   Nostrant, Robert F. *Chronology of Paper Mill Point* 1/9/1998

10

Tanneries, Shoemakers, Harness Makers & Rawhide Gears

Tanneries

Tanneries are an almost forgotten industry but once were thriving enterprises that were important to all residents. The tanneries turned animal hides into leather that provided boots, shoes, harnesses, saddles and a variety of other needed items. Figures are not available specifically for Lysander and Van Buren until the 1835 census, but the *US 1810 Census of American Manufacturers* notes there were 31 tanneries in Onondaga County. These 31 tanneries processed 1,855 hides and 7,076 calfskins that year.

The *1835 New York Census* states there were three tanneries in Lysander and two in Van Buren. In the *1845 New York Census* the number in Lysander had increased to five and decreased to one in Van Buren.

The significance of the tannery is not in the number of tanneries that existed or the number of employees, but that they provided a market for the hides from the hundreds of farms in the area, which in turn provided local shoemakers and harness makers with the necessary raw materials for their products. The shoemakers and leather workers provided services for every resident in the area.

Tanning is defined as the conversion of the skins of cows, oxen and other animals into leather to prevent its putrefaction. Skins of animals were used for thousands of years as a covering for man, but they had to be kept dry as moisture would cause the skins to rot. The discovery of tanning goes back over 2,000 years with the principles well established, but it was not until the 19th century that the chemistry of tanning was understood. It is interesting to note that rawhide was the "duct tape" of the frontier. Rawhide could be cut into strips, soaked and then wrapped around items, binding them as one. As the rawhide dried, it shrunk, holding the pieces tightly together.

Tanning receives its name from tannin, which is found in many plants, but tree bark was commonly used as the source of tannin for tanning hides. Tree barks were composed of approximately 10% tannin and often a mixture of more than one bark was used to obtain the desired tanning effect for a particular leather.

In Europe oak bark was the principle source of the tannin for the tanning process. In the United States several different barks were used including oak, chestnut and hemlock, often depending upon what was available. Hemlock trees were prevalent in the Baldwinsville area and hemlock bark was commonly used here. Trees were cut in the late spring when the sap was flowing from the roots to the branches, permitting the bark to be readily removed. An axe was used to split the bark lengthwise and then a bark spud was used to remove the bark in slabs. The slabs of bark were dried and then ground in a bark mill to make them ready for use in a tanning solution.

The dry bark was usually crushed, until it became a coarse powder, by a large stone wheel powered by an ox or a horse. The finer the bark was ground the more tannin was available. It is likely that the earliest tanners, in a newly settled area, crushed their bark by pounding, but because of its coarseness more bark was needed for the tanning process.

Tanneries were almost always located on a stream. All of the waste flesh and hair were dumped in the stream and carried downstream away from the tannery. Tanneries normally smelled badly because of the decomposing flesh and the presence of vermin. In warm weather they were not popular with nearby neighbors.

Portions of meat and fat that clung to the hide needed to be removed before the tanning process began. The hides were then soaked in a lye solution so the animal hair could readily be removed. Sometimes the hides were soaked in a vat or a small pond until bacterial action loosened the hair from the hide. After rinsing, the hides were ready to be soaked in the tannin solution, which killed the bacteria and shrunk the skin pores, changing it from rawhide to leather. The tanning process varied with the type of skin being tanned and its eventual use.

Tannery Creek, a well-known creek in Baldwinsville, received its name from the tanneries that were located along its bank. Aaron Jerome operated a tannery near what is now the corner of E. Genesee St. and Albert Palmer Lane. The tannery must have been established at an early date as Jerome conveyed his property and business to Stephen Baldwin by deed on January 5, 1818 for the sum of $1,900. The tannery was owned in the following years by Thompson Riddle, followed by H. Stilwell and then by Elisha Hickok.[1]

Another A.J. Christopher article states that in the summer of 1854 the principle tannery on Tannery Creek, owned by Phillips & Bentley, burned to the ground. It must have been rebuilt because in 1860 Stark & Co. was doing business on the same site. Eight years later, Stark & Kaulback are listed as proprietors. In 1879, the property was owned by Williamson Brothers of Syracuse, but was unused and in poor condition. A creamery was next located on the site. Another tannery is shown on an 1860 village map and was operated by R. Hitchcock. It was located between Tannery Creek and the railroad, north of E. Genesee Street.

The New Process Rawhide Co. came to Baldwinsville in 1888, locating on Papermill Island and manufactured rawhide gears. The company at first made rawhide canoes and then went into rawhide gear production. They had a private leather-tanning department and continued in business until a fire in 1898 destroyed their building Their tanning process was designed to produce tough leather. They also made their own glue as a by-product.[2]

The earliest tannery in the area appears to have been built at Ionia in 1807 by a man named Mead. It was later sold to Daniel Betts who continued the business for many years. David Tillotson purchased 10 acres of land on Lot 40 near Warners in 1816 and operated a tannery. Amon Dayton and Ambrose S. Worden succeeded him and continued the business until the 1840s.[3]

In 1836, David Tillotson left Warners, and with his son Sanford, purchased 100 acres a mile south of Plainville for $920.14. He operated a tannery for a number of years and was succeeded by his son-in-law, Nathan Ward. Later Nathan Ward moved to Phoenix, but the Tillotson family continued to operate the tannery for some time. Near the building foundation were several round, stone tanning vats. Harlo Tillotson, great- grandson of David, told Mr. Christopher that his grandfather's diaries showed the price of tanning a large hide was 50 cents. He also said that some work was done on shares with no money changing hands.[4]

Onondaga's Centennial notes that there was a tannery in Baird's Corners operated by Samuel Richards, which was later purchased and run by Leander Ballard & Co. The *1868 Onondaga County Directory* shows Smith & Sutfin and William C. Biggs, both in Lysander, as operating tanneries. The *History of Onondaga* lists a tannery in Jacksonville operated by B. Hazard. Pearl Palmer, in Part 150 of her book *Historical Review of the Town of Lysander*, mentions D.P. Rice of Jacksonville as tanner and currier as well as boot and shoe manufacturer.

The tanning business left the local area more than a century ago. It, like many other industries, moved closer to the source of its raw materials and to large manufacturing facilities where there was

---

1 Christopher, A.J. *Churchill Kin Ran Old Creamery* February 17, 1966

2 Ibid *Tanneries in Old B'ville* September 19, 1973

3 Scisco, Louis Dow *Early History of the Town of Van Buren* p. 43

4 Christopher, A. J. *Tanneries Were Quite Common* February 24, 1966

increased quality control and greater efficiency. The tanning industry was, for over 50 years, an important aspect of the self-sufficiency in the developing towns.

Shoemakers

The moccasin is probably the oldest type of shoe. Sandals, from a variety of materials, were the common foot protector worn by the people of Egypt, China, Greece, Rome and many other countries of the world. During the Middle Ages, the open-toed shoe was replaced in Europe by clumsy shoes made of leather or wood to hide the foot. Heavy, boxy-looking shoes called "batts" were worn in America until the end of the 18th century. The first shoes to open in front and lace with a shoestring were made in New England about 1790. During the 19th century boots were the most popular footwear for men and boys. Women and girls wore "gaiters", ankle-high shoes fastened with lacings or buttons up the side.[5]

The shoemaker (also referred to as a cobbler) also made boots, which extended further up the leg than a shoe. He had a variety of different sized lasts, which were forms shaped like a foot, that the leather was worked around. The shoemaker measured the customer's foot and then picked the appropriate sized last to use as a pattern. There was no danger of putting your shoe on the wrong foot, as a last was symmetrical and without toes, permitted the finished shoe to fit either foot. In fact, the user often reversed his shoes each day to make them

---
5 Arbor, Marilyn *Tools & Trades of America's Past* p. 86

In sparsely settled areas, the shoemaker or cobbler as he was often called, traveled from home to home making shoes for each family member. As communities grew the shoemaker became an important resident of the community, making shoes not only to fit his customer but also of the style the customer desired. Photo at Old Sturbridge Village by the author

wear more evenly. In rural areas it was common for the shoemaker to travel from home to home, making whatever shoes the family needed. At times the family might furnish the leather, the hide of which had come from the family's retired ox, prior to processing by the local tanner. The alternative was for the shoemaker to bring tanned hides with him to provide the necessary raw material.

As the population in a community increased, the shoemaker set up a shop, often a room in his home, for customers to come, to have their foot measured and then return in a day or two to pick up their shoes. The number of cobbler's benches that have survived to this day is amazing. They are often offered for sale at antique shows. It is additional evidence of the number of cobblers needed to supply the needed shoes prior to mass production by shoe factories. By the middle of the 19th century the shoe and boot industry employed more workers than any other branch of American manufacturing.[6]

Few realize that early shoemakers used small wooden pegs, cut from maple or beech, to fasten the soles of shoes to the uppers. These little pegs were an important product from early sawmills even though the volume of lumber used was barely measurable. The pegs were about three-quarters of an inch long and about the size of a matchstick. The pegs were used in place of hand stitching. When machine stitching came into use, wooded shoe pegs were no longer used.

Until into the 20th century, it was quite common for young boys to go barefoot from early spring into late fall. This was economical for families and also pleasurable for boys. Boys even were barefoot in the schoolroom. If a shoe that was worn during the winter survived for further use and was too small in the fall, it was likely passed on to a younger child in the family.

In all likelihood the first shoemakers in the area were part-time in conjunction with land clearing, farming or some other early occupation. Joseph P. Brown of Baird's Corners is mentioned as an early shoemaker.[7] In the 1850s, Dennis R. Rice had a cobbler's shop in Jacksonville.[8] A. Carpenter is listed for boots and shoes in the *Onondaga Gazette* of October 20, 1846 and also L. Van Velzar as a dealer in boots and shoes.[9]

The listing in the 1846 *Onondaga Gazette*, of a dealer in boots and shoes, indicates the local shoemakers are beginning to have competition. By the end of the Revolution, shoemaking had been established on a commercial basis, but we know from the listings of local shoemakers that the cottage industry of shoemaking continued until the beginning of the 20th century. Change came slowly in the 19th century compared to today and it came even more slowly in the rural areas.

The appendix of this book lists the shoemakers between 1859 to 1881 as shown in a variety of business directories. Without doubt some shoemakers were missed, but in 1859 there were 13 listed with four of them in Baldwinsville. In 1881, there were also 13 listed, but six of those were in the village. The shoe industry was moving gradually from low-density population areas toward greater density populations, a shift that has been continuing many years. Two shoemakers were listed in the *1909 Baldwinsville Business Directory*: Archie Baker at 2 Oswego Street and Albert Piton at 19 Syracuse Street, but none are listed after that date.

Occasionally a shoemaker plied his trade in a community for many years. Horace Ells is listed in Lysander from 1859 to 1881 and Chauncey Hubbard in Plainville from 1859 to 1886. It's not known how much sooner than 1859 that they started their business in these communities or how much longer than the last date on record that they continued in business. The author's mother once told him that Chauncey Hubbard made shoes for her family. The time came, however, when the local shoemaker evolved into a shoe repairman when he could no longer meet factory competition.

Harness and Saddle makers

Since there were only 326 horses in the Town of Lysander in 1825, and likely no more than that number in Van Buren, (Van Buren was still part of the Town of Camillus in 1825.) there were not a great number of harness makers at that time. There was, however, a need for a harness maker in almost every community to repair and make new harness for existing horses. Oxen, which were the common source of power on farms in the early 1800s, did

---

6 Ibid p. 86
7 Bruce, Dwight *Onondaga's Centennial* p. 750
8 Palmer, Pearl *Historical Review of the Town of Lysander* Part 149

9 Ibid Part 118

not require harness. A heavy wooden yoke over the oxen's neck with a chain passing between the oxen, from the yoke to the implement being pulled, was all that was necessary. As horse numbers dramatically increased during the middle and late 1800s, harness makers became more numerous.

Horses required a collar, usually leather covered and stuffed with straw. Also needed were leather traces extending from each side of the collar to the implement being pulled, leather lines to direct the horse and several other straps of leather to complete the harness.

In the Amish communities of New York and other states, the harness maker is still an active and important member of the community. The author remembers going to a harness shop in Syracuse with his father to purchase harness and also has purchased harness for his own horses from harness makers near Ovid, New York and in Intercourse, PA. A well-made harness for a workhorse today costs over $1,000 and a fancy show harness can go for as much as six times that figure.

A harness maker normally started out as an apprentice and was given the simpler task of making thread by coating long flax fibers with beeswax. He also was given the chore of using a stitching awl, which today has been replaced by a heavy-duty sewing machine. A wooden clam or clamp was used to hold the leather firmly in place as it was being worked. The harness maker needed a good understanding of leather to select the correct grain and proper thickness to insure appropriate strength.

Occasionally a harness maker would also make trunks and saddles, but these were usually made at larger facilities in heavier populated areas. Sleigh and carriage makers often called upon the harness maker for leather they needed to cover parts of the wooden frames. In early America leather fire buckets were a staple in almost every home and used in bucket brigades to fight fires.

Although there were certainly harness makers in the area prior to 1850, no record was found of any prior to the October 20, 1846 *Onondaga Gazette Business Directory* listing of R. E. Allen, E. M. Robinson and Tibbits Nichols. Dart & Goble are listed in the August 8, 1850 *Onondaga Gazette Business Directory*.[10]

Boyd's Onondaga County Directory of 1859 lists, in the village of Lysander, John Irvine who continues to be listed regularly through 1881. It also lists in Baldwinsville Michael Dowdall and C.H. Segar. Oscar Allen is listed for Little Utica in *Boyd's Onondaga County Directory of 1870*. Harness makers are listed for Baldwinsville regularly through the Baldwinsville Directory of 1915. John McGonegal, located on Bridge Street, was listed in 1878 and continually listed for 37 years with the last listing in the *1915 Baldwinsville Directory*. In 1915, his location was shown as 16 Oswego Street, which could have been the same location as Bridge Street later became both Syracuse St and Oswego St. in downtown Baldwinsville. (See appendix for other listings.)

Rawhide Gears

It seems like it would be erroneous to hear that gears were made out of rawhide, but Baldwinsville had a major rawhide gear industry, the New Process Rawhide Company, doing exactly that from 1888 until the plant burned on December 19, 1898. After the fire, the business moved to Syracuse where it prospered and in 1912 became the New Process Gear Corporation. In the 1950s it became a wholly owned subsidiary of the Chrysler Corporation and employed 3,000 people in 1973.[11]

Thomas W. Meachem of Syracuse and originally from England, was president of the company. The original Baldwinsville plant employed 30 people and was housed in a four-story wooden building between the Hotaling flourmill and Jacob Kenyon's paper mill. All three businesses were destroyed in the 1898 fire.

The company was originally named the New Process Rawhide Company and was formed with the intent of producing leather canoes. An article in the June 28, 1888 *Gazette* stated that one of the canoes they would be producing was on display in front of M. Johnson's Baldwinsville store and that the manufacture of those boats would take place in Baldwinsville if $5,000 of stock was subscribed. The article went on to say that the rawhide prepared by their process was as flexible as steel and seemingly quite strong.

The New Process Rawhide Factory utilized a patented process that produced rawhide gears, mallets, chisel handles and other rawhide specialty

---

10 Ibid Parts 118 and 119

11 Chrysler Corporation *The Gear Box* June 1973

items. The rawhide gears, which were noiseless and durable, were used for electric railway drives. The company made some rawhide gears until 1915 but with the advent of automobiles their gears shifted from rawhide to steel, brass & cast iron.[12]

Power, electricity and steam heat were supplied to the rawhide factory from Kenyon's adjacent paper mill with mechanical and electrical energy originating from the paper mill's water wheels. Hides, which arrived on the adjacent train spur on Water Street, were processed on the first floor. The gears were made on the second floor and the specialty items were made on the third floor. A number of discs of leather were bound with brass, then riveted, drilled and turned to the proper size. Teeth were then cut on a gear machine and then completed with a coat of shellac or varnish.[13]

Leather products continued in popular use after the tanneries and manufacturers of leather goods left Lysander and Van Buren. First the leather industries gravitated to the larger cities in the United States and then to foreign countries. The use of leather continues to increase with great quantities now used for furniture and automobile seat covers. Leather continues to be the material of choice for shoes but the local shoemaker has become a remnant of the past.

---

12 Christopher, A. J. *Rawhide Firm Forerunner of New Process Gear* October 19, 1965

13 Ibid

11

Local Industries Utilizing Minerals from the Earth: Stone, Brick, Pottery, Stoneware, Fertilizer, Plaster and Cement

Transportation was slow and difficult when this area was settled in the early 1800s. To the greatest extent possible, whatever was available locally was utilized to meet the communities' needs. As transportation improved, materials for manufacturing and manufactured products that were superior or could be transported and sold more economically than locally produced products, replaced those local items. Thus many small industries, once of importance to our local residents, gradually disappeared.

The variety of important products that came from the earth to meet the needs of residents is quite amazing. The settlers, coming from other areas of the country and world, brought with them a broad knowledge of manufacturing and their resourcefulness created the birth of many small industries.

Stone

Today most of us think little of the stones we see scattered around the countryside, and, if they are considered at all, it is as a nuisance. In the 19th century local stone was an important building material. The first buildings were log cabins, but as soon as a sawmill became available, frame structures were constructed with a foundation made of stone. Often these were cobblestones shaped by nature, but as more substantial buildings were constructed there was demand for square or rectangular shaped stones to provide a more sophisticated look to buildings. The stone dam in Baldwinsville is a daily reminder of the importance of stone.

There is a ridge of limestone bisecting much of New York, extending west to east many miles. The limestone rock was exposed two miles north of Baldwinsville, near the intersection of Route 48 and Church Road. There were four stone quarries developed in that area. We do not know when the first stone was quarried, but there is a written record referring to a stone quarry at that location in 1834. It is likely that a number of the older buildings in the area have stone from one of those quarries.[1]

In 1836-7, Sanford C. Parker constructed a huge stone gristmill with stone from those quarries. The mill was 100 feet long by 60 feet wide and four stories high. The large, tall, stone building was an impressive sight against the Baldwinsville skyline. It was described by Joshua V. H. Clark in his 1849 book, *Onondaga*, as the best mill in the area. The mill was located at 4 Syracuse St. to the west of the current Red Mill Inn. The Parker Mill survived a fire in 1861 but finally succumbed on December 19, 1898 when it was destroyed in a fire along with the Kenyon Paper Factory and the Rawhide Gear Plant, both adjacent mills.[2]

We can only imagine the men mining the rock from those quarries with simple but effective hand tools: hammers, steel wedges, stone chisels and levers. Occasionally, some coarse blasting powder may have been used to help break out sections of the layered limestone. The blocks of stone were all shaped by men using stone hammers and then

---

1 Palmer, Pearl *Historical Review of the Town of Lysander* Part 98
2 Christopher, A. J. *Stone or Hotaling Mill* January 28, 1965

were hauled by oxen to the mill site two miles away to be finished cut and put into place by masons.

Bricks

Brick making goes back hundreds of years. Mud bricks will suffice in an arid climate but clay bricks, properly made, are building components of beauty that will last for many years. There are a number of areas where red clay is available in the Baldwinsville area, making the production of bricks a natural local industry. The only other ingredients needed, in addition to clay, are sand and water. Wood was used for the brick moulds and also to furnish heat for the kiln.

There were several steps in the production of bricks. The first was mining or removing the clay from the ground. This was done with hand shovels at the time bricks were made in Baldwinsville. The clay could be mined at any time, but an ideal time to do the mining was in the autumn. Leaving the clay exposed to repeated freezing and thawing during the winter made it softer for working in the spring. The clay was then ground, similarly to grinding grain, by using large stones to break down coarse particles, and then it was screened, if necessary, for removal of coarse particles.

The clay was then mixed with water to give it the right consistency and then shaped into appropriate size lumps. The lumps of wet clay were placed in wooden molds that had been lightly sanded to permit easy removal of the bricks after firing. The bricks were partially dried in the sun before being placed in a kiln for further drying at a low temperature. After drying, a higher temperature was needed to harden the clay into a lasting brick. Not every brick came out perfect in shape and color. Bricks of uniform color and shape were used in the facing course on buildings and bricks of less uniformity were used in the interior courses of the walls.

Edith Hall in her book, *History of Baldwinsville*, writes that the brick used to build the Baldwinsville Academy on Elizabeth St. in 1867 came from the brickyard of John Hax on East Oneida Street near Tannery Brook. (This schoolhouse was torn down around 1970. An addition constructed around 1920, closer to Elizabeth St., remains and continued to be used as an elementary school for a number of years but now is part of a church)

In 1882, John Hax advertised in the *Syracuse Journal* that he had 100,000 bricks ready for sale at his old yard on the Munro farm[3] (on E. Oneida St. near the Baldwinsville Schools bus garage). This advertisement must have appeared after John Hax discontinued making bricks as evidenced by excerpts (as follows in the next paragraph) from a newspaper article written by Charles A. Hall of the recollections of Fred L. Mawhinney regarding his father's, John Mawhinney's, brickyards.

John Mawhinney operated brickyards in Jordan and New Bridge (Belgium) before reopening the Hax plant in Baldwinsville in 1879. He operated the Baldwinsville plant until his death in 1890.

The business continued for some years under the direction of his widow. The old records showed that the property for the brick works was leased from Squire Munro for $50 a year, which included all of the clay that was used. Also recorded was the sale of 89,900 bricks for the sum of $360 or about $4.50 per thousand. The article lists many of the businesses and houses in Baldwinsville that were constructed with bricks from his yard. The largest single order was for one million bricks that were used to construct the H.A. Moyer Carriage Factory in Syracuse. He noted that the clay was ground in a pug mill by a horse going round and round, attached to a sweep. The article goes into great detail about harvesting the clay, sanding the molds, drying the bricks and firing the bricks in the kiln.[4]

Just below Belgium, on the east bank of the river, there was a fine bed of red clay. Walter Crawford opened a brickyard there in 1828, which was run by his family for 40 years. Dudley Breed became the next owner of the business, which produced both brick and tile. A Mrs. LaGarry said that in the last years of operation clay was loaded on barges and sent to a business in Geddes. Later, when the river channel was improved by dredging for the Barge Canal, dredges filled the discarded clay pits.[5]

Possibly the oldest and the longest in operation of the brickyards was the Warners Brick Co. at Warners, very close to the Van Buren town line. The red clay for the bricks was obtained from the hillside north of Brickyard Road.[6] In a separate article

---

3   Christopher, A. J. *Events of 1882 Recorded* March 14, 1973
4   Gazette & Farmers' Journal September 26, 1940
5   Ibid *Belgium Hamlet was Once Known as New Bridge* May 19, 1966
6   Christopher, A.J. *Brickyards Once Flourished Here* January 20, 1966

by Mr. Christopher, *Warners Boasted Clay Industries*, he notes that there is a state marker near the site referring to Thomas Marvin coming to the locality in 1811 and "making the first bricks from native clay trod by oxen".

A fourth known brickyard was located on Lot 3 in Van Buren, west of Baldwinsville on the riverbank. It operated for less than 20 years and carried several names including Seneca River Brick Co. and Riverside Brick Co. This brickyard made common brick, ornamental brick and tile. Its origin dates back to 1891 when George Babcock sold Riverside Brick Co. 35 acres from his farm. When the brickyard was dismantled in about 1910, Baker Bros. tin shop bought much of the metal used in the brick manufacturing along with surplus bricks and transported them to their business location north of the dam. These items were used in a variety of projects around the village.[7]

Many of the older brick buildings in the Baldwinsville area are made from bricks produced locally. There are undoubtedly other Baldwinsville area locations where bricks were made that are not recorded.

Pottery and Stoneware

Clay, which was very common in the Baldwinsville area, is the main component in pottery. Preparation of the clay for pottery, often referred to as earthenware and sometimes redware when formed from red clay, is similar to the preparation of clay in making bricks. Both grinding and screening

---

7   Ibid January 20, 1966

This shows a potter forming his clay on a potter's wheel using a foot-powered treadle, very similar to the way clay would have been formed in Baldwinsville in 1840. Note the clay objects curing on the shelves behind the potter prior to firing. Photo taken at Old Sturbridge Village by the author

This is a pug mill for grinding clay prior to forming the clay on the potter's wheel. Water is added to the clay and knives protruding from the shaft of the pug mill cut the clay into fine particles. This pug mill is powered by a person turning the handle and is used in Old Sturbridge village in MA depicting the 1840 time period.

remove lumps in the clay. Water is then added to the clay to make the clay pliable. Pottery, however, normally is formed on a potter's wheel, layered in rope form or molded by hand to produce a hollow container, often for food or drink.

It is critical that any air in the clay be removed and that was accomplished by a process called "wedging" where the clay was forcefully manipulated, similarly to removing the air in preparing bread dough prior to rising. The next process was called "throwing" where a rough ball of clay was centered on the potter's wheel and by a combination of pressing, pulling and squeezing, the clay was shaped as the wheel turned. The shaped items were set on shelves for drying. After drying, the pottery was placed in a kiln for firing and wood was burned to bring the temperature to approximately 1700 degrees Fahrenheit.

Stoneware production was similar to pottery manufacturing except that a variation of clays were used and a salt glaze was added. A higher firing temperature of 2100 degrees was needed to provide the desired finish. Often a blue cobalt decoration was added to make the stoneware more attractive. Stoneware with cobalt decorations is quite beautiful and these articles have become sought after collector's items.

In Baldwinsville, John Darrow started producing pottery around 1845 on the north side of the dam, between the river and the Baldwin Canal. In 1848, the pottery moved to near the sulfur spring in the area of Van Buren Road in Lot 14, where there were readily available deposits of red clay. Darrow produced red earthenware pottery until 1852 and then became a stoneware pottery, which was run under the name of J. Darrow & Son until 1876. Some of the clay used in the stoneware pottery came from New Jersey.[8] Competition from glass containers cut into Darrow's business so they diversified into making clay flowerpots. This did not produce the necessary sales and they closed their doors in 1876.

In a paper, *Darrow Pottery* written by Dorothy

---
8   Scisco, Louis Dow, *Early History of Van Buren* p.43

Local Industries Utilizing Minerals from the Earth

Three examples of stoneware produced by the Darrow family in Baldwinsville beginning about 1845. For several years John Darrow produced pottery at the north side of the dam and west of Oswego St. In 1848, he moved the business near what is now the intersection of Rt. 690 and Van Buren road and in 1852 began producing stoneware there.

E. Mann in 1982, she states that the local clay was combined with Amboy clay, which was brought to Baldwinsville by the canal and river to a dock on Cooper Street (now Maple Road) and from there to the pottery shop by wagon. She also noted that the stoneware produced prior to 1855 was marked as Darrow/B'ville, from 1855 to 1872 as Darrow & Sons/B'ville, from 1872 to 1876 as L.S. Darrow/B'ville and 1876 or later as Baldwinsville Stoneware.

The brand identification, along with the cobalt decorations on stoneware, have given a long lasting identity to this relatively small business that existed in Baldwinsville over a century ago. Its name and products continues to be well known long after many much larger area manufacturing businesses have been forgotten.

Lime, Plaster, Cement and Fertilizer

Limestone was readily available in the area as evidenced by the previously mentioned four stone quarries north of Baldwinsville. Lime is produced

A pottery kiln made of bricks and used at Old Sturbridge Village for firing the pottery. Next to the kiln notice the wood, which was used to provide the necessary heat.

The Warners Portland Cement Works, located in the very southern part of Van Buren, commenced production in April 1890. It produced 200 barrels of cement daily and provided employment for 90 men. A fire destroyed much of the building in 1893. Although the plant was rebuilt, financial difficulties brought business to an end a few years later. Photo courtesy of OHA Museum & Research Center

by heating limestone in a kiln and was produced in Lysander for use in making plaster for application on the interior walls of local buildings and also for use as a fertilizer. When used as a fertilizer its benefit was not so much as a nutrient for the plants but as a means of reducing the acidity of the soil to make existing soil nutrients more readily available for plant use. For wall plaster, water is added to produce slaked lime, which is sold as a white powder. When the slaked lime is applied to walls and ceilings additional water is added to form a paste. Animal hair obtained from tanneries was often added to minimize cracking of the plaster after application.

Joshua V. H. Clark in his 1849 book, *Onondaga*, notes that there were two plaster mills in the Town of Lysander at that time. No names or locations are mentioned but they were likely in or near Baldwinsville and provided the plaster for new homes being constructed in the area, a number of which were replacing log cabins. Limestone, the main ingredient other than water and animal hair, was readily available. It is likely that kilns for heating the limestone to make plaster were adjacent to the plaster mills.

Apparently the plaster business continued for some time in Baldwinsville as the shipping news in the Baldwinsville paper for the first week of May 1880 noted that the boat "Stella" arrived with 114 tons of plaster stone for the Frazee Plaster Mill.[9]

The village of Lysander had an early and long history of lime and fertilizer production. The only side street existing in the hamlet today is named Phosphate Alley. As mentioned in the chapter on asheries, Chauncey Betts established an ashery there at a very early date. Most of the ashes, which were high in potash, were processed and sold but some were applied to the land as fertilizer. Pearl Palmer, in Part 128 of *Historical Review of the Town of Lysander*, mentions a resident of the village born in 1860 remembering a lime kiln in the hamlet. *Boyd's Onondaga County Directory of 1859* lists Albert A. Vedder as a lime producer in Lysander village and in 1881 Casper Dietrich is listed as a lime

---

9 Christopher, A. J. *Port of Baldwinsville once Figured in Canal Commerce* January 27, 1966

manufacturer. In 1868, the *Onondaga County Directory* shows Thomas and George Hammond as lime manufacturers.

Indications that the fertilizer business of the hamlet of Lysander might be diminishing is indicated by a comment in the *Gazette & Farmers' Journal* of April 16, 1903 stating, C.H. Tillotson has moved his storehouse from Phosphate Avenue to his lot in the village for a workshop. An advertisement in the same paper on April 8, 1920, showing limestone coming from external sources, states, Solvay pulverized limestone is sold by H.J. Eason of Lysander New York. Charles Ridall and his family, who have been longtime residents of Lysander, told the author that there were at one time three fertilizer storehouses on Phosphate Alley.

Originally, cement was non-hydraulic or unable to harden under water. It was a similar product to plaster and when used to bind stones for a building foundation was referred to as a "dry wall". About 1820, when the Erie Canal passed through the area, methods had been developed to produce hydraulic cement, which would harden under water and was much stronger. This was accomplished by adding specific impurities to the pure calcium carbonate in limestone. Portland cement, commonly used since the middle of the 19th century, is hydraulic cement.

In 1877, Thomas Millen & Sons, who had a Portland cement plant at South Bend, Indiana, purchased 45 acres of land adjoining the Erie Canal south of Warners and commenced producing Portland cement. They utilized the naturally existing white marl and the blue clay from the Warners property to produce the Portland cement. It was a large operation using six domed kilns. In 1890, the Millen Co. sold the plant to the Empire Portland Cement Co., which marketed the cement under the *Empire* and *Flint* brands. During 1901 the plant was totally remodeled but on February 13, 1902 there was a serious fire. The plant was rebuilt with its capacity increased from 750 to 1,000 barrels of cement a day. The plant closed in 1908 because the raw materials, on their now 150 acres of land, had all been used and they were unable to purchase additional land. Although this plant was just south of the Van Buren line, its success induced a Syracuse group to form the Warners Portland Cement Company.[10]

By 1889, the Warners Cement Company owned 48 acres and was attempting to purchase more. The Town of Van Buren tax assessment for 1891 showed they owned 46 acres, all in Van Buren. Construction was commenced and by April 1890 the plant was producing first-class cement. On January 30, 1893 a fire broke out destroying the main building with a loss of $120,000 ($2,236,000 in 1999 $). At the time of the fire the plant was producing 200 barrels of cement a day and employing 90 men. The plant was rebuilt and resumed production in January 1895 but shortly was forced into receivership and ceased operations.[11]

Boyd's 1892 Directory of Onondaga County lists Bentley & Son of Warners as a manufacturer of cement pipe. It is likely that the cement used in the concrete came from one of the Warners producers.

---

10 Nostrant, Robert F. *The Erie Canal and Cement* p. 7-10
11 Ibid p. 11-12

12

Foundries

Iron, first produced about 4000 years ago, was needed even more when the Baldwinsville area was being settled than it is today. Cooking utensils, guns, knives, nails and a multitude of other everyday items were made of iron. There was no plastic or aluminum to rely upon; everyone needed iron every day.

The settlers brought numerous iron tools with them, but, with time, tools break or wear out and need to be replaced. Blacksmiths made small items like hinges and fasteners and did many iron repairs, but when it came to making an iron kettle or a plow it was beyond their capabilities. Small quantities of iron could be produced by a blacksmith in a hearth, called a bloomery, by urging the fire in a mixture of iron ore and charcoal with a simple bellows. This fire was not of a sufficient temperature to melt the iron, but the iron accumulated in pasty particles that could be merged into a lump. This iron was low in carbon and could be forged by the blacksmith. This process was not efficient or very productive so most blacksmiths turned to a foundry to supply their needs.[1]

A foundry is a place where metals are cast, thus the name, cast iron. Much of the reddish color in rocks and soil comes from the presence of iron. Normally the percentage of iron is too low to make separation of the iron from the other rock components practical. Local sources of utilizable iron ore include the Marcellus shale formation at the surface near Marcellus and bog iron ore along Scriba Creek in Constantia. It is likely that an occasional early blacksmith used some source of local iron ore, but for the most part the iron came as pig iron or wrought iron from larger foundries with blast furnaces some distance away.

Blast furnaces were large, tall brick structures filled from the top with alternate layers of charcoal, iron ore and limestone. The limestone served as a flux to give increased efficiency to the process. Air from large bellows, usually operated by waterpower, was forced up through the charcoal and iron ore. As the charcoal burned and the iron melted, the liquid iron was drawn off into large open sand molds called pig beds, thus the name pig iron. (Note the drawing of the furnace in this chapter). Furnaces were located where there was a good source of wood for making charcoal and ready access to iron ore and limestone.

Pig iron is high in carbon and brittle as it comes from the blast furnace. Baldwinsville area foundries purchased pig iron, which was often melted and poured into sand molds to produce cast products. The founder, the person heating the iron to a liquid and then pouring and forming it, used charcoal and forced air from a bellows to obtain the necessary heat for melting the iron. Charcoal, basically pure carbon, burns at a much higher temperature than wood causing iron to reach a sufficiently high temperature to melt. A foundry could also control the amount of carbon and the brittleness of iron through a process called fining. To fine the iron, it was remelted in a small charcoal-fired hearth with a bellows. The air blast gradually burned out the

---

1 Chard, Jack *Making Iron & Steel, the Historic Processes 1700-1900* p.2

This is a replication of the Saugus Iron Works north of Boston, a national historic site operated by the National Parks Service. The two different types of waterwheels are similar to the ones used in the Baldwinsville area in the 1800s. Photo by the author

desired amount of carbon leaving an iron product with the correct amount of carbon for the product being produced. Iron used by a blacksmith was wrought iron. It was low in carbon, which made it malleable and easy for the blacksmith to heat, pound into desired shapes and weld in his forge.[2]

Foundries came to the area at an early date. The *1824 New York Gazetteer* shows one ironworks in the Town of Lysander. It is difficult to know whether the term ironworks used at that time designated the business as a bloomery or a foundry. Levi Elsworth operated a small foundry at Memphis as early as 1829.[3] The 1845 New York Census shows one ironworks in Van Buren and two furnaces in Lysander.

A foundry was erected in the village of Lysander in the 1840s. It was an early user of steam power and was noted for its manufacture of plow points, castings and cultivators.[4] A listing in the 1868 *Onondaga County Directory* gives the name of the foundry as Peck & Brown. A report by the Dun financial rating firm in 1869 indicated that Peck & Brown had been in business eight years. This foundry apparently changed hands often, as you will note by the following list of foundry owners in Lysander village, since it is doubtful if there was more than one foundry in Lysander village at any one time. Dun shows visits to a Bidwell Schermerhorn foundry from 1876 to 1883 and to Mrs. Maryiette Spratt's foundry in 1882 and 1883. In the January 6, 1887

---

2 Ibid p. 7
3 Bruce, Dwight H. *Onondaga's Centennial* p. 730

4 Shapiro, Missy Eileen *People, Life, and Landscape in Northern Lysander During the 19th Century* p. 61

Gazette and Farmers' Journal, the sale of the foundry owned by Mrs. John Spratt to Gaylord brothers for $1,000 is mentioned. A.F. House, listed as a pump manufacturer in Lysander, was visited by a Dun representative at various times between 1871 and 1881. There is no way of being certain but it is likely that castings for these pumps were poured in the nearby foundry.

In Baldwinsville, John Humphrey had a foundry on Bridge Street, which he sold in 1855. In the 1850 *Gazette* his card advertised plows, points and castings. Humphrey's foundry must have been established prior to 1837 as Edith Hall's *History of Baldwinsville* describes an ice jam in the river that year being broken up by firing a nine-pound cannon ball through an opening in the side of the bridge, the cannon ball having been cast by Humphrey.

There was a foundry constructed of bricks, south of the village near Van Buren and Maple Road, established by John Gayetty and Alexander Rogers in about 1845 that continued for nearly 20 years.[5] An advertisement, in an 1851 *Onondaga Gazette & Farmers' Journal*, offers to make castings to order as well as offering a variety of stoves, kettles, plow points and other items. During the same year there were advertisements in the *Gazette* by M. VanAllen, owner of the Baldwinsville Novelty Works, offering iron turning, boring, finishing and repairing. The ad stated that they were located adjacent to the stone foundry and that there were all kinds of patterns for mill and factory gear at the foundry. Patterns, to provide exact shapes, were essential for pouring molten iron when making parts for iron tools or when making items like plows and kettles

Another foundry in Baldwinsville was White and Lankin, which in 1868 became Warren White. Although a Dun representative visited the foundry in 1868, no other mention of the business has been found. Possibly it is the same foundry as the one

---

5   Bruce, Dwight H. *Onondaga's Centennial* p. 730

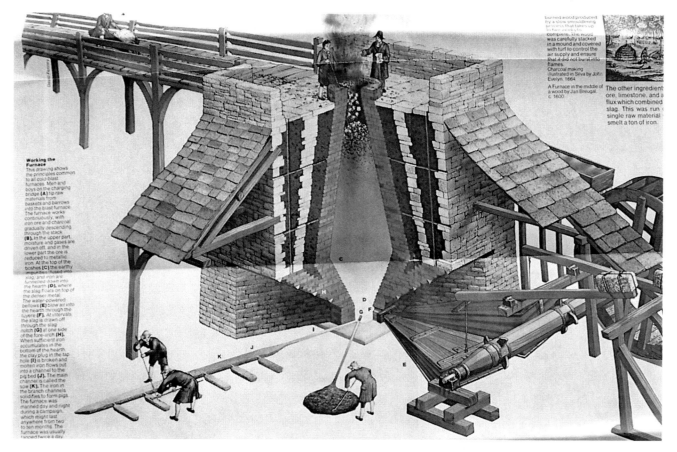

This is a diagram, provided by the National Parks Service, of an early iron foundry showing how it functioned. It was loaded from the top with iron ore, charcoal and limestone. Bellows forced air into the chamber creating sufficient temperature to melt the iron ore, which collected at the bottom. The limestone served as a flux, which combined with the impurities in the iron ore to form a slag.

sold in 1855 by John Humphrey.

Baldwinsville, with its various pump and other metal manufactured products, often had foundries connected to the manufacturing plants. In 1870, a fire destroyed 13 buildings on the south side of the river including the works of Heald, Sisco & Co. along with their patterns, stock and machinery. The following spring they purchased the Fink property at the corner of Canal (now E. Genesee St.) and Virginia Streets, utilizing the existing buildings on the site and erecting a foundry and other structures. It is likely that they had also operated a foundry at their previous location. Heald, Sisco & Co. was the forerunner to what later became Morris Machine Works. In 1900, two lots with frame houses east of Morris Machine Works were purchased and the houses moved to make room for a new foundry.[6]

In the 1940s, Morris Machine Works purchased a bronze foundry located at approximately 82 East Genesee St., behind the Baldwinsville Farmers' Cooperative. Later Morris sold it to James Jardine who operated it as the Jardine Bronze Foundry. This business closed around 1990 and the building was subsequently demolished.

An unknown number of blacksmiths and manufacturers in the Baldwinsville area used metal from our local foundries to produce a large variety of products. During the last half of the 19th century, foundries gradually left smaller communities as competition from large producers in cities with ready access to ore, limestone and power became both specialty and low cost producers.

---

6   Hall, Edith *History of Baldwinsville* p.52 and 68

This is the outlet for the molten metal from an iron foundry. The long, large excavation in the sand is called the sow, and the smaller depressions running from it are called the pigs. Molten iron flowed from furnace to the sow and into the pigs and later was recast into usable iron objects. Sometimes the molten iron flowed directly into sand molds forming the end product, such as a kettle. Baldwinsville had several foundries but it is likely that most of them purchased pig iron to be melted, poured and shaped at their foundries. Photo at the Saugus Iron Works by the author

There were dozens of water wheels in the Baldwinsville area. Shown are two types of waterwheels. Water enters the further waterwheel near the top and it is called an overshot wheel. Water enters the one in the front near the bottom and it is called an undershot wheel. Where water is moving rapidly with little fall the undershot waterwheel is the most effective. Photo at the Saugus Iron Works by the author

On the left is a forge where the cast pig iron from the sow and pig is heated to change cast iron to wrought iron by lowering its carbon content. Wrought iron can be worked into desired shapes by heating and pounding. On the right are two waterwheel-powered bellows. The large round shaft with protruding cams, powered by the water wheel, operated the bellows. A similar system would have been used in our local foundries. Photo at the Saugus Iron Works by the author

This is a triphammer that goes up and down by the power from cams on a shaft powered by a water wheel. Triphammers varied in weight with this one weighing several hundred pounds. The constant banging of the triphammers shaping red-hot iron into ax blades, scythes and other iron objects was a normal sound in 19th century Baldwinsville. Photo at Saugus Iron Works by the author

13

Textile Industries

Until about the middle of the 19th century, in rural and developing communities, the textile industry was largely a cottage industry. The wool from sheep and linen from flax both came from local sources, often on the same property where the women of the family turned the fibers into thread or yarn and then into cloth.

The *1825 New York State Census* shows 4,289 sheep in the Town of Lysander and 14,450 in the Town of Camillus, which at that time included the towns of Elbridge and Van Buren. Ten years later the number was similar in Camillus, Elbridge and Van Buren, but had almost doubled in Lysander, which was settled somewhat later. Local sheep numbers remained fairly steady up to the Civil War but then dropped dramatically as the fiber industry became commercialized and shipments of the fibers came to factories, where clothing was produced, rather than in the home. In the early 19th century, the majority of flax used to make linen was grown in small plots for home use. Thus, the total acreage grown, similar to acres of vegetables in gardens, is not recorded. The 1845 New York Census shows 1,064 acres of flax grown in Onondaga County, much of which was for commercial use.

The first movement toward industrialization of the textile industry, in this area, was the presence of carding and fulling machines. These machines appeared where waterpower was available. For centuries carding of wool had taken place in the home. Carding was a process of breaking up clumps of the woolen fibers to align them somewhat parallel with each other in preparation for spinning. In the process, foreign matter, including plant burrs that had attached to the sheep's wool, were also removed. Hand-powered carding machines had been invented in Europe during the 18th century but were much slower than the water-powered carders. Taking the fleece of wool to the carder eliminated the long tedious process of carding the wool at home.

Teasels, affixed to small wooden paddles called cards, were commonly used to card wool in the home. The neighboring towns of Skaneateles and Marcellus were noted for their large production of teasels. In commercial establishments teasels were fastened to large revolving drums powered by water to raise the fibers from a cloth's surface to form a nap. They were used extensively into the 20th century. In later years teasels were replaced with closely spaced wire pins on the revolving drums. Today home crafters who enjoy spinning their own wool use a pair of cards with protruding hooked pins. For removal of foreign matter from flax and to align the fibers, the long flax fibers are drawn over a piece of wood holding many sharp prongs, called a hetchel.

The carding of a quantity of wool was a long slow process. When a carding machine came to a community many of the residents were eager to take their wool to the carder, usually paying for the service with part of the wool. The remaining wool was then taken home for spinning and weaving.

Fulling is a process used to treat woven or knitted wool and is sometimes referred to as felting, which is similar but takes the process a bit further.

Fulling involves three basic steps: cleaning the fabric, agitating it and then stretching it so it will take on a desired shape. During fulling, moisture and friction cause the scales on the wool to open up and then to interlock creating a denser fabric. The greater the agitation or friction, the thicker the cloth becomes. Felting provides a cloth that is not only denser, but is also more durable. It is not a reversible process and requires care to provide the appropriate amount of agitation. It is basically a controlled shrinking process with up to a fifth of the volume of the product lost during fulling.

Upstate New York with its numerous rivers and varied elevations provided the waterpower for many 19th century industries. Up and down the Mohawk, Seneca and Oswego Rivers, as well as along numerous smaller streams, the textile industry flourished. The textile industry did not escape the Baldwinsville area, but did not become as large or persist as long as in many other Upstate locations. Baldwinsville had waterpower, but not to the extent of cities like Utica and Amsterdam. Eventually the industry moved to the southern states for cheap labor and then to other countries for the same reason.

The 1835 New York Census indicates that there was one fulling machine in each of the towns and two carding machines in Van Buren. There was also a woolen factory in Lysander. The 1845 New York Census shows one fulling machine, one carding machine and one woolen factory in Lysander. It also showed two carding machines in Van Buren.

Steps in the progression of industrialization of the textile industry in Lysander and Van Buren came fairly early. The 1824 *New York Gazetteer* states that Lysander had one fulling and one carding

A view, to the north, of the 4th bridge across the Seneca River in Baldwinsville, constructed in 1900. A single trolley track runs across the bridge providing convenient and rapid transportation to Syracuse. Trolley transportation expanded the opportunities of Baldwinsville area residents for both employment and shopping in Syracuse, one of the initial causes of the demise of local industry and businesses. The large building on the left is the J.C. & J.C. Miller knitting mill.

machine. Both Edith Hall in *History of Baldwinsville* and Pearl Palmer in *Historical Review of the Town of Lysander* refer to a carding and cloth dressing factory in 1826 or 1827 owned by James Marshall. This mill was located between the Baldwin Canal and the dam near the north end of the bridge. The building was originally constructed by Dr. Baldwin as Baldwinsville's first gristmill and later converted for use as a woolen mill. The building was later converted into a mill for the manufacturing of veneering and burned November 11, 1841.[1]

After the fire, a new building for use as a woolen factory was constructed on the same site by Kellogg & Farr. This new building was also destroyed by fire in 1851 or 1852. In Part 118 of *Historical Review of the Town of Lysander*, taken from the 1846 *Onondaga Gazette Business Directory*, the Seneca Woolen Factory of Kellogg & Farr is listed, and in Part 215 of the same book a reference is made to the Woolen Mill Company making, in 1865, about 400 yards of plain and fancy cashmere daily.

Stephen Tincker came into Van Buren about 1830 and built a mill for carding and fulling at Bangall where waterpower was available. His mill drew custom work from miles around and was an important feature of the area. In 1839, he sold the mill to Timothy J. Handy who continued it some time, and when the mill passed to Albion J. Larkin it was turned into a gristmill.[2]

In 1872, John Armstrong started a cotton mill in Bangall but the mill lasted only a few years. The cotton came to the mill by railroad.[3]

The *Onondaga County Directory* of 1868 lists a woolen mill owned by James Frazee & Co. In the 1878 *Onondaga County Business Directory* Robert Miller, Jr. is listed as having a hosiery manufacturing business and J.C. Miller as manufacturing knit underwear. The Dun & Co. financial records show visits to the Downer & Voorhees woolen factory in 1868 and also to the woolen factory of S.A. Groves & Co. in 1874, which was the successor to Clark Woolen Mills.

Members of the Miller family who came to Baldwinsville in 1876 from Amsterdam, NY had a significant impact upon the Baldwinsville manufacturing scene. Amsterdam, at that time and well in to the 20th century, was a major textile-manufacturing city. The Millers purchased the former woolen mill property, north of the bridge between the dam and the Baldwin Canal. Later they also purchased the property of the Morris Axe factory with its water rights. The abundant waterpower, and the good rail and water transportation facilities drew the Millers to Baldwinsville. The business headquarters remained in Amsterdam and they had a large warehouse in New York City. The principles were James C. Miller, John Charles Miller and Robert Miller. The firm operated under several names during its lifetime including J.C. Miller & Co., J.C. & J.C. Miller Knitting Co. and Miller Knitting Mill.

The Miller manufacturing facility was large and at its height employed close to 200 people, mostly women and young girls, with an annual payroll reaching $75,000. (At this time female workers received less than a dollar for a 10-hour day.) It was in operation for over 20 years. In 1898, it filled its final large order, which was a contract for 200,000 shirts. The organization failed and the only bidder at the auction of the property was John Charles Miller who ran the operation for a short time. In 1900, much of the machinery was removed.

Both wool and cotton were purchased for use in the mill with washing, bleaching and dyeing done in separate buildings outside of the mill. Lint and dust from the knitting process often started fires. The plant had a high-pressure pump and many feet of hose to control any small fire that broke out. The finished product was packed in wooden boxes and transported by horse and wagon to the train depot. In 1887, an associated company was founded and a generating plant was built to provide the village with electric lights. Interestingly, as the business grew, two 30 horsepower steam engines with boilers from Morris Machine Works were installed to supplement the waterpower.

The knitting mill stood unused at the site for many years. The electric company associated with the mill, known as the Edison Illuminating Company, was sold to George M. Pulver of Syracuse and later became known as the Seneca River Power Company.[4]

In 1913, the West Brothers of Syracuse leased a building on the south side, owned by Warren

---

1 Hall, Edith *History of Baldwinsville* p. 10 and 15
2 Scisco, Louis Dow *Early History of the Town of Van Buren* p. 43
3 Ibid p. 43

---

4 Christopher, A.J. *The Miller Enterprise* April 2, 1975 and *Knitting Mill Prospered* April 9, 1975

J. Abbott, in the old Gardner and Davis block. The building was to be used for making finished garments from material produced by the company in Syracuse. They anticipated hiring about 50 women and girls.[5]

In 1932, it was announced that the Dixie Knit Products Corporation of Syracuse acquired sales rights to the products made in the Tappan Mills in Baldwinsville. Several new products had been developed for national sale under the brand names of "Dixie Cloth" and "Velvetknit". Products to be sold include dishcloths, dusting cloths, and wiping and polishing cloths.[6]

It is likely that the business described in an April 15, 1971 article in the *Baldwinsville Messenger* by Anthony J. Christopher entitled *'Velvetknit' – A Financial Failure*, is the same one. He states that in 1931 several businessmen came from Oswego to set up a firm called Velvetknit Corporation. They set up business in the old Amos Mill, located between the river and 10 E. Genesee St., to make polishing and cleaning cloths. The article also stated that they ran into financial difficulties and were out of business within a few years.

At the time this is being written, further information regarding Tappan mills, West Brothers in Baldwinsville or Dixie Knit Products in Baldwinsville couldn't be found. Without a doubt there were other manufacturers of textiles in the community but records may have been lost. There is no question

---

5 *The Gazette & Farmer's Journal* October 2, 1913
6 The *Gazette & Farmers' Journal* October 6, 1932

The invention of the wool-carding machine relieved the housewife of the tedious chore of carding her wool by hand in preparation for spinning. Carding straightens the wool fibers and removes any foreign matter that might be present in the wool. This machine, which is of the early 1800s era, is carding wool at Old Sturbridge Village.

that the Baldwinsville area had a significant textile industry in the 19th and early 20th century.

Custom manufacturing of clothing for individual family members was part of the duties of women for thousands of years, a practice that was ongoing at the time the Baldwinsville area was settled. This practice gradually evolved into one where specialists, seamstresses or tailors, produced custom clothing in their homes for neighbors. The ones who were successful, either male or female and with a talent for business, often opened their own shop in the business community, which might specialize in ladies dresses, millinery or men's suits. These types of custom clothing stores existed until the middle of the 20th century. The millinery portion of the textile industry will be discussed in a later chapter.

As with most small manufacturing businesses, local clothing manufacturers either went out of business or moved to larger cities where clothing could be produced at a lower cost. This trend has continued to the point where much of the clothing we wear is made in China, India or some other country. Today we occasionally find an individual with exceptional talent, who finds enjoyment in sewing, making clothes for their family. These people are rare individuals, a remnant of our past, providing us with a glimpse of yesteryear.

14

Cigars

Although cigar manufacturing in the towns of Lysander and Van Buren is now an almost forgotten part of the past, it provided employment for a significant number of people for half a century. This area was the center of the tobacco industry of Central New York with production of tobacco continuing until the middle of the 20th century, although local cigar manufacturing faded away in the early part of the century.

Columbus is credited with taking tobacco back to Europe when returning from his voyage to the Americas. His sailors had noted that the natives smoked twisted tobacco leaves wrapped in other leaves. Tobacco smoking took hold in Europe, and many thought tobacco had medicinal properties. With the establishment of European settlements in the Virginia colony, tobacco production was encouraged with the bulk of the crop shipped to Europe.

Cigar smoking became very popular in the United States during the 19th century. Cigars, popular with many men at that time, found a ready local market. Cigarettes increased in popularity after our soldiers had observed their use in France during World War I with cigar usage gradually dropping after the war. The National Health Interview survey of 2005 estimated that 2.2% of the US population smoked cigars. The US is the top cigar-consuming nation, followed by Germany and the UK.

Cigars are composed of three grades of tobacco. The filler is poorer quality tobacco, made up of small leaves and pieces of leaves. The filler is enclosed with larger leaves that have imperfections, called binder, and finally the very best leaves, the wrappers, are used to cover the cigar and give it an attractive appearance.

Cuba produced cigars from an early date. Cigar making gradually spread north from Cuba to Key West, continuing northward to Tampa. Increased population in the northern states attracted tobacco production and the manufacture of cigars further north. Locally, tobacco production started in the town of Marcellus in about 1845, spreading to Lysander and Van Buren a few years later. When it was determined that the climate and soils of the area were conducive for the profitable production of tobacco, the industry flourished. Peak production in Lysander and Van Buren reached over 1,000 acres in 1865. By 1940 tobacco production had decreased to 400 acres and quickly disappeared in the following years. The local production of tobacco, the relative ease in learning how to make cigars and the limited expenditure required for cigar production provided the incentives for a fast growing industry in the Baldwinsville area. Without question the Civil War, which limited tobacco imports from the South, was an important factor in the rapid growth of the tobacco industry in the North.

Although tobacco was grown in each of the towns in Onondaga County as well as in neighboring Cayuga and Oswego counties, it thrived the greatest and longest in Lysander and Van Buren. Cigar making became a vocation for many individuals in Baldwinsville and surrounding communities.

Arthur Hudson is stringing mature tobacco plants on lathe with his son Gates by his side, circa 1918. The lathe, with its tobacco, was hung in a drying barn and the leaves were later stripped from the stalks and manufactured into cigars. Gates later became one of the founders of Hudson & Mowins on E. Genesee St.

In 1886, Syracuse had 96 cigar makers and dealers along with three cigar box factories. In Baldwinsville, Allen & Chubb manufactured tobacco and cigar cases at about the same time. When specialty manufacturers develop for an industry, it signifies the industry is thriving.

Cigar production, like almost all other industries, gradually moved from the Baldwinsville area to other locations where costs were lower. Cigarettes, which were produced cheaply in large manufacturing plants with automated machinery, gradually replaced cigars bringing the cigar manufacturing business in the Baldwinsville area to a grinding halt.

Edith Hall in her 1936 book, *History of Baldwinsville*, provides an interesting summary of the tobacco industry in Baldwinsville. "The cultivation of tobacco was introduced in this section in 1850. This had a far reaching effect upon the growth and prosperity of the village, for Lysander and Van Buren were recognized for many years as comprising one of the outstanding tobacco producing districts in the country. In the early days of Onondaga tobacco, all crops were packed by the growers and shipped in the cases as purchased. Then came warehouse sorting and packing which greatly enhanced the value of the crop. The first

A tobacco shed where the tobacco stalks on lathes were hung in early September to dry until winter and then taken down for stripping of the leaves in preparation for making cigars. There were dozens of tobacco sheds like this one scattered around the Baldwinsville area and some are remaining today even though they haven't been used for tobacco for over 50 years.

Circa 1870 engraving from W.W. Clayton's book, The History of Onondaga County, showing the tobacco business of William Wilson of Plainville. Note the long vertical ventilation doors on the barns for drying the tobacco. Mr. Wilson also owned a large tobacco warehouse on his farm, constructed after this engraving was made, and a cigar factory, which employed about a dozen people.

warehouse for this purpose was opened in 1878 by E.W. Tucker, in a large red building that stood on the site of the Town of Lysander building, on East Genesee Street. Soon after this, Herrick's Hall was moved below the railroad by J.W. Upson, while the Fuller warehouse stood across from the old Frazee Mill on East Genesee St., and Michael Tobin built on the same street just east of the American Hotel. Between 1884 and 1890 the crop value exceeded a million dollars each year, and the money thus placed in circulation had much to do with the general prosperity of the merchants of the community."

The earliest reference of a cigar maker I have found in the Baldwinsville area was in Pearl Palmer's Part 149 of *Historical Review of the Town of Lysander* referring to an unidentified cigar maker in Jacksonville in the 1850s. There were very likely other cigar makers in the two towns at that time but they are not mentioned. W.A. Allen is mentioned as a tobacconist in Little Utica in the 1876 *New York State Business Directory*.

Plainville had a thriving tobacco industry. The previous noted directory names Thomas McCall, William C. Ward and William Wilson as tobacconists. William Wilson built a thriving business a short distance south of Plainville, an engraving of which is included in this book. He traveled to Cuba where he became impressed with the quality of the tobacco produced but found that tobacco seed could not be legally exported. Since tobacco seeds are very small he was able to paste seeds on the paper of letters he sent home to Plainville. He planted these seeds and built a thriving business, not only selling tobacco, but also selling tobacco seeds and making cigars, which he marketed throughout Central New York. A story is told that he left 1,000 cigars in his sleigh when he hitched his horse in the Seneca House barn one winter's day. He then went to several local places of business to solicit sales, but when he came back the cigars were missing. The culprits were located and ended up spending a few weeks in the Jamesville Penitentiary.[1]

The author's father purchased the William

---

[1] Christopher, A.J. *Cigarmaking Thrived Here* February 4, 1965

Wilson farm some years back. On the farm there was a special building, which had housed up to 17 cigar makers, a three-story tobacco warehouse containing an elevator and two large tobacco sheds along with other farm buildings, none of which were being used at that time. In the hamlet of Plainville west of the four-corners there was another tobacco business that sorted and graded tobacco. This building had many windows to provide good lighting for sorting and grading since its use was prior to the time that electric lights were available.

The *New York State Business Directory* of 1876 lists the following tobacconists in Baldwinsville: Tappan & Allen on Canal Street, Tucker & Crippen on Canal Street and Wm Weller at 40 Bridge Street. There are several other cigar makers listed in other directories in the Appendix. The last year that a tobacco listing was found was in the 1915 *Baldwinsville Directory*. The listing was 'tobacco & cigars', so there is no indication whether they actually made cigars. The businesses listed were Edward L. Beebe on Oswego Street, L.R. Sheldon on Oswego Street and T.H. Shoens at 25 Water Street.

Several Baldwinsville cigar makers must have had a good businesses because the following were visited by the Dun Financial rating firm in the 1870s and 80s: J.M. Scoville, William Miller, McGuigan Bros., and John Scoville. Also visited by Dun & Co. were Allen & Chubb, a manufacturer of tobacco and cigar cases, and Knapp & Williams who were cigar makers in Memphis.

Anthony J Christopher relates a significant bit of Baldwinsville cigar history in *Sketches of Yesterday* article, *Cigarmaking Thrived Here*, published on February 4, 1965 in the *Baldwinsville Messenger*.

"Cigarmakers were scattered about, Elmer E. Brooks, who kept a cigar store and pool room where Joe Glass'

Circa 1900 tobacco warehouse and sorting room on Rt. 370 at the western edge of Plainville. Notice the many windows in the sorting room to provide natural light, since no electricity was available until many years later. The buildings were razed in the 1940s. Photo courtesy of Virginia Billings

furnishings store is now located, also made cigars. His brands were 'Try-Me' a 5 cent smoke, and 'Mi Corona', which sold for 10 cents."

"The Gazette of January 7, 1892 carried the news that 'Richard Pelton has started to make cigars in Van Buren'. The same publication of May 1, 1883, tells of a strike in J.M. Scoville's cigar shop. The workers wanted a $1 per thousand increase. Their demands were met and they returned to work."

"E.L. Montague & Son manufactured several brands in the village. 'White City' and '777' were 5 cent cigars. The Montagues also assembled a special smoke, the 'Sagawatha' cigar, which was sold only at the boat club by that name and at their establishment. This was before 1910."

In the same article Christopher gave a detailed description of the Gifford cigar making business.

"Lawerence Gifford and his son made cigars for a long time at their barn at 71 Downer Street. Their plant was fitted after the fashion of an oldtime tobacco factory. It consisted of an office, a large manufacturing room and smaller rooms heated by coal stoves. Work was done under a high degree of humidity to permit the tobacco to remain pliable. Gifford's employees were four girls. According to Mrs. Bi Minnoe, they were the Socia girls, the present Mrs. Celia Kingsley and herself, ages ranging from 16 to 18 years. The young helpers had become proficient in the art of 'rolling' cigars through the direction of their eye, but the craft was fascinating. After a few weeks the operator became accustomed to the damp tobacco atmosphere in the factory. Wages ran 15-16 dollars for a week of 50 hours. Mrs. Minnoe remembers working for Mr. Gifford a few years in the 1912 times. 'The core was made of a cheaper or poorer tobacco, rolled into proper shape,' said Mrs. Minnoe. "then a binder was

Farmers are lined up on E. Genesee St. in Baldwinsville, circa 1897, waiting to unload their year's production of tobacco on railroad cars for shipment to the buyer's destination. The wagons will cross the bridge over the Baldwin Canal, on the left, and load the tobacco on what was originally the Baldwinsville & Syracuse Railroad. Although a great deal of the tobacco grown was used locally in the manufacture of cigars, the majority was shipped to other destinations.

rolled oblong, and this was followed by a final layer, the wrapper. White paste cemented the last layer, and the ends were carefully tapered. These wrappers were cut to a pattern, from choice autumn-gold leaves. The damp cigars were placed in a gang mould to attain a uniform shape. Afterwards, one end of the cigar was cut off, the other left sealed. They were usually packed in boxes of fifty. The Gifford brand read 'Alberts'."

The above description of cigar manufacturing came directly from one of the participants. Many of our old, long disappeared industries are gone with no detailed descriptions of their operation. Tobacco growing and the cigar manufacturing businesses in the Baldwinsville area likely contributed a greater percentage of the total income and employment, between 1860 and 1920, than any other single industry has contributed in the more than two centuries since the first settlers arrived in Baldwinsville. Tobacco was an important part of our economy at a time when its use was yet to be recognized as detrimental to a person's health.

15

Dairy Products

What was the manufacturing business in the towns of Lysander and Van Buren that had the greatest number of locations and the greatest number of personnel during the 19th century? You may be surprised to learn that, by a very large margin, it was the manufacture of butter and cheese. In 1855, on several hundred farms, there were 341,238 pounds of butter and 62,378 pounds of cheese produced. Butter and cheese production began upon the arrival of the first settlers and increased as the land was cleared and the population expanded. The butter and cheese was sold to anyone in the area who did not have cows and transported by water or roads to adjacent communities where there was a market. Fluid milk was not consumed to any great extent and instead was converted to butter and cheese. Butter and especially cheese have a longer shelf life than milk and weigh less to transport since it takes approximately three gallons of milk to make a pound of butter and 1.2 gallons of milk to make a pound of cheese.

Cheese making goes back more than 4,000 years. According to legend, cheese was made accidentally by an Arabian merchant who put his supply of milk into a pouch made from a sheep's stomach as he set out on a day's journey across the desert. The rennet in the lining of the pouch, combined with the heat of the sun, caused the milk to separate into curd and whey. That night he found that the whey satisfied his thirst, and the cheese (curd) had a delightful flavor that satisfied his hunger. Eventually cheese making flourished in Europe and later moved to America's shores with the new settlers. At the current time more than one-third of all the milk produced each year in the US is used to manufacture cheese.[1]

Cheese factories came to this area shortly after the middle of the 19th century about 25 years prior to creameries, which manufactured butter. The first cheese factory in the US was built in neighboring Oneida County in 1851. There was great variation in the quality and flavor of cheese coming from the dozens of farms in any area. Cheese buyers wanted a product that was not only of good quality but was consistently the same flavor, texture and color. The cheese factory provided a greater standardization of product that buyers could depend upon. With the arrival of railroads cheese could also be transported more rapidly to distant markets.

The equipment needed for a cheese factory was minimal. Tanks were needed to warm the milk to the desirable temperature and allow it to coagulate into curd. The curd was cut into small squares, heated to the appropriate temperature for the curds to harden. The liquid (whey) was drained and the curds put into a press to form blocks of cheese. The whey was usually used to fatten cattle or poultry but if a market wasn't readily available it was dumped into an adjacent stream. Often the farmer delivering his milk would take the previous day's whey back to the farm to feed his livestock.

We don't know where the first cheese factory was in our area or when it was established but there was an early cheese factory in the village

---

1 International Dairy Foods Association *History of Cheese*

The Baldwinsville Creamery straddled Tannery Creek, and faced E. Genesee St. approximately at Albert Palmer Lane. Elmer E. Fisher and Ovid Garrett started the creamery in 1884. Later, when Fisher retired, John Snell became a partner, it became known as Garrett & Snell Baldwinsville Creamery. Farmers delivered their milk to the creamery daily, and the creamery turned it into cheese and butter. A number of other creameries were located throughout each of the towns so farmers wouldn't have to haul their milk more than two or three miles.

of Lysander. Prior to 1865, the Lysander Cheese Manufacturing Co. leased a piece of land along Ox Creek, west of the four corners. The operator, John Coppernoll, reported that in 1865 the factory had processed milk and cheese worth nearly $25,000.[2] It appears to have changed hands several times. The Dun financial reports indicate the cheese factory was operated by Mrs. Ann Alexander in 1869 and sold to John Coppernoll in 1870. Further reports indicate it was operated by Ovid Brown during the years 1880 to 1883.

The Plainville Cheese Mfg. Co. was operating east of the four corners from 1872 to January 23, 1877 when it was destroyed in a fire. A.R. Jaycox was president of the company and L.H. Norton was Secretary and Treasurer. A creamery was constructed on the site at a later date. Prior to 1874 another milk manufactory (probably a cheese factory) was constructed on the Mud Lake outlet northeast of the Little Utica four corners. Both of the above facilities are shown on maps in *Sweet's 1874 Atlas*. The *Dun & Co.* financial rating firm also mentions visiting a cheese factory in Memphis, owned by Henry Daboll, during the years 1881-3. Daboll's cheese factory was also listed in the 1876 New York State Business Directory.

There was a long, red building on Marble Alley in Baldwinsville that manufactured cheese. A "Town News" column of July 26, 1867 mentioned the Baldwinsville Cheese Factory had 15 tons of

---

2 Shapiro, Missy Eileen *Time Past, People Life and Landscape in Northern Lysander During the 19th Century* p. 107

cheese curing.[3] There was also a cheese factory in Belgium on the site previously occupied by the boat works of Rome VanWagner. The cheese factory was managed by a Stebbins and later run by Fred and Charles Church.[4]

After 1875 cheese production on farms dropped very rapidly due to greater consistency of cheese by the cheese factories and their increased marketing skills. By 1900 farm production of cheese had all but disappeared. Cheese factories were also moving through the same competitive cycle of all types of manufacturing and were gradually absorbed or put out of business by larger and more efficient cheese factories. An additional factor in their demise was the gradual increasing profitability for dairy farmers to market their milk for the production of butter and sale as fluid milk. This change brought creameries to the Baldwinsville area.

The origin of butter is credited to the nomadic tribes of Asia around 3,500 B.C. Its use spread and by the Middle Ages butter had become a staple in the diet of many Europeans. The colonists brought cattle with them and, as with cheese, also brought the knowledge of butter making.[5] Butter is approximately 80% fat and retains about 20% water. Salt is normally added to give the butter better flavor and to aid in preservation.

Initially, farmers put their milk in pans to let the cream rise and skimmed the cream from the milk as they had done when making the butter on the farm before delivering the cream to the creamery where it was churned into butter. The skim milk was retained on the farm and fed to the farmer's livestock. About 1880, the cream separator

---

3 Christopher, A. J. *The Baldwinsville Creamery* November 28, 1963
4 Christopher, A.J. *Belgium Hamlet was once known as New Bridge* May 19, 1966

5 How Products are Made *Butter and Margarine*

The interior of the Garrett & Snell Creamery looks much different than today's spotless dairy interiors filled with stainless steel equipment. For its time, this creamery was state of the art. Note the 10-gallon milk cans in the foreground that were used by farmers to ship their milk to dairies until the 1960s.

was invented, which permitted rapid and more complete removal of the cream from the milk on the farm. Since the milk now did not have to set in pans for a day to allow the cream to rise, the quality of the cream delivered to the creamery improved.

Because the farmer delivered his milk to the creamery only once a day, he now had to build an ice house to store ice for cooling the evening milk from his cows. Many farmers accepted this added burden while others decided to discontinue dairying, and still others continued to make butter on the farm until it became impractical.

In addition to cream for the production of butter, a creamery in a village the size of Baldwinsville usually accepted whole milk to provide fluid milk for retail customers. Eventually, as we moved toward the middle of the 20th century, cream separation on the farm disappeared and whole milk went to the creamery. The author remembers often going with his father to local creameries and purchasing several hundred gallons of inexpensive skim milk to feed to his turkeys. At that time almost no person would have even considered drinking skim milk.

A creamery operated by Elmer E. Fisher and Ovid Garrett of South Granby started business in Baldwinsville in 1884. They first rented a building that stood near what is now East Genesee Street and Albert Palmer Lane at Tannery Creek. Later they added cheese making to their business and in some years processed over a million pounds of milk. When Fisher retired from the firm John Snell, a cheese maker, joined with Garrett and the business became known as Garrett & Snell, Baldwinsville Creamery.[6] In lists of manufacturers of various years the author did not find a creamery listed until Garrett & Snell at 37 East Genesee

---

6   Christopher, A.J. *Creamery Served Local Farmers* March 1, 1972

This picture taken in Lysander village circa 1900, shows a creamery on the left and a gristmill on the right. Lysander village was a small community but these two manufacturing businesses played an important role for local residents and neighboring farmers. The nearest large villages, Baldwinsville and Cato, were both more than seven miles away, which was too far to travel daily either on foot or by wagon. Photo courtesy of Frances Van Wie

Street was named in the 1909 *Baldwinsville Directory*. The Dairyman's League had a cheese factory and a butter creamery adjacent to the railroad tracks and south of the Baldwinsville Farmer's Cooperative at 82 E. Genesee St. in the early part of the 1900s.

There were several other creameries in the area, scattered to make it convenient for farmers to make their daily deliveries of milk or cream without having to drive their horses more than three or four miles. There were creameries at various times in Plainville, Lysander, Belgium, Jack's Reef, Bangall and Warners in addition to Baldwinsville. The 1915 *Baldwinsville Directory* also listed the Seiler Brothers Creamery at the D.L. & W. station on E. Genesee St.

There were a number of dairies in the Baldwinsville area well into the 20th century. Their business was primarily pasteurization and homogenization of milk for retail sale. Barnes Dairy, located on Salina Street just south of the railroad tracks, did make ice cream and perhaps there were others that also did manufacturing in a minor way. Byrne Dairy with plants in Syracuse and East Syracuse, currently operates convenience stores, carrying their dairy products, on Salina Street and Route 370 west of Baldwinsville. None of their manufacturing is done in the Baldwinsville area. The manufacture of butter and cheese, once an important area industry involving hundreds of people, has moved to distant locations because of lower costs, market availability and economy of scale. Even the number of dairy farms in Lysander and Van Buren has dramatically decreased from several hundred farms in the 1800s to fewer than the number of fingers on one hand today.

16

Wagons and Carriages

Baldwinsville had become a thriving little community before wagons or carriages appeared in the area. The only highways were the Seneca River and trails through the forest. Sleds, pulled by an ox, predated wagons and a person on horseback predated the carriage due to the difficulties in traveling by land.

As wider paths were cleared through the forests, sleds that could hold sizable quantities of goods were used. They were well utilized all 12 months of the year and were especially valuable during the winter when they could be pulled over snow easily. Another advantage of the sled was that it could made by anyone. All that was needed was an appropriate crotch from a tree with the larger limb beveled by an adz and then some split branches fastened across the two branches of the crotch. This type of sled could be made by a man in a few hours and was very durable.

When a sawmill came to a community the sled was improved by fastening several planks side by side. These sleds were turned up at the front and could glide over the rough terrain without dumping their load. Oxen effectively pulled a sled over rough terrain, since oxen moved more slowly than horses, and could be easily maneuvered around obstructions. This type of plank sled was still used on most farms well into the 20th century. It was often referred to as a stone boat.

Early settlers sometimes came with their goods piled on a two-wheeled cart pulled by an ox. As roads were improved, wagons gradually made their presence in the area. Settlers began to arrive with their goods on four-wheeled wagons pulled by horses. A settler, driving a wagon pulled by horses, showed substantial wealth.

Initially, a blacksmith often made the needed repairs for a wagon or oxcart but it was an unusual blacksmith that could construct a new wheel. As roads improved there was a need for wagons and carriages in the community. To provide these needs, wagon makers and carriage makers set up businesses in the area. Looking back at historical records it was very often the person gathering information for a directory that determined whether the business was called a wagon maker or a carriage maker as most businesses made both types of vehicles.

Actually, both wagons and carriages needed wheels with a carriage to which to attach the wheels. They both also needed a body, although in the case of a wagon it was often only a few boards. Even though a wagon is a carriage for a great variety of items, common terminology referred to a vehicle that carried people as a carriage. There is no question, however, that certain businesses specialized in vehicles that carried passengers and that some made only vehicles designed to carry merchandise. In all cases it was necessary to have a wheelwright who was an expert in making wheels.

It was often a talented blacksmith, who also had the skills of a wheelwright, who was the first manufacturer of wagons in a community. He had gathered experience in repairing wheels, but more likely had been indentured to a blacksmith who also made wagons, in a previously settled community.

The wheelwright made the wheels from a

combination of wood and iron. The wood components were the nave (hub), spokes and fellies. Holes needed to be accurately placed and sized in the nave to accommodate the spokes. Each felly, commonly made from elm or oak, received two spokes. The fellies were attached to each other and a red-hot iron band (tire) was fitted tightly to the circumference of the fellies. The hot tire burned away any small high spots in the fellies and pulled the wheel components tightly together as it shrunk while cooling.[1] A knowledgeable well-trained wheelwright was essential to make wheels that would last on the rough roads of the 19th century.

Wheels came in all diameters and widths. Wide heavy wheels were needed for wagons carrying heavy loads and light narrow wheels were used on carriages to provide a faster, more comfortable, ride. Whereas wagon carriages and bodies were quite simple, the carriage and the body of a coach (carriage) could be quite complicated. The carriage often had leather springs to ease the bumps and leather for the top and sides. Thin light wood was commonly used for the body, which was painted or varnished. A blacksmith was necessary to forge the iron components needed to give the carriage and body strength. Seats for the passengers were made from woolen cloth and stuffed with horsehair.

Most wagon and carriage manufacturers made sleighs (cutters) that were superior to carriages for traveling when snow covered the ground. Cutters had a body attached to runners and were pulled over the ground by a horse with little effort. They provided a smooth ride as the long runners eliminated most of the bumps in the roads. Early sleighs had heavy wooden runners with a strip of iron attached to the bottom. Later 19th century cutters were designed from lighter materials and had small, stylish iron runners.

As local families prospered they often purchased a fancy carriage, which parallels the 20th century when a family purchased an expensive automobile. In 1867, a local businessman purchased a

---

1 Stockham, Peter *Old Time Crafts & Trades, the Wheelwright* p. 84-87

The Haywood Wagon Works was located at the west corner of Lock and E. Genesee Streets, approximately where Dunkin Donuts is now located. The company produced a variety of commercial wagons including dump, garbage, coal and asphalt between 1903 and 1914.

This is a wheel stone, found outside many blacksmith and wagon shops throughout New York during the 19th century. The hub of the wheel, with spokes and the fellies attached, was placed in the hole in the center of the stone. The tire, a circular band of iron properly sized, was heated red hot and placed around the wheel. As it cooled the iron tire shrank and pulled all parts of the wheel tightly together.

custom-made family carriage from a local artisan for $750. With a fine pair of horses and fancy harness the cost was well over $1,000. (Remember that the common workman was earning less than a dollar a day at this time.) Another former Baldwinsville resident who had moved to Denver had a similar carriage made in Baldwinsville and shipped to Denver.[2]

Between 1825 and 1845 the population of the two towns almost doubled. This influx of population coupled with increased prosperity for the existing residents brought significant demand for wagons and carriages. Edith Hall in her book, *History of Baldwinsville*, stated that there were four carriage shops in 1849. *Boyd's Onondaga County Directory* of 1859 names wagon and carriage makers in Lysander, Jacksonville, Plainville, Van Buren and Baldwinsville. At various times there were also carriage and wagon shops located in Belgium, Warners and Memphis. (Due to the number of these shops most are named only in the appendix.)

Some wagon and carriage makers had a lifetime career in the local community with even a second generation continuing the business. In the village of Lysander Clark Berry is listed as a carriage maker in various directories from 1859 through 1881. In Jacksonville Alanson Fancher was making carriages in 1859, and Fancher & Son were still making carriages in 1881. Ebenezer Allen was named as a carriage maker in Plainville in 1870, as a wagon maker in Plainville in 1886 and as a carriage and coach manufacturer in Baldwinsville in 1881. A quote from A. J. Christopher's article, *Wagonmakers Were Many*, published in the *Baldwinsville Messenger*, states,

"Ebenezer Allen manufactured vehicles, with a shop and business in Plainville. His small factory burned to the ground in March 1879 and he decided to locate in Baldwinsville. After acquiring a lot on Syracuse St. in front of the red mill he procured lumber in Lysander, sending it down the river on a raft. The building was completed in October, and through the numerous years his shop was in operation, as many as five workmen were employed."

Another carriage manufacturer that moved his business from Plainville to Baldwinsville in the 1890s was Dunham & Son. He located his business in a new building at approximately 18 E. Genesee St.[3]

An interesting article from a January 17, 1889 paper is in the Van Buren files. Because it provides a candid insight into business during that time it is worth quoting. *"Mr. J.W. Fugett, our south side carriage dealer and blacksmith, has formed a partnership with Mr. Warren A. Burgess, of North Syracuse, and the business will continue to manufacture first-class wagons, cutters and sleighs, and carry a full line of whips, harnesses, robes, etc. Their blacksmithing department will continue to keep up to the high standard of work maintained by Mr. Fugett, and our readers know how good this has been. Mr. Burgess is a gentleman who understands all the business details of an establishment of this kind, while Mr. Fugett*

---

2 Christopher, A.J. *Wagonmakers Were Many* April 18, 1973

3 Christopher, A.J. *Wagonmakers Were Many* April 18, 1973

This is Harvey A. Moyer's first shop, which was located on the Oliver Moyer farm on Patchett Road. Mr. Moyer founded his carriage shop in 1876 and developed a large and successful carriage business. He produced automobiles in Syracuse from 1908 to 1914 but was not successful in that endeavor. Photo courtesy of OHA Museum & Research Center

is well known as a careful, conscientious manufacturer of A No. 1 vehicles. The new firm solicits a share of the trade of this locality. We know that Mr. Fugett can give you the best of satisfaction in every department, and with this addition to the head of the concern we bespeak a liberal patronage for the firm of Fugett & Burgess."

A very large and successful wagon business came to Baldwinsville in 1903. The Haywood Wagon Co. located on the site formerly occupied by the Bliss & Suydam sash and blind factory at approximately what is now 34 E. Genesee St.. They developed a prosperous business in the production of industrial wagons but moved to Newark, NY in 1914. They made contractors' dump wagons, the predecessor to today's dump trucks, asphalt, garbage and coal wagons, and stone spreaders. They employed about 40 men with a weekly payroll of $300 and produced 15 wagons a week. An interesting bit of trivia is that they also made a speedy, steel-bottom motorboat named the "Haywoodia" and a heavy fast bobsled designed to coast down Oswego Street. Morris Machine Works later operated a bronze foundry in the old Haywood building. [4]

Harvey A. Moyer started his successful carriage career in the Town of Lysander and moved his business to Salina and then to Syracuse. He was one of many successful carriage makers at the beginning of the twentieth century who saw the carriage business was soon to be doomed by the advent of the automobile. Like most, he found the challenges of the automobile industry greater than those of the carriage industry and did not obtain success with the automobile.

By 1915 there are no carriage makers listed in the *Baldwinsville Directory*. Perhaps an occasional blacksmith in the community made wagons, but the carriage industry went the way of the buggy whip industry. Farmers still needed wagons and continue

---

[4] Christopher, A.J. *The Haywood Wagon Works* October 11, 1962

to use them today; however, the wheels, carriages and even bodies are mass-produced in distant cities and shipped to our area. Today, about 50 miles southwest of Baldwinsville, is an Amish community where wagons and carriages are made and restored by individual craftsmen. Since this community still uses horses for transportation of goods and people, the talents of wagon makers and carriage makers are still needed.

Wagons and carriages were to the Baldwinsville area residents of the 19th century what trucks and automobiles are to people today. They were but one step in the gradual evolutionary process of transportation.

This is an image of downtown Baldwinsville in the 1880s on the day of the dedication of the Civil War monument (October 12, 1887) that is now located in Riverview Cemetery. Note the wagons and carriages, most of which were the products of local carriage and wagon manufacturers. Baldwinsville manufacturing was at its prime until the late 1800s. Most products were manufactured for local consumption and purchases were made from local manufacturers.

17

Pumps

Unquestionably, of all the single manufacturing businesses in the Baldwinsville vicinity during the last 200 years, Morris Machine Works has had the greatest impact. The company originated in 1864 as Heald & Sisco, later becoming Heald & Morris in 1875, a few years later becoming Morris Machine Works and finally in 1972, Morris Pumps. The pumps manufactured by this firm were of the highest quality and were used in all corners of the world.

One generally accepted version of the idea for the centrifugal pump is that it came from the mind of John Boley. Mr. Boley was working at a forge in the Heald plant in 1862 when a fire broke out. Some of the water used to extinguish the fire found its way into the blower, which was being driven by a belt from a lineshaft. The water was ejected from the blower in the same manner as the air, giving Mr. Boley the idea of adapting the principle of the air blower to make a similar device for pumping water. He successfully adapted the blower into a pump to move water, which marked the beginning of the pump industry in Baldwinsville. Experimentation followed with the issuance of patents and in 1864 the firm of Heald & Sisco was formed to manufacture and market pumps.

Gradually improvements to the pumps were made and a flourishing business developed. Disaster, however, struck in 1870 when fire destroyed all of their buildings, patterns, machinery and stock. Mr. Sisco died the same year and in 1875 his widow sold her shares to William F. Morris who later purchased the shares owned by Mr. Heald. William F. Morris was a son of Ezekial Morris who founded the Morris Axe Factory in 1850.

After the fire the company purchased property at the corner of Canal (now East Genesee St.) and Virginia Streets. This site, along with later additional nearby land purchases, became the home of Morris Machine Works for over 100 years. The company later produced steam engines with some connected directly to their pumps.

The company continued to expand its line of pumps and awards were won at several expositions.

Until 1895, Morris machinery was powered by steam engines but in that year water rights were purchased from James Frazee who had a flourmill directly across the street from the pump factory. Since the plant was located some distance from the canal, an overhead steel-rope drive carried the power to the plant. About this same time, Morris Machine Works sold steam engines to the Frazee Mill and also to J.C. Miller's knitting factory. A number of 120 horsepower engines were also manufactured to power the boats being constructed in Baldwinsville by Captain Melvin Brown.

By the 1890s Morris pumps were being sold in many locations for varied uses. Pumps were being used for the mining of phosphate in Florida, mining in Alaska, for use in the Sault Ste. Marie Falls Canal and for draining, irrigation and dredging in numerous states. The business continued to grow with additional buildings constructed and an increase in employees from 75 in 1896 to 170 in 1903. During the period prior to World War I, Morris pumps were purchased for use on several of

Heald, Sisco & Co. centrifugal pump works was established in 1864 on the south side of the Seneca River in Baldwinsville. A fire destroyed its buildings in 1870 and the company purchased property on Canal St. (now E. Genesee St.). In 1875, William F. Morris purchased Mr. Sisco's shares after his death, and the firm later became known as Morris Machine Works. This engraving was made between 1870 and 1875.

Morris Machine Works originated on the south side of the Seneca River in 1864 as Heald & Sisco. A fire in 1870, destroyed their buildings and they moved to the location of this circa 1890 picture at the corner of Virginia and East Genesee Streets. In 1895, the firm purchased water rights to power one water wheel that replaced the steam boilers they had been using for power. The large pulleys you see at the side of the building were likely there as part of this change in power. You will note that these are the same buildings as are in the previous Heald, Sisco engraving. Photo courtesy of OHA Museum & Research Center

the newly constructed US battleships. Sales passed the million-dollar mark in 1919 and employee numbers reached 350. In 1920, William F. Morris died and Windsor Morris became president.

The depression of the 1930s was difficult for the firm but as business in the world improved, Morris' record of consistent quality combined with the dedication of its employees pulled the company through those lean years. Windsor Morris died in 1936 and Carl Lager assumed the presidency but died a few years later and was succeeded by Gary Hotaling who was later succeeded by Alfred G. Forssell.

During World War II the company formed a subsidiary to procure contracts for the manufacture of defense materials. They made an important contribution to the war effort by subcontracting part making to other manufacturing plants and then assembling the parts at the Morris plant. During this time Morris purchased a bronze foundry at 82 East Genesee St., which was later sold to James Jardine. During the latter part of the war, pumps were produced for a top-secret project, which was later identified as the Atomic Laboratory at Oak Ridge, TN. In 1957, John C. Meyers became president.

In 1964, Morris Machine Works celebrated its 100th anniversary. During an open house the public was invited to view a 60 inch mixed flow centrifugal pump that weighed 55,000 pounds. This pump had been built by Morris for the Dow Chemical Company of Freeport, TX. At this time Morris manufactured a complete line of centrifugal pumps of from one to sixty inches in diameter. There were pumps for water, slurry, dredge, sewage, drainage, paper stock and general industrial use, not only in the United States but also in many parts of the world.

At the time of the Morris Machine Works Centennial, C. Alan Baker, editor of the *Baldwinsville Messenger*, in the September 24, 1964 edition, very succinctly conveyed the thoughts of the residents of the Baldwinsville area regarding Morris Machine Works.

"Whenever we think of industry, too often we emphasize the help that factories give us in terms of taxes. This is a valuable contribution obviously, but by no means is it the only measure of the importance of an

The Morris Machine Works office building at the corner of Virginia and East Genesee Streets was constructed in 1906. The adjacent buildings were also part of Morris Machine Works. The office and adjacent building were replaced in 1960 with a new office and production building. Photo courtesy of OHA Museum & Research Center

Ted White of White Signs is shown installing a spark arrestor on the stack at Morris Machine Works, circa 1946. At this time, prior to the day of the bucket hi-lift truck, ladders were the only means of reaching the necessary height. It was common practice for manufacturing firms, when they had a project that they were not equipped to handle in house, to rely on other local businesses. Photo courtesy of Ted White

industry like Morris Machine to a relatively small community such as Baldwinsville, NY.

Steady employment for the Morris labor force has meant security for their families, as well as for local business. Expansion of their business through new product lines has meant new jobs.

Over the years Morris has attracted scores of new people to our town. These new talents, and new leaders have taken their places in bolstering our churches, our schools, our lodges and our clubs.

All the folks at Morris—those who design the product, those who make it and those who sell it—have good reason to take pride in their company and the Morris reputation. One hundred years in the business represents a lot of pioneering, together with determination, vision and the ability to do the job well.

Here at this centennial observance we are certain that William F. Morris and Windsor Morris, men of vision, would be just as proud of Morris Machine Works as the rest of Baldwinsville is proud."

In 1972, the company changed its name to Morris Pumps, which more accurately described the products of the business. The business continued to expand in both physical facilities and product line. In 1981, the majority of the stockholders of Morris Pumps decided that the sale of the business to the Gould Pump Company of Seneca Falls would be in the best interests of the company. Control of the company was now removed from the realm of the local community. During its 117 year history of local control the company had been a stalwart community supporter. Its relationship with the village, schools, towns and residents of the community had been supportive. It had not only provided hundreds of well-paying jobs but had also provided benefits to its employees beyond those of most businesses of the same era.

Gould Pumps continued operating the business but gradually the number of employees in Baldwinsville declined. Gould Pumps is still listed as having a business in Baldwinsville in 1991 but by 1994 is no longer listed. In 1996 the Gould Pump Co. sold the Morris Pump Division to Yeomans Chicago Corporation of Aurora, IL. Yeomans is still producing and marketing Morris pumps for use around the world.

The Morris property and buildings in Baldwinsville were sold and later demolished. A spacious

This picture circa 1900, was taken inside Morris Machine Works. Note the large pulleys and belts to operate the machinery. Although working conditions look difficult and the equipment appears crude, it was the state of the art in manufacturing for this period in our history.

new community library was constructed on the site as well as a new shopping center. Although gone from the community, the name Morris is close to the hearts of many residents of the area and Morris pumps are continuing to move a great variety of products throughout the world.[1]

The pump industry has been gone from the Baldwinsville area for about two decades; however, the Morris name still exists on pumps performing their original duty in many locations throughout the world. The inventive minds and the creativity of several men a century and a half ago had a profound influence on the Baldwinsville community for well over a century.

---
1 Connell, Ruth M. *A Pure Gold Enterprise, Morris Machine Works and Morris Pumps* 1981. Most of the material in this summary of Morris Machine Works came from the paper written by Ruth when she was both the Town of Lysander and the Village of Baldwinsville Historian.

Following is a summary of the name changes in the development of Morris Pumps.

- **Heald, Sisco & Co.,** 1864, founded in Baldwinsville and in 1875 became Heald & Morris
- **Heald & Morris**, 1875, on Canal (approximately 33 E. Genesee St.) in Baldwinsville and in 1892 became Morris Machine Works.
- **Morris Machine Works**, 1892, on Canal Street in Baldwinsville and in 1972 became Morris Pumps.
- **Morris Pumps**, 1972, still at 33 E. Genesee Street (formerly Canal Street) and in 1981 became a subsidiary of the Gould Pump Co. of Seneca Falls.

Although Morris Pumps and its predecessors made Baldwinsville famous for its centrifugal

A view of the interior of Morris Machine works circa 1900. Notice the electric lights, which supplemented the natural light from the windows. Morris was one of the first businesses in Baldwinsville to generate their own electricity.

pumps, there were other manufacturers of pumps that need to be mentioned.

- Perry & Boley was formed by John Boley, who is credited with the idea of a centrifugal pump, and Eli Perry. John Boley developed the air blower into a centrifugal pump and received three patents. He had been a builder of grain cradles and joined with Eli Perry to manufacture pumps. The firm of Perry & Boley was succeeded by White, Clark & Co. in 1876.[2]
- White, Clark & Co., successor to Perry & Boley, was established in 1876 in the building formerly used as an axe factory. It employed eight workmen and was located on Bridge St. in Baldwinsville. The firm later became Clark & VanWie.
- Clark & VanWie moved from Baldwinsville to Syracuse in 1881.
- A.F. House, 1881, Lysander village

The pump manufacturers listed above are actually only three different firms as two of them had name changes following changes in ownership. One stayed in Baldwinsville for well over 100 years, one moved to Syracuse and the third, a small company in the village of Lysander, discontinued operations.

---

2 Christopher, A.J. *Two Pump Firms Originated Here* November 20, 1969

Pumps

This picture is of the last Morris Pumps office building, constructed in 1960 and located along E. Genesee St. This building, with the other remaining Morris buildings, were demolished in the 1990s after the company was sold to Gould Pumps in 1981, who in 1996 sold it to the Yeomans Chicago Corporation.

A large Morris pump ready for shipment to any of the four-corners of the world, circa 1964. Morris made centrifugal pumps of many sizes, from one to sixty inches, and for many uses including mining, dredging, drainage and irrigation.

113

Aerial view of Baldwinsville circa 1950. Morris Machine Works is the series of buildings on the right side of E. Genesee St. Tappan Lumber Co. is in the lower left and is located on the old Baldwinsville & Syracuse railroad yards. Note the Baldwin Canal, in the lower portion of the image parallel to E. Genesee St. The lower road crossing the Baldwin Canal from E. Genesee St. connects to the old Frazee Mill.

A 1960s aerial view of Baldwinsville showing the Morris Pumps new building, which included both manufacturing and offices. The two large brown buildings in the lower right, owned by Morris, were formerly tobacco warehouses. The Elizabeth St. School, formerly Baldwinsville Academy, is shown in the upper right. The Presbyterian Church is in the background and the large brick building to its left was formerly a tobacco warehouse.

18

Paper Mills

Paper dates back about 2,000 years ago, where it was made in China from hemp. Papyrus, which was used much earlier in Egypt, is not considered paper. Vellum and parchment, which also are much older than paper, were made from calfskin and sheepskin.

Production of paper gradually moved westward to the Arab countries and displaced papyrus. The first European paper mills came to Italy and Spain during the 11th century. Old clothes, supplemented with hemp, cotton and linen, were the primary source for paper in Europe and the western world until late in the 19th century. Beginning about 1840, straw became an important material for paper. There are about 400 different cellulose fibers that can be used for making paper including corn stalks and sugar cane but most of them have drawbacks that have prevented their use.

Straw from wheat, oats, barley and rye are all suitable for use in the production of paper. Straw was often mixed with old rags and other materials to produce paper. By varying the ingredients, different qualities of paper could be produced. The explosion in the production of magazines and books during the 19th century tremendously increased the demand for paper. Prior to and during the Civil War, with limited cotton shipments from the South and the need for cotton for bandages, the price of straw increased substantially.[1]

One of the drawbacks of straw is that its bulk makes storage and transportation difficult. In addition, straw is only produced in the summer, which increases the need for storage. Straw was readily available in the area around Baldwinsville during the 19th century. The soils were productive and the farmers grew large quantities of wheat, oats, barley and rye. The farmers had limited use for the straw from these crops and papermaking made a market for the straw.

It wasn't until the last half of the 19th century that wood was discovered as a source for paper. Wood produces much more paper for its bulk than does straw. Today about half of the trees cut annually are used in paper production. It is unlikely that paper made in Baldwinsville contained wood until late in the 19th century. Unlike many other local industries that lasted only a few years, paper was produced in Baldwinsville for about 100 years. Both the frequent changes in ownership and the numerous fires indicate that papermaking was a risky business. Under the right conditions and at the right times, it could also be profitable.

In 1866, C.G. Kenyon and Co. purchased what has been known as "paper mill point", between the Seneca River and the present west entrance to the Barge Canal Lock 24. This property was first occupied by sawmills and later by the distillery of Wetherby, Cook & Co. The owners of the paper mill were Charles A. Kenyon, John S. Kenyon, Peter Mumford and J.P. Shumway. The product manufactured was primarily a coarse wrapping paper. Production started early in the next year with about 20 employees. During the first year the mill was enlarged and an additional engine, boiler

---

[1] Peter Hutchinson *A Publisher's History of American Magazines* p.6

and bleaching equipment were installed. In 1874, the property was listed on the Van Buren assessment roll as Schoonmaker & Co. The mill burned on September 3, 1879. In 1885, the Van Buren tax assessment roll shows Kenyon & Dixon as owners of the paper mill. On December 22, 1898 it was reported that the Kenyon Paper Mill was destroyed by fire. On June 19, 1903 the paper mill burned again. The paper mill was rebuilt and from 1903 to 1909 was listed as the Kenyon Paper Co. in the Town of Van Buren records. The *1909 Baldwinsville Directory* lists E.H. Hoffman as proprietor and the product of the mill as tissue paper. The paper mill burned for the fourth time October 27, 1914 and by 1917 the mill was known as the Hoffman, Youmans Paper Co. In 1925, the death of paper manufacturer Richard S. Hoffman was listed in the *Gazette & Farmers' Journal* and later that year W. H. Hoffman Paper Mill was sold to Beebe Mills, Inc. of New York City. A notice in the April 7, 1927 *Gazette & Farmers' Journal* stated that Beebe Mills, Inc. was undergoing a process of liquidation and in the future would operate under the name of National Cellulose Corp.[2]

There is some confusion as to the ownership of the company indicated by the records of Dun & Co., which regularly sent representatives to assess the financial strength of businesses. In 1869, the Dun Co. mentioned H. Monroe as principal of a paper mill, S. Fox in 1871, Lefever & Palen in 1873 as successors to Kenyon and Dixon & Kenyon in 1882. There were likely at least two generations of Kenyons involved considering the differing initials between the 1866 mention of C. G. Kenyon and the fact that Jacob C. Kenyon was listed as owner in 1892.

The National Cellulose Co. manufactured facial tissue, toweling, cellulose wadding and napkins. The company had as many as 110 employees at its peak. During the later period of its operations the company purchased pulp to make the paper from outside sources. In 1936, National Cellulose moved its conversion operation to Eastwood, in Syracuse, while continuing operations on "paper mill point". In 1945, the Eastwood property was sold to Bristol Labs and the conversion operation moved back to Baldwinsville, locating it in the old tobacco warehouse directly across the street from the Presbyterian Church. In 1954, the property on Oswego St. was sold to Baldwinsville Furniture and Appliance Co. The National Cellulose Co. ceased all operations in Baldwinsville in 1956.[3]

In the Van Buren history files is a handwritten article, with the date March 18, 1886, describing the Kenyon Paper Mill. There is no identification as to the author or of the date it was written; however, excerpts of the article are worthy of recording.

"The mill initially manufactured tissue and manila paper. After about two years the partnership was dissolved and the mill was leased to Henry Munroe of Cazenovia and refitted for the manufacture of straw wrapping paper. Munroe continued until 1870 and then leased the mill to Lewis A. Fox of Middleburgh, Schoharie County. After running the mill about a year Mr. Fox was joined by John S. Kenyon as a partner. In 1872 this firm sold to Le Fevre & Palen who continued until 1873 when A.S. Schoonmaker purchased their interest. In 1874, Jacob C. Kenyon and Theodore Haines bought an interest in the mill known as Schoonmaker & Co. On September 3, 1879 the mill burned destroying the machinery. A new brick building was constructed on the site to manufacture 1st class straw wrapping paper. In 1882, J.C. Kenyon purchased an interest and admitted Isaac Dixon as a partner with the firm now being known as Kenyon & Dixon."

"Two tanks were used to bleach the straw, each holding 14 to 15 tons. Limewater was added and the whole batch was boiled with steam. The bleached straw was moved by an elevator to two smaller tanks, which contained a cylinder with knives to cut the straw into fine particles. At this point the pulp resembled paper that has been thoroughly soaked. It was conveyed to a storage from where it was pumped to a series of rollers that determine the size and thickness of the paper. Finally it passed over steam-heated rolls to dry the paper and then the paper was wound onto rolls for cutting into proper sizes. The production was approximately 80 tons of paper a month and was marketed in the eastern states. The paper had a fine glossy finish and could be handled without crushing or breaking. A 125 horsepower boiler furnished the steam for bleaching. Water powered three turbine wheels and one center discharge wheel to provide a total of 80 horsepower. A gentleman by the name of Abram Carpenter had the contract to furnish the

---

2   R.F. Nostrant *Chronology of Paper Mill Point* January 9, 1998

3   A. J. Christopher *Paper Mill's Long Existence* December 4, 1974

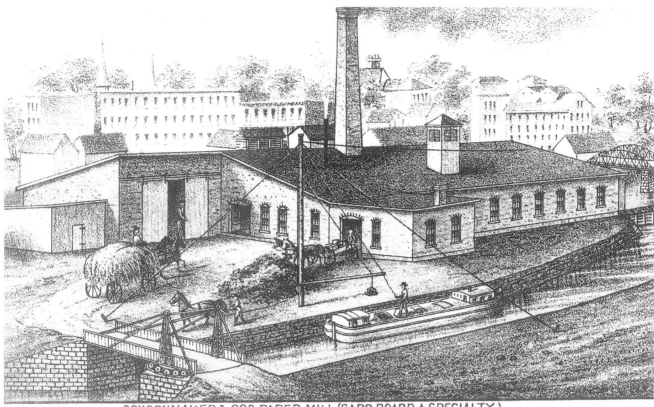

SCHOONMAKER & COS, PAPER MILL (CARD BOARD A SPECIALTY.)

The Schoonmaker & Co. paper mill was located on "paper mill point", circa 1874, before the construction of the Barge Canal turned it into 'paper mill island". It first became used for a paper mill in 1866 when the property was purchased by C.G. Kenyon & Co. There were several fires that destroyed the buildings and also several owners during the property's existence as a paper mill. Notice the farmers bringing loads of straw, which was used to make paper. The paper mill continued in operation until 1956 when the National Cellulose Company closed the plant. Image courtesy of OHA Museum & Research Center

mill with 2,000 tons of straw annually. Eleven men worked at the mill, which operated day and night."

Waterpower, a ready access to straw and access to the canal for procurement of supplies and marketing of products brought the paper mill to Baldwinsville. By the 1950s all of these advantages had disappeared and competition from other areas of the country brought almost a century of paper making in Baldwinsville to a close.

West Phoenix, with its access to the waterpower of the Oswego River had three large paper factories from the late 1800s until well into the 1900s.

- Judge Avery and John Waugh established the Phoenix Toilet and Paper Manufacturing Co. in 1875 under the name Phoenix Paper Manufacturing. The company later opened a second factory on the east side of the Oswego River and was considered the second largest toilet paper manufacturer in the country. They sold their product in all of the United States, Mexico, Cuba and Europe.[4] Their factory in West Phoenix was destroyed by fire in 1948.[5]

- Edmund Merry, John O'Brien and M.C. Murgittroyd constructed the Oswego River Paper Mill in 1889. The mill was 44 by 140 feet and three stories in height. It commanded one-quarter of the waterpower of the river and had capacity to produce two and a half tons of paper a day. It first produced toilet paper in reams but by 1902 the paper was cut into toilet rolls, which was

---

4 Grip, *Grip's Historical Review of Phoenix* p. 85
5 Sauers, Evelyn L. *The Story of Schroeppel (Oswego County NY)* p. 132

Lino Scusa, a noted West Phoenix toolmaker, is shown with a toilet paper making machine he invented. He founded the Phoenix Gage Co. in 1910 and made many inventions of value to the paper milling industry. Photo from The Story of Schroeppel *by Evelyn L. Sauers.*

the main part of their business. Their paper was sold throughout the United States.[6]

- The third paper mill in West Phoenix began operations in 1891 and was owned by Frank Dilts of Fulton. Mr. Dilts purchased the building constructed in 1868 by A.W. Sweet that had previously been the Phoenix Coffin and Cabinet Works.[7]

Paper factories changed hands from time to time. Other names associated with one of the West Phoenix paper factories were the River Valley Paper Co., Woods Paper Co. and Velvet Tissue Co. A significant contribution to the West Phoenix toilet paper industry was the invention of a toilet paper making machine by Lino Scusa.[8] Scusa had formed the Phoenix Gage Co. in 1910 and was a notable toolmaker.[9]

The tremendous power of the Seneca and Oswego Rivers brought papermaking to both Baldwinsville and West Phoenix. Paper manufacturing companies are now part of our history but during their time brought many jobs and made a significant contribution to the economy of the area.

---

6 Grip, *Grip's Historical Review of Phoenix* p. 85
7 Grip, *Grip's Historical Review of Phoenix* p. 5

8 Sauers, Evelyn L., *The Story of Schroeppel (Oswego County, NY)* p. 94
9 Ibid, p. 92

19

Electricity and Gas

Electricity

In 1886, three Baldwinsville manufacturing businesses lighted their shops with electricity generated on their premises: J.C. & J.C. Miller knitting mills, Morris Machine Works and the Amos Milling Company.

The Miller Company contacted representatives of the Edison Electric Company and purchased an adjacent property (at approximately what is now 7 Oswego St.), including water rights, from the J.M. Young's Fork Company for a hydroelectric plant site. The existing water wheel was replaced with a modern turbine wheel to drive their generators, which produced direct current rather than the alternating current that we use today. The name of the new company formed was the Edison Illuminating Company of Baldwinsville.[1]

A proposal by the Edison Co. to furnish electricity to the village and an expenditure of $500 for street lighting was approved by the voters on October 13, 1887. The Edison proposal to supply 85 incandescent lights to run all night, every night, for $1,000 was accepted and the generating plant was installed.[2] The village's streetlights were illuminated with electricity for the first time on February 4, 1888. At about the same time a number of merchants made arrangements for lights in their stores and numerous residents replaced the oil lamps in their homes with electric lights.[3]

In 1886, W.F. Morris ran a line from his plant to the Grace Episcopal Church, which became the first church in the United States to be lighted with electricity. In November 1887, Morris Machine Works connected electric power to drive a pump in their shop, which is likely the first use of an electric motor to power a machine in the village of Baldwinsville.

In 1902, the Edison Illuminating Company of Baldwinsville was sold to George W. Pulver who made improvements to the powerhouse and named the new business the Seneca River Power Company. Only when the Syracuse Lighting Company took over the operations in 1925 did electric service extend significantly beyond Baldwinsville.[4] Later, the electrical service to Baldwinsville was supplied by the Niagara-Mohawk Power Company and currently is supplied by National Grid.

It took almost 50 years after electricity came to the homes in Baldwinsville for it to reach all of the rural areas of the towns of Lysander and Van Buren. It reached the author's home near Plainville in 1928 and was even later in some of the more remote areas. As a boy the author remembers his father stopping to pay his monthly electrical bill at the Syracuse Lighting Company's office at 5 Syracuse Street.

Electricity is still being generated from the waterpower provided by the dam in Baldwinsville. Niagara-Mohawk was required to divest some of their generating facilities by the US government

---

1 Christopher, A.J. *Electric Company is Organized* February 14, 1973
2 Bruce, Dwight H. *Onondaga's Centennial* p. 767
3 Hall, Edith *History of Baldwinsville* p. 63
4 Christopher, A.J. *Edison Illuminating Company of Baldwinsville* May 18, 1961

An image of the old Syracuse Lighting Company electric generating plant constructed in the early 1900s, and adjacent to the dam on the north side of the Seneca River. It is currently owned by Brookfield Power Co. and its two generators produce 0.6 megawatts of electricity.

and sold the generating plant on the north side of the Seneca River to a company by the name of Orion, who later sold it to a firm by the name of Reliant. The plant was sold in 2004 to the current owner, Brookfield Power, which owns hundreds of electric generating plants in North America. The plant is 0.6 megawatts and has two generators. In Van Buren, Wave Hydro LLC owns the hydro power plant located between the Barge Canal and the Seneca River. In West Phoenix a hydroelectric plant producing 3,500-kilowatts is operated by Algonquin Power Systems.

Natural Gas

With the oil well boom in PA in the late 1800s many local residents wondered if there might be oil deep in the ground in the Baldwinsville area. Near Warners there was a pond in the woods covered with an oily film and south of Plainville there was a spot where a lighted match held over a pool of water caused a slight explosion. Today we recognize that the decay of organic matter can create such situations. Natural gas had been discovered and put to use near Sandy Creek, so why not Baldwinsville?

In 1895, a dozen local businessmen and some outsiders started leasing land in and adjacent to Baldwinsville with the idea of drilling for oil and gas. Contacts were made in PA and a German named Gustav Leopold came to Baldwinsville in a democrat wagon, a light wagon used to carry either passengers or merchandise, pulled by a team of horses. Part of his cargo was bottles of nitroglycerin suspended from springs to minimize the danger of an inappropriate explosion. Drilling commenced for the first well in March 1896 on the Munro farm, currently where the Baldwinsville High School and district offices are located. In late June, at a depth of over 1,000 feet, gas was located with 1,200 pounds

This is the electric generating plant on the Oswego River in West Phoenix operated by Algonquin Power Systems. It produces 3,500 kilowatts of electricity. There have been numerous manufacturing facilities at and near this site since a sawmill was constructed in 1829.

of pressure at the wellhead.[5] A flame 20 to 30 feet in diameter and 20 feet high burned for more than a week.[6]

Drilling continued for other gas wells around Baldwinsville, and natural gas was located from a depth of 1,000 feet to more than 2,000 feet. A stock company called the Baldwinsville Light and Heat Company was formed to market the natural gas. Numerous village homes were supplied with gas, and lines were run to Phoenix and Fulton. Later the lines were extended to Syracuse, Jordan and Elbridge. A Fulton newspaper of 1898 stated that the Baldwinsville gas was satisfactory and economical, the price being 25 cents per thousand cubic feet and a top pressure of 200 pounds was registered at the city.[7]

By 1908 the supply of gas started to dwindle and supply to the more distant locations was cut off. By 1910 only the local users had access to the gas. Low-producing wells were gradually abandoned to the farmer on whose land they were located and were used by them until the flow was exhausted. The Virklers on Canton Street Road continued to use gas from a well on their farm past the middle of the 20th century. Edward Loveless and Albert Johnson drilled a well for their own use at their own expense, for $1,500, adjacent to the old East Sorrell Hill road in the edge of the village. The well did not meet their expectations but a small amount of this gas was used in the Albert Johnson household until about 1955. By 1930 when the supply of local gas had almost disappeared, the Niagara-Mohawk Company brought an ample supply to the village from Syracuse. It is quite possible that in 2011 there still may be an unknown homeowner or two in the

---

5 Christopher, A. J. *Gas Wells were Plentiful in Early Baldwinsville* March 2, 1961
6 Hall, Edith *History of Baldwinsville* p. 65
7 Christopher, A.J. *Gas Wells were Plentiful in Early Baldwinsville* March 2, 1961

This is an image of the American Knife Works and the derrick for its gas well located between the Baldwin Canal and the Seneca River off Lock St. In the 1890s natural gas was discovered in Baldwinsville at a depth of from 1,000 to 2,000 feet and the Baldwinsville Light and Heat Company was formed to market it. About a decade later the gas supply began to diminish and eventually the gas wells were abandoned. There is still a pipe from this old gas well that has been capped, protruding from the ground on the east side of the former Town of Lysander office building on Lock Street.

Baldwinsville area still using gas from one of the old gas wells.

In the latter part of the 1900s gas wells were drilled to a greater depth in the Town of Lysander on Tater Road and on Dog Harbor Road. Natural gas was located but not in sufficient quantity to utilize the wells. Recently, firms have been securing gas leases in the area with the hopes of drilling deeper into the Marcellus shale and using a process of hydrofracking to release large quantities of gas. This method has been very successful in PA. It is possible that some time in the future the Baldwinsville area will again be producing natural gas and in much greater quantities than a century ago.

20

Millinery and Beyond

Millinery businesses, like blacksmiths and shoemakers, did not employ more than one or two persons in any shop but played a needed role in most 19th and early 20th century communities. Millinery shops were the first commonly found manufacturing enterprise owned and operated by women. The dictionary defines a milliner as a person who designs, makes, trims or sells women's hats. Millinery shops appeared in Baldwinsville and surrounding area by the middle of the 19th century and continued well into the 20th century.

Although milliners' main product was hats, the talent and individuality of the milliner would often expand her offerings to include one or more of the following: neckerchiefs, caps, cloaks, hoods, petticoats, shirts, shifts, ruffles and trim for gowns. When it comes to ladies' hats, the raw materials were varied to provide hats that were not only functional but were elegant and unique. Some of the materials used were artificial flowers, feathers, muslin, gauze, crepe, lace and ribbons. All of these materials came in a wide variety of colors and shapes to ensure that even if 1,000 hats were produced, each one would be different.

A successful milliner needed to be flexible and ready to change her line of hats to follow the changes in style occurring in London, Paris and New York City. Although Baldwinsville was well removed from these cities that set the trends in the millinery industry, it was important to not fall too far behind or a local millinery competitor would pirate away some business. Locally produced materials, although important, were not sufficient to maintain a successful business. Exotic materials needed to be imported: muslin from the East Indies, spangles from France and Germany, crepe from England and unusual feathers from all corners of the world.

In 1886, Paul Chapman, ornithologist for the American Museum of Natural History in New York City, during the course of two walks in Manhattan noted feathers from 40 different species of birds on the hats of the ladies on the streets. Of the 700 hats he observed, three quarters of them were decorated with bird feathers. The great egret and the snowy egret of the heron family were extremely popular. The male of these birds had especially beautiful feathers during the mating season, which were highly prized. There was a period in the early 1900s when egret feathers for use in ladies' hats were worth more than gold. In 1902, there were 1,608 thirty-ounce packages of heron feathers sold in London. These feathers came from almost 200,000 herons that had been indiscriminately killed in rookeries. There was serious danger of the extermination of the species, and the Audubon Society, along with preservationists, mounted a campaign to make the slaughter of these wild birds illegal. By World War I the practice had been discontinued and feathers for hats were either artificial or came from domestically raised birds.

The milliners of Baldwinsville and surrounding areas were numerous from 1850 until World War II. A list of some of these feminine entrepreneurs found in local directories follows.

Mrs. E. Cardell, milliner and dressmaker, Baldwinsville, August 8, 1850 *Onondaga Gazette*

Listed in the *1876 New York State or the 1878 Onondaga County Directory* as milliners:
  Miss Laura Bowman, 5 Canal St., Baldwinsville
  Mrs. J. M. Scoville, 54 Bridge St., Baldwinsville
  Mrs. Lizzie Lindon, White block on Bridge St., Baldwinsville
  Mrs. Charles Woodford, 35 Syracuse St., Baldwinsville
  Mary E. Wormuth, Canal St., Baldwinsville
  Mrs. E.H. Wooster, Lysander
  Mrs. Harriet Buck, Memphis
  Mrs. Louisa M. Gilley, Memphis

Boyd's 1892 Business Directory of Baldwinsville lists these milliners:
  Mrs. Charles Root
  Miss Emma Seager
  Nettie J. Turner

Boyd's Business Directory of 1909 and 1915 list the following milliners:
  Miss S.T. Costello, 42 Oswego St., Baldwinsville
  Miss Ada Pierce, 11 E. Genesee St.

Beyond Millinery

As this author explored the history of manufacturing in the Baldwinsville area, he realized that an important aspect of manufacturing was being overlooked. During the 1800s and well into the 1900s America was a male dominated society. Wives took a back seat to their husbands with the male member of the family generally receiving any recognition that might come in the family's direction, regardless of which member really deserved the recognition. Today this is changing and the distaff side of the family has greater opportunity and generally receives recognition that is earned. A brief review of a few facts from the past will substantiate this overlooked side of manufacturing.

In 1835, there were 17,187 yards of cloth manufactured in homes in the Town of Lysander and 16,530 yards of cloth in Van Buren homes. Women were the ones who prepared the flax and wool, spun it into thread, wove it into cloth and turned the cloth into clothes. At that time the total population of the two towns was only 6,801. This equates to approximately five yards of cloth produced for each person in the two towns. Five yards of material provided a major part of the clothes worn by the residents during that time period. This was a major manufacturing business employing close to 3,000 women on a part time basis.

In 1855, there were 207,813 pounds of butter produced in the Town of Lysander and 133,425 pounds of butter produced in the Town of Van Buren. The women in the families produced almost all of this butter in the homes on the farms with cows since creameries did not come into existence for another several decades. There were about 700 farms in the two towns at this time. If 500 of these farms had cows, each farm produced an average of almost 700 pounds of butter annually. Women generally milked the cows and churned the butter until late in the 19th century. This was another manufacturing business employing approximately 500 women part time. In addition to producing butter, these same women also produced over 60,000 pounds of cheese in 1855.

It wasn't until the last half of the 19th century that textile mills became prominent and began employing women. The Miller family came to Baldwinsville in 1876 and their textile factory employed up to 200 people, mostly women and young girls, during the 1880s to 90s. Women were always paid less than men, receiving less than $1 for a 10-hour day. When the canning factory came to Baldwinsville in 1898 most of its employees were young women.

As the 19th century progressed fewer and fewer women were employed in the homes producing cloth and making butter but were instead working in factories in the mass production of manufactured goods. While these changes were taking place there were also women showing their entrepreneurial spirit by starting their own business.

Often when a woman's husband died the widow continued the business, sometimes without skipping a beat and continuing the business indefinitely, while at other times continuing the business until it could be sold. An example of this is demonstrated in the history of Morris Machine Works. After Windsor Morris died in 1936, Mrs. Morris continued her connection with the company, later becoming Chairman of the Board of Directors. The company continued its success in Baldwinsville for another half a century.

In perusing through the various Directories we find women as the owners of a variety of manufacturing businesses in the 1870s. Mrs. L. Warner of 1 Charlotte St. is listed as a cabinetmaker in 1876. Mrs. Maryiette Spratt is listed as the owner of a foundry in the village of Lysander and Mrs. Alexander is shown as the owner of the Lysander Cheese Factory. During the same period Mrs. Lucy Wilson is listed as owning a business providing waterpower in Phoenix. In the *1915 Baldwinsville Directory*, Eva Brown of 33 Canton St. is listed as a baker.

The role of women in manufacturing, although generally overlooked, played an important part in the development of Baldwinsville and the towns of Lysander and Van Buren. Recorded in this chapter are just a few of the names of thousands of women who dedicated a substantial part of their lives in the production of manufactured goods.

21

Other 19th and Early 20th Century Industries

In the 19th century, if there was a local need for a product someone set up a business to manufacture it. Early in the century, transportation of products from one part of the country to another was slow and expensive. Most manufacturing facilities tended to be small with a localized market area. Occasionally, proximity to raw materials, a readily available supply of labor, business expertise and marketing acumen enabled a business to prosper and compete effectively against competitors from other localities. Eventually most small businesses passed by the wayside when they became unprofitable or when the owner died. The majority of the manufacturing firms in this chapter and most of the other chapters had a productive life of less than 40 years.

We know very little of the many small industries of the 19th century other than at some time they were mentioned in a directory of businesses. The industries varied but provided items needed by local residents. Some may have existed for only a few months while others found a niche and continued for years. Manufacturers between 1800 and 1950 that are not discussed in other chapters are mentioned here. Name of manufacturer, date of mention and location are as follows. Unfortunately and unquestionably, some manufacturers are lost to posterity.

Agricultural implements
- James Gaylord, 1881, Lysander village
- Fairbanks & Co., 1881, Baldwinsville
- C.C. Nagley & Son, 1892, Memphis. Charles Nagley is mentioned as a blacksmith in Memphis as early as 1876. He became a manufacturer of tools for the tobacco industry in the 1880s and patented a transplanting machine on January 19, 1892 and a tobacco cutter on August 5, 1885. He also made tobacco presses.

Axes
Morris Axe Co. was founded by Ezekial Morris in 1850 when he came to Baldwinsville from Little Falls. After his death in 1869, he was succeeded by his sons H.D. and W.F. Morris. The firm later changed its name to Morris Axe Edge Tool Co. The firm continued to make axes into the 1870s. In 1871, it received shipment of 31 grindstones, each weighing 150 pounds, by canal boat.

Barges
James Stewart Co., 1918, used the yards of the Barge Canal at Baldwinsville to make war barges.

Barrel bungs, broom handles and hand-spikes
R. Rogers, 1846, Baldwinsville. Robert Rogers operated a lumberyard and claimed he stocked 25,000 to 30,000 broom handles. He bought hickory and beech logs to make the handles.[1]

---
1 Christopher, A.J. *B'ville Had Broom Industry* October 8, 1970

In the late 1800s, the M.P. Brown boat works constructed large passenger boats measuring 18 feet by 90 feet that could carry more than 250 people. These boats were fitted with steam engines, often from Morris Machine Works, and were constructed at two different locations, the foot of Lock St. and the foot of North St. Photo courtesy of OHA Museum & Research Center

Baskets
John & A. Blakeman, 1875, Plainville

Batteries
William Letterman, circa 1930s -1960s, West Genesee St., Baldwinsville

Bed springs
James E. Decker, 1876, Lysander village

Bluings and ammonia
So-jer Manufacturing Co., 1915, 4 Syracuse St., Baldwinsville

Boats and boat frames
- Valley Boat Works, 1909, on Canton Street in Baldwinsville
- M.P. Brown built large boats, in the 1880s and 90s, for passenger and freight traffic on the Central New York waterways. Some were constructed at the foot of North St. and others at the foot of Lock St. between the Baldwin Canal and the river. Most of the boats were 90 feet long by 18 feet wide and could carry 250 people on excursions from Baldwinsville to resorts on Onondaga Lake. Some of his boats were powered with high-pressure boilers manufactured by Morris Machine Works.[2]

Boring machines
Kenyon Manufacturing Co., 1881, Baldwinsville

---

2   Christopher, A.J. *Brown Crafted Packet Boats at B'ville Location* February 1, 1968

Brooms
- John Virginia, 1881, Baldwinsville south side
- Judson Smith, 1885, River St., Baldwinsville
- Jessie Palmer, circa 1900, 4 Walnut St., Baldwinsville

Cabinets
- A. Simmons, 1846, between the two bridges in Baldwinsville
- George S. Wells, 1846, Charlotte Street, Baldwinsville
- Seth Brown, 1859, Baldwinsville
- J.G. Dundore, 1859, Baldwinsville
- Jerome S. Mosely, 1859, Baldwinsville
- William E. Huntington, 1859, Baldwinsville
- L.E. Warner, 1868, Baldwinsville
- E.R. & E.C. Brown, 1881, Baldwinsville
- Avery's Cabinet Works, 1852, West Phoenix

You will note the majority of the above cabinetmakers who were listed in the various directories are dated prior to 1860. It is an indication that cabinets and furniture manufacturing was moving to larger centers of population by 1860 and were being mass-produced rather than one piece at a time. There continued to be a need for cabinetmakers for special projects, fancy carriages and caskets.

In 1898, the Mack-Miller Candle Company purchased the property that was previously the Bamboo Furniture Co., between the paper mill and the Riverview Cemetery, near what is now the west end of Barge Canal Lock 24. The state took their property by eminent domain in 1907 and the company moved to Syracuse. Notice the rail spur, in the foreground, that came along the south side of the river to the factory. Photo courtesy of OHA Museum & Research Center

The cider mill and sawmill located on the south side of Ellsworth Road, circa 1940. This is the probable spot where Hiram H. and James A. Scoville built a sawmill on Crooked Brook in 1824. Orlando Houghtaling was the last to operate the sawmill, cider business and ice business on this site. Photo courtesy of OHA Museum & Research Center

Candles

The Mack-Miller Candle Company, in 1898, purchased the property between the paper mill and the cemetery that had previously been used by for production of bamboo furniture. The company employed about 25 girls and 35 men and operated a successful business. It also made tailor's chalk, incense burners and synthetic charcoal in a building at the rear. The state took the property by eminent domain for the Barge Canal in 1907. Inability to locate on a suitable property in Baldwinsville resulted in their relocation to Syracuse.[3]

Churns

(no name available), 1878, Lysander village

Cider

- W.A. Wright, circa 1876, Jacksonville
- James Nostrand, 1868, Memphis
- Jerome Snyder, (also vinegar) 1881, Baldwinsville
- F. L. Mahoney, 37 E. Genesee St., Baldwinsville, 1923
- Orlando Houghtaling, 1936, Ellsworth Road, Baldwinsville

Edge Tool Manufacturers

- Sharp & Co., scythes, 1859, Baldwinsville
- Harris, Baldwin & Co., (axe heading machines) 1872, Baldwinsville
- Young & Frazee Tool Co., 1883, Baldwinsville
- American Knife Co. In 1901, Addison Tooley and W.F. Marvin moved their knife manufacturing plant from Fulton to Baldwinsville. They purchased the Wilkins mill site (southwest corner of Lock and E. Genesee Streets). A 40 by 150 foot one story building was constructed with a water powered line shaft. A gas well was drilled to furnish heat for the building and for the furnaces. Twelve men were employed with sometimes as many as 30. A variety of knives were produced but the company's specialty was ensilage cutter knives, used by farmers to chop corn stored in silos. The business was purchased in 1945 by W.B. Colitre, T.S. Seifert and G.C. Dutton and modernized at that time. The business closed in around 1960.[4]
- Central City Knife Co. was founded in the latter 1800s, in West Phoenix by J.I. Van Doran. He brought workmen from England to work in his factory. An 1885 photo shows over 50 employees in his factory. Later the business moved to the east side of the Oswego River.[5]

---

3 Christopher, A.J. *The Mack-Miller Candle Factory* August 16, 1962

4 Christopher, A.J. *Tooley Operated Knife Works on Old Island Site* Sept. 29, 1966

5 Sauers, Evelyn L., *The Story of Schroeppel (Oswego County, NY)* p. 51

Other 19th and 20th Century Industries

The American Knife Co. was located between the Baldwin Canal and the Seneca River, south of E. Genesee St. on the site of the former Wilkins mill, and southeast of where the present Dunkin Donuts is located. The author can remember the clanking of the planks on the bridge as he crossed the Baldwin Canal to reach the knife works. The business was in operation producing knives, including ensilage cutter knives, from 1901 to about 1960. The author also remembers the large number of worn-out grindstones lying outside the building.

(right) This is an advertisement for a steam engine manufactured in the 1870s by White and Fox who were located on Bridge Street in Baldwinsville. These steam engines were used as a source of power where waterpower was unavailable or as supplemental use during periods of drought when water levels were low.

Engines
- Heald, Sisco & Co., 1881, Baldwinsville
- White & Fox, 1878, Bridge Street, Baldwinsville

Emery Wheels and Emery Powder
Frank Symansky and Joseph Jacques, 1903, Baldwinsville south side. (They were induced to come here by A. J. Tooley of the American Knife Factory. They had an emery factory in North Tonawanda where they employed 75 men and anticipated employing 25 men here. Emery was made by crushing ore imported from Turkey.) (Newspaper November 5, 1903)

Flexible shafts
Fancher Machine Co. was established in 1901 at Baldwinsville's Downer Street and Canton Streets by Aaron P. Clark, R.I. Fancher and W.H. Tappan. They produced flexible shafts and flexible boring and drilling machines for the carriage manufacturing and the

This image shows the excavation, which began in 1907, for the Barge Canal Lock 24 in Baldwinsville. A number of businesses were either moved or razed for the canal. Note the arrows on the photograph pointing out the Mack-Miller Candle Factory and Papermill Island.

mining industries. They also patented a tomato scalder for canning factories. This company was listed in the *1909 Baldwinsville Directory*.[6]

Folding boxes

Breroha Paper Box Co., 1909, 8 Syracuse Street, Baldwinsville

Forks

- Otsego Fork Co., 1869, located north of the bridge and east of Oswego St. in Baldwinsville. The building burned on February 22,
- Young & Frazee, 1882, John M. Young's fork and rake factory started circa 1877 in a portion of what was the axe factory north of the river between the bridge and dam in Baldwinsville.

Furniture

- J. Holcomb, 1876, Memphis
- Syracuse Bamboo Furniture Co. purchased property between the paper mill and the cemetery in 1891 from Jacob Kenyon and erected a building 150 feet long by 54 feet wide and 34 feet high. The D. L. & W. Railroad extended their Water St. branch along the south side of the building almost to the cemetery. Products manufactured were bamboo furniture and fishing tackle

---

6 Christopher A.J. *Fancher Machine was a South Side Industry* April 1, 1971

Other 19th and 20th Century Industries

Circa 1910 ice delivery wagons of E.E. Ellsworth of Baldwinsville. The sides of the wagon advertise Spring Brook Ice, which was very likely cut from the millpond that was fed by water from Crooked Brook. Mother nature froze the ice, which Ellsworth cut and packed in his icehouse for delivery to Baldwinsville homes during the warm weather of spring, summer and fall.

with the bamboo coming from Japan and Calcutta. 50 people were employed but business languished and the company was sold in bankruptcy in May 1893. Subsequently the property was sold to the Mack-Miller Candle Co.[7]

- Avery & Northrup Furniture Factory was located in West Phoenix and had been converted from a lumber and stave mill, which was on the site.[8]
- A. Wayne Sweet opened a coffin and casket manufacturing firm in West Phoenix in 1868. Later he took in two partners and added furniture to the company's line. The building was later converted to a paper mill.

Gas motors
American Gas Motor Company, circa 1905, on Canton St. in the former canning factory, Baldwinsville

Grain cradles
Nicholas and John Boley, 1852, near the Warners-Ionia Road in Van Buren

Hub boring and box setting machines
Monarch & Eureka Co., 1892, on Canal Street in Baldwinsville

Iron products
Seneca River Iron Works, 1917, Baldwinsville

---

7 Ibid *Bamboo Furniture* January 5, 1972
8 Sauers, Evelyn L., *The Story of Schroeppel (Oswego County, NY)* p. 48

Kettles
Gayetty & Randall, 1851, Herrick's Corners (corner of Maple and Van Buren Roads)

Launches and 2-cycle engines
American Gas Motor Company, 1906, Baldwinsville, south of the Seneca River

Machinists
- Isaac U. & Stephen Baldwin, 1859, Baldwinsville
- Heald & Sisco, 1865, Baldwinsville

Marble products
- Chase & Blanchard, founded circa 1863, Baldwinsville
- Blanchard & Frazee, 1875, Baldwinsville

Oar locks
Montague, Stewart & Montague, 1909, 27 Syracuse St., Baldwinsville

Pickets
Sawmill on the outlet of Beaver Lake near Jacksonville

Planing and molding
Osborn & Ford, 1881, Plainville

Plows
Gayetty & Randall, 1851, Herrick's Corners (corner of Maple and Van Buren Roads)

Pump logs and log pipe
Horace Baldwin and James L. Voorhees between the Canal and River, south of Canal Street (E. Genesee St.), prior to 1830

Rakes
- John Pardee, 1869, Lysander village
- J.M. Young, 1878, Baldwinsville

Sash, blinds and doors
- Milton Goble started a sash and blind factory in 1834 in conjunction with a carding and woolen factory in Baldwinsville.
- Martin Peelor, 1859, Baldwinsville
- Fuller & Bliss, founded in 1866 by William L. Fuller and C.N. Bliss, employed 20 men, on Canal St., adjacent to Lock St. and later became Bliss & Suydam.

In 1872, the Delaware, Lackawanna & Western Railroad succeeded the original Syracuse and Oswego Railroad, which opened in 1848. This image was taken in the late 1800s, looking west toward the river bridge. The freight station is in the lower right and the large white building in the middle is the Amos mill. Photo courtesy of OHA Museum & Research Center

- George Ellison, 1868, Baldwinsville*
- Charles Ringe, 1868, Baldwinsville*

  It is probable that George Ellison and Charles Ringe worked in the Fuller & Bliss factory.

Almost every home in the 19th century had outside shutters to help keep out wintry blasts and to enhance the beauty of the home. Interior blinds were used to suppress sunlight. Window sash and doors could be manufactured more efficiently in a plant than on a construction site. These needs kept sash and blind factories operating in Baldwinsville until 1902 when the Bliss & Suydam property was sold to the Haywood Wagon Works. Fuller & Bliss began business in Truxton in 1830 and moved to Baldwinsville in 1866. The firm later was known as Bliss & Suydam. The plant obtained water from the canal to power its machinery.

Salt

Fairbanks & Co., 1881, (The author is suspicious that even though this company is listed as a manufacturer in Baldwinsville, the salt probably came from Liverpool)

Soft drinks

- E.S. Darrow, 1909, 11 Oswego St., Baldwinsville
- Baldwinsville Bottling Works owned by Silas Otts, 1930s to the 1950s, Corner of Elizabeth and Mechanic Streets

Spinning wheels

Alvin Bostwick, about 1807 until 1858, Lot 27 in Van Buren where Bentley Brook crossed an early trail.

Scythes

Sharp and Co., 1860, Baldwinsville

Springs

Penn Spring Works was a major manufacturing business in Baldwinsville from the 1880s to 1930s. It was located on Lock Street between river and canal at the foot of Margaret Street. The business originated in Canada and moved to different locations in Upstate New York before coming to Baldwinsville in the 1880s. The waterpower from the river was an inducement to locate here. The business was allowed two flumes of water to power the plant. (A flume was the amount of water that would pass through a 24 x 24 inch opening.)

After coming to Baldwinsville the Penn Spring Works was purchased by three

An image of the Penn Spring Works on Lock Street between the Seneca River and the Baldwin Canal near the foot of Margaret Street. From the 1880s to the 1930s it made springs, first for carriages and later for automobiles. It was a huge manufacturing plant employing as many as 200 people. Photo courtesy of OHA Museum & Research Center

Tin shops were an important segment of manufacturing in many communities prior to the 20th century's mass production. This tinsmith is holding a tin can that he has made. Initially all tin cans, millions of them, were individually cut and soldered by hand. The opening in the top was smaller than the can's diameter to facilitate soldering the top after filling. Millions of this type of can were made and soldered by hand in the last quarter of the 19th century. Many other commonly needed items such as sprinkling cans, food containers and metal roofs were made by the local tinsmith. Photo at Old Sturbridge Village by the author

Robinson brothers who operated it until 1931 when it was sold to the Detroit Steel Products Co. Three years later the buildings were destroyed by fire. (There had been a fire in 1908 that had destroyed the buildings but they were replaced.) Originally the plant had made springs for carriages and wagons but with the advent of the automobile they made springs for a number of automobile manufacturers including the Franklin and the Ford. Business peaked during the World War I period with approximately 200 employees, increasing to 300 during periods when two shifts were required to meet the demand. Raw materials and finished products were transported between the business and railroad, first by horse and wagon and later by a truck. Competition and the cost of shipping to their major market in Detroit brought the local business to an end.[9]

Stoves
- Gayetty & Randall, 1851, Herrick's Corners (corner of Maple and Van Buren Roads)
- G.W. Morley, 1875, Baldwinsville

---
9   Christopher, A.J. *The Penn Spring Works* July 26, 1962

Tinsmiths
- Wilson & Warren, 1855, Baldwinsville
- Baker Brothers, 1881, Baldwinsville
- C.M. Burtch, 1881, Baldwinsville
- S.M. Dunbar, 1881, Baldwinsville
- Voorhees & Son, 1881, Baldwinsville
- G.W. Wilson Jr., 1881, Baldwinsville

Urico
- Smith Drug Co., 1909, 28 Oswego St., Baldwinsville (the author believes that urico was likely a blend of herbs and was sold as a product to support normal urinary function)

Vegetable canning
Baldwinsville Canning & Preserving Company, circa 1898 to 1912 when it was destroyed by fire. It was formed by a group of area farmers and village industrialists and employed about 100. It was located south of the Seneca River along Water St. The factory opened on July 14, 1898 principally for the canning of tomatoes. 75 acres of tomatoes were contracted. Anticipated profits did not materialize and the plant was leased in 1900 to David Hunt Canning Company and to the Lane Bradley Company in 1902.[10]

Veneer
Moses Beach and Tompkins Bolles used the building previously owned by James Marshall for carding and cloth dressing in 1826-7, north of the dam between the river and Baldwin Canal in Baldwinsville.

Wire sieves and screens
O.B. Herrick, 1830s to 1870s, Herrick's Corners (corner of Maple and Van Buren Roads) (Note: Edith Hall wrote that the sieve factory was established about 1820.)

Wood turnings
Jonathan Birge, 1830s, Bangall

---

10 Christopher, A.J. *Canning Factory Flourished* September 22, 1971

A circa 1890 view from left to right of the Kenyon Paper Mill (established in 1866), New Process Rawhide Co. (established in 1888) and Hotaling & Co. Millers (originally established as a stone mill by Sanford C. Parker in 1836. All were on the south side of the river near the dam. An 1898 fire destroyed these three buildings. Photo courtesy of OHA Museum & Research Center

An aerial view of downtown Baldwinsville circa 1970s. The abutments for the former Baldwinsville and Syracuse Railroad are in the lower right. Tappan Lumber Co. buildings are in the right foreground and the Baldwinsville Fire Department is in the lower left. The Morris Pumps buildings are in the back of the picture.

22

The Ordnance Works

Shots were being fired around the world and the biggest shot to hit the Baldwinsville area in its history came during the winter of 1942. The United States of America, acting under "eminent domain", ordered with very short notice, 170 land owners, mostly farmers, to vacate their homes, land and buildings as soon as possible. The Town of Lysander, a rural town of less than 8,000 residents, along with its village of Baldwinsville was about to see the transformation of 6,800 acres, over 10 square miles, of farmland into an industrial site of major proportions in less than 12 months! Only the power, enterprise and wealth of the United States could bring this to fruition so quickly.

World War II, with the United States deeply involved, was being waged on multiple sites throughout the world. Millions of young Americans were risking their lives, many of them giving the ultimate sacrifice, to maintain freedom for not only the citizens of the United States but for the citizens of many other countries throughout the world who had been oppressed by the tyranny of aggressive dictatorships. Massive amounts of munitions were needed to fight this aggression and the Town of Lysander was chosen as a site to produce munitions as part of the battle to save freedom for the world.

The Lysander site was chosen for several key reasons: a ready supply of labor trained in the use of chemicals, abundant raw materials, an adequate power supply, a large source of water and a central railroad shipping point.

On April 6, 1942, construction on the site commenced. A four-strand barbed wire fence was placed around the entire perimeter. Over six miles of railroad track were installed and 13 ½ miles of new roads constructed. Twenty-eight guard houses, each standing nearly 30 feet high, were placed at 1500 foot intervals around the exterior of a designated critical area lined with floodlighted cyclone fence. A patrol road was constructed around the interior of this fence for rapid access to all points. A border, designed as a safety section of one mile, was reserved on three sides of the site. A natural hillside to deflect a huge explosion protected the fourth side. The community learned that explosives were to be manufactured on the site and were told that the dangers of an explosion are "practically negligible".

The public knew little of what was happening on the site and referred to it as the "government project". Hereafter, although the official name became "The New York Ordnance Plant" the local community always referred to it as "the project".

The Army Ordnance Department and the Corps of Engineers signed a contract with the National Aniline Defense Corporation for the construction and the operation of the plant. The plant was to cost $11,274,630 and the yearly operating expense was established at $5,250,000. The end product, ammonium picrate, an explosive for army and navy armor-piercing shells and bombs, was to be produced at a cost of 2/3 of a cent per pound. The plant was designed for a daily capacity of 75,000 pounds.

By April, less than a month after the community first heard about the project, all of the farmers had moved from the property and there were 600

A view of a few of the many buildings of the New York Ordnance Works, locally named "the project", constructed during World War II for the production of munitions. The photo is taken to the north with Rt. 31 in the foreground. The US government took about 6,800 acres of land by eminent domain. A large portion of this property is now Radisson.

construction workers putting the project together. By late summer there were 3,100 construction workers on the site with the number dropping to 1,955 by the end of the year and rapidly moving to none by one year after the start of construction.

In addition to roads and railroad tracks, other infrastructure constructed included: six ammonium picrate lines in six separate buildings, warm air drying houses, production facilities for highly concentrated nitric and sulfuric acid, 14 in-ground storage magazines, a boiler plant with over three miles of steam distribution lines, an administrative center, medical center, warehouses, laundry, employment office and dozens of other buildings, all in less than a year! The number of principal buildings was 88, all constructed of wood and designed to be temporary. The cost of the project had exceeded the agreed-upon price by about 25%. Part of the extra cost was due to a national shortage of phenol, one of the basic raw materials, that required the insertion of a substitute ingredient and substantial changes in the manufacturing equipment. (The cost of living index has increased by a multiple of 14 since 1942, making the cost in 2010 dollars approximately $200 million.)

This change required the start-up date to be moved from January 1, 1943 to January 20, and on January 22 the first batch was produced and was ready for shipment on February 3. By the end of March there were 938 employees with 384 directly involved in the production of the explosive. The peak number of 1,078 employees was reached in June. Among the support employees were 30 for the fire department, 122 in engineering and maintenance, 10 for first aid, 35 in transportation, 71 groundskeepers, 14 for laundry, 29 janitors and 35 in administration and accounting.

There was great emphasis placed on both discipline and safety. Production employees were provided with a set of clean white of clothing each day and required at the end of their shift to put all of their clothing in the laundry and to shower before they could put on their street clothes. They passed through security and were bussed to and from their cars to the buildings where they worked.

In August of 1943, the production of ammonium picrate reached 3,143,100 pounds, 140% of the design capacity for the three shift, 24 hour, 7-day production schedule. Production was so successful that by September 30 the storage magazines were almost filled with 3.3 million pounds of explosive. Because of the successful production and other outside factors, the production lines were gradually shut down, and on March 4, 1944 all production ceased. The total production of ammonium picrate had been 26 million pounds. The plant was put on "standby" at that time and by the end of June there were only 128 workers remaining and 22 of the 28 sentry towers were dismantled and sent to the Syracuse command to be used for guarding prisoners of war.

On August 15, 1945 the Japanese accepted the Allied surrender terms, nine days after the atomic bomb was dropped on Hiroshima, and a few days later the Army Ordnance Department and the Army Engineers declared "the project" excess. There was a great deal of speculation as to what would happen with the old New York Ordnance Works. There was consideration given to use it as a new site for the New York State Fair. The Baldwinsville School District considered it as a site for temporary classrooms. Early in 1946 the government contracted with the Lawrence Warehousing Co. of San Francisco to maintain and guard the property. In the summer there was a proposal by New York State to purchase over 3,000 acres of the project, which was accepted and it became known as the Three Rivers Game Management Area.

In the summer of 1946, Syracuse University renovated eight administrative buildings to house 625 single men along with 13 apartments for couples. The return of servicemen from the war had increased the university's enrollment and housing was seriously needed for them. In October of that year the Hamilton Co. and the L.B. Foster Co. purchased 156 acres containing 150 structures

Construction of the building housing the boilers at the New York Ordnance Works in 1942. Hundreds of workers constructed all the buildings with the facility starting production in less than one year.

An aerial view of the six ammonium picrate production facilities at the New York Ordnance Works north of Rt. 31. The site was arranged to provide a one-mile buffer zone on three sides and a natural drumlin for protection on the fourth side. The US government assured local residents that the danger of an explosion was minimal.

for $529,000 on condition that the companies decontaminate both the land and the structures. Dismantling of the structures began immediately.[1]

In 1952, the trustees of the William Waldorf Astor (William was the great grandson of John Jacob Astor who had amassed a great fortune first in trading furs and then in buying, selling and leasing real estate, mostly in New York City) estate purchased 2,030 acres of the project from the Fosham Realty Corporation for $325,000. It was stated that the Astor Estate trustees desired to have the property developed for industrial business and residential purposes.[2]

Little happened on the site for a number of years. The wooden buildings on "the project" were weathering and beginning to rot. In 1959, Del Nero Homes had leased part of the administration buildings to produce pre-fabricated homes. The homes were constructed in two halves, which were moved to the home site on trailers. In 1969,

A fire destroyed the buildings used by Del Nero and arrangements were made by the company to lease some of the other buildings on "the project".[3] Del Nero continued to build manufactured homes on the old Ordnance Works until the early 1970s.

In 1968, the 1001 E. Genesee Corp., owned by Sol Spector, a Syracuse car dealer, purchased approximately 2,300 acres of "the project" from the Astor Estate for $1 million. Nine months later, in June 1969, Spector sold 2,100 acres of the site to the New York State Urban Development Corporation (UDC) for $1.5 million. Spector retained 201 acres adjacent to the area designed by the UDC as an industrial park.[4]

The UDC designated the name "Radisson" for the property, and moved forward with the purchase of adjacent properties to meet their needs for the property's development. In the 42 years since Radisson was a name on the UDC's drawing board it has become a substantial residential, business and manufacturing community that has added much to the Baldwinsville area. The manufacturing companies of Radisson will be discussed in the next chapter.

---

1 All of the above material comes from a seven part series of articles in *The Baldwinsville Messenger* beginning on February 11, 1981 by C. Alan Baker, editor of the paper
2 *The Baldwinsville Messenger* July 17, 1952
3 *The Baldwinsville Messenger* January 30, 1969
4 *The Baldwinsville Messenger* September 15, 1971

23

Manufacturing in Radisson

The New York State Urban Development Corporation (UDC) was formed in 1968. It purchased 2,100 acres, which had been part of the New York Ordnance Works in June of 1969. Although the UDC was designed primarily to build state-subsidized housing projects to help stem urban decay, its project in the Town of Lysander, which they named Radisson, also included large industrial sites. After the initial land purchase the UDC made a number of additional purchases of adjacent land making a total of close to 3,000 acres with about one-third of that designated for industrial use. One of these purchases was for land west of Sixty Road for a 25-acre railroad freight yard capable of holding up to 300 railroad cars.[1]

Many of the same factors that had made the site desirable for the Ordnance Works appealed to the UDC in establishing the planned community of Radisson. There was an adequate supply of power and water for a large planned community and the presence of the railroad would help to attract large industrial plants. Even though the UDC had the power of eminent domain, the availability of over 2,000 acres of open land made the site even more attractive. Onondaga County was growing, providing a strong market for new homes as well as industrial growth. All of these factors combined in attracting the UDC to the town of Lysander. Manufacturing in the towns of Lysander and Van Buren had been on the decline for many years, and hope for new industries was appearing on the horizon. The UDC brought a number of other businesses to Radisson, including distribution, storage and other services, which are not mentioned since this book deals with just manufacturing.

A great deal of planning needed to be accomplished before the infrastructure for the new community could be constructed. In 1973, construction began for a 12,000-square-foot industrial plant for Technical Fabricators, a metal fabricating plant with 30 employees that decided to move from N. Franklin St. in Syracuse to Radisson. During the same period the UDC moved ahead with a 40,000-square-foot structure labeled as an inventory building.[2]

The Breweries at Radisson: First Schlitz, then Anheuser-Busch

There had been rumors for some time that the UDC was bringing a large manufacturing business to Radisson but almost everyone was shocked to hear that it was a business that would employ over 600 people and cost $150 million to build. The Schlitz Brewing Co. of Milwaukee, WI had chosen Baldwinsville to be the site of the largest and most modern brewery in the world.

The new brewing facility was designed to produce 5.8 million barrels, 31 gallons to the barrel, of beer annually. Schlitz's reasons for choosing Baldwinsville paralleled the reasons of the Ordnance Works in 1942: access to a railroad, a good electrical supply, central location close to two interstate highways and a bountiful supply of water. The water was a key factor as the right water

---

1 *The Baldwinsville Messenger* March 5, 1976

2 Ibid, January 10, 1973

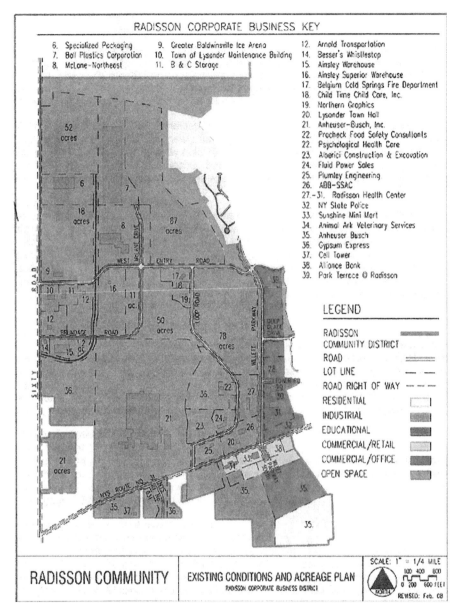

A map of the Radisson business community. Rt. 31 goes diagonally across the bottom of the map with Sixty Road on the left and Willett Parkway on the right.

is necessary in producing the best beer. Onondaga County had tapped into Lake Ontario for water some years earlier, and all that a brewery would ever need was readily available.

Planning and construction took several years prior to the plant's opening in late 1976. There were over 500 workmen involved in the construction of the 1,300,000 square feet brewery.

The brewery had been founded in 1849 by August Krug and was acquired by Joseph Schlitz, his son-in-law, in 1858. The Schlitz Brewing Company became the world's top beer producer in 1902 and exchanged that status, from time to time, with Anheuser-Busch into the 1950s.[3]

Schlitz made changes to its methods of making beer in the 1970s at the time it opened the Baldwinsville plant. The changes did not please its customer base and sales volume dropped. Production decreased at Schlitz's Baldwinsville plant and it was sold to Anheuser-Busch in 1979. Anheuser-Busch paid $100 million for the plant, closing it for over a year to make necessary modifications costing over $100 million.[4]

Anheuser-Busch began as a small struggling brewery in St. Louis and was purchased by Eberhard Anheuser in 1860. Anheuser's son-in-law Adolphus Busch became a partner in 1869. The company was an innovator, becoming the first to use pasteurization to keep the beer fresh, the first to use both artificial refrigeration and refrigerated railroad cars and the first to bottle beer extensively.[5]

In 1957, Anheuser-Busch became the largest brewer in the United States and in 2008 had almost half of the US beer sales. Its growth in business was mirrored in its Baldwinsville plant as demonstrated with several additions since 1979, now encompassing over 1,500,000 square feet.

The Baldwinsville plant has received numerous awards for its efforts in reducing its impact on the

---

3   Tremblay, Victor J. and Carol Horton *The United States Brewing Industry* p. 68 and taken fromWikipedia
4   *The Baldwinsville Messenger* November 7, 1979
5   Wexler, Sanford *From Soap Suds to Beer Suds: How Anheuser-Busch Became the Largest Brewer in the World* , Financial History December 2002, pp. 30-34

The Anheuser-Busch plant on Rt. 31 east of Baldwinsville. The Schlitz Brewing Company constructed the brewery in 1976. It was purchased by Anheuser-Busch in 1979 and substantially remodeled.

A view of the Anheuser-Busch brewery looking southeast from Sixty Road. The large silos for the storage of grain are on the right. The plant encompasses over a million and a half square feet.

environment. In 1995, it received an award from New York's governor for its use of a "comprehensive, energy producing pollution prevention system-bio energy recovery-to treat wastewater from the brewing process". The brewery also sets goals to reduce energy consumption and to increase the use of renewable fuels. The company recycles billions of aluminum cans, actually more than it produces.

The brewing process starts in stainless steel mash tanks where ground barley malt is mixed with water. Milled rice is mixed with water in a cooker, boiled and then mixed with the malt in the mash tank. Natural enzymes in the malt break down the starch into fermentable sugars. The mixture from the mash tanks is then strained, separating a clear sweet amber liquid called wort from the spent grain husks. The wort is transferred into brew kettles, brought to a boil and natural hops are added while the boiling continues. After cooling the wort to the proper temperature, yeast is added to convert fermentable sugars into carbon dioxide and alcohol. This process can take up to six days changing the wort to beer. A lagering process, utilizing beech wood chips accompanied with other steps, makes a beer that is unique to Anheuser-Busch.

In 2008, Anheuser-Busch merged with the Belgium brewing company of InBev and became known as Anheuser-Busch InBev. This almost $52 billion deal created the world's largest brewing company. Anheuser-Busch operates 11 breweries in the United States in addition to its plant in Baldwinsville. The North American headquarters is in St. Louis. The Baldwinsville facility has over 800 employees and is by far the largest manufacturing facility in Lysander and Van Buren. It has a significant economic impact upon the local community as well as the entire Central New York area.

An asterisk (*) indicates manufacturing businesses or their successor operating in Radisson in 2010.

* **Anheuser-Busch**: Schlitz Brewery at 2885 Belgium Rd. occupied 1,300,000 sq. ft in Radisson from 1976 to 1979. The Schlitz Brewery was purchased by Anheuser-Busch, Inc. in 1979 for $100 million. Modifications to the plant made during the next year were estimated to have cost over $100 million and increased the size of the plant to 1,372,478 sq. ft. Additions to the plant in 1990 increased its size to 1,437,518 sq. ft., and further

This is a photograph of the Anheuser-Busch railroad siding to the west of Sixty Road. Railroad cars filled with grain wait here for unloading and are shunted back here after emptying.

additions in 1993 increased its size to 1,510,871 sq. ft. It had 828 employees in 2010.

* **Commodity Specialists Co**. located at 2904 Belgium Road contracts to market the brewer's grains from the Anheuser-Busch brewery. Brewer's grains have significant nutritional value and are delivered from the brewery to dairy farms throughout Central New York. The parent company is located in Minneapolis, MN and has two employees at the Baldwinsville location.

Ball Plastic Container Corporation, at 2900 Mc Lane Drive, came to Radisson in 1996. In April of 2009, Ball announced that it was permanently closing its Baldwinsville plant as well as one in Watertown, Wisconsin. The Radisson plant employed 113 people but was one of Ball's smaller plants. The company stated that Ball's larger more efficient plants would supply customers of the Baldwinsville plant. Another factor in the closing was the decreasing demand for the plastic bottles produced at the Baldwinsville plant. Ball originated in Buffalo in 1880 as the Wooden Jacket Can Co. A few years later it moved to Muncie, Indiana and began making glass fruit jars.

* **Central Industrial Packaging Supply Inc**. at 8255 Willett Parkway moved from Molloy Rd., north of Syracuse, in 2009. It occupies 30,000 square feet in Radisson and has 16 employees. The company was founded in 1982 and manufactures and distributes a broad line of packaging materials and janitorial supplies. Its customer base extends from Utica to Rochester and from Binghamton to Ogdensburg.[6]

* **Fluid Power Sales, Inc.**, 8257 Loop Road, came to Radisson in 2005. It was founded in Syracuse in 1968. The company produces hydraulic valve manifold systems and has 35 employees. Its market area is New York and Ontario, Canada.

Goetz Dolls came to Radisson in 1989 and continued there until 2005. Initially they occupied 6,250 sq. ft., increasing it to 16,450 sq. ft. in 1990, to 18,700 sq. ft. in 1993 and in 1994 to 30,300 sq. ft. Franz and Marianne Goetz formed Goetz Dolls in Germany in 1950. Their first dolls were made of paper mache and crafted with the help of five family members. Later the company moved into collector

---

[6] The Post Standard *Packaging Firm Expands Despite Tough Economy* January 7, 2009

The Fluid Power Sales, Inc. is located at 8257 Loop Road. The company makes hydraulic valve manifold systems and has 35 employees.

This is a picture of ABB/SSAC at 8242 Loop Road. It manufactures electronic devices and employs over 100 people.

Central Industrial Packaging Supply, Inc. is located at 8255 Willett Parkway. The company manufactures and distributes packaging and janitorial supplies.

dolls, which were relatively costly. The Radisson facility included manufacturing, distribution, a Goetz doll shop and a visitor center. Demand for the dolls gradually decreased with both the German facility and the Radisson plant closing. The dolls remaining after production was discontinued were sold at discounts to Goetz retailers and also at the store in Radisson.

Harland Simon Control Systems, Inc. at 8255 Willett Parkway was in Radisson from 1993 to 1999. It occupied the 40,993 sq. ft. building previously used by Morris Pumps. The company produced turnkey engineered industrial drive systems for a broad array of companies involved in pulp and paper, plastics, textiles, mining and converting industries. Harland Simon was acquired by Spartec of Canada in 1996 and left Radisson in 1999.

* **Lawson Mardon**, 8800 Sixty Road, came to Radisson in 1993 and occupied a 158,821 sq. ft. building. It produced printed and folding cartons for the US and Canadian markets. In 1983, previous to coming to Radisson, Lawson Mardon formed a global alliance with Specialized Packaging to market its international capabilities throughout North America. In 1998, Specialized Packaging acquired Lawson Mardon, which at that time had four other manufacturing plants in North America in addition to the Radisson plant. Specialized Packaging was formed in Connecticut in 1983, and in 2009 had annual sales of approximately $175 million. During the last decade the company has had an annual growth rate of over 9%. In 2009, Specialized Packaging merged with Paper Works, which is headquartered in Pennsylvania. There are 167 employees at the Radisson plant.

Morris Pumps leased 40,993 sq. ft in Radisson from 1977- 1987. This leased space was needed for an increase in the line of pumps Morris produced in their plant in Baldwinsville. (Information about Morris Pumps is in the chapter, Pumps.)

Northern Graphics at 8435 Loop Road in Radisson was a screen print manufacturer occupying 19,800 sq. ft. from 1991 to 2009 and had 33 employees.

* **Patient Portal Technologies** at 8276 Willett Parkway provides programs and strategy for the

The Specialized Packaging plant located at 8800 Sixty Road. The company produces paper cartons and has over 150 employees.

healthcare industry (software). It was established in 2006 and has 65 employees.

* **SSAC,** located at 8242 Loop Rd., manufactured a great variety of electronic devices and came to Radisson in1987. It occupied 39,182 sq. ft., which was decreased to 22,562 sq. ft. in 1989. In 2005, SSAC became known as ABB/SSAC, and has 120 employees in the Radisson plant. The company states that its research and development group provides the vehicle for bringing forth new innovative products that meet today and tomorrow's equipment requirements. They offer many standard products and will also develop a specialized new product to meet a customer's needs in quantities of one piece or 100,000 pieces.

Technical Fabricators at 8265 Loop Rd. were custom metal fabricators and came to Radisson in 1974. Technical Fabricators occupied 12, 822 sq. ft., had 27 employees and became Lambert Fabricators in 1978. Lambert Fabricators left Radisson in 2005.

In 2011, Radisson is growing with new houses still being constructed and a Northern Onondaga County area YMCA soon to break ground. Whether Radisson's manufacturing component will stagnate or continue to grow is yet to be answered. Looking at Radisson's manufacturing growth over the last two decades, with its relative status quo, may be a clue into its future.

24

World War II to 2011 Manufacturing

Little is recorded of manufacturing in Lysander and Van Buren from the 1940s to the current time. It seems as though there is not an interest in what has happened until three-quarters of a century has passed when there are few people remaining to share what transpired. The *Baldwinsville Messenger*, however, is a valuable resource and much can be learned by exploring the stories related to manufacturing in its pages of the past. Even with this resource, small manufacturers will be overlooked as they often did not make a large enough splash to hit the news.

Consolidation of manufacturing was taking place in this country and other parts of the world even before Baldwinsville was first settled. Sparsely populated newly settled areas like Baldwinsville, without convenient transportation, needed a large variety of locally produced manufactured goods so consolidation arrived later. The rapidity of consolidation has accelerated with each decade following World War II. Super highways appeared, transportation of goods by air became common and larger freighters were constructed, gradually bringing all of the world's manufacturing and markets closer together. The number of local manufacturing facilities declined and manufacturing has moved to larger population centers and to areas of lowest cost production.

Radisson became the bright spot for manufacturing in our towns. The UDC had a desirable site and the financial resources to construct an infrastructure to attract large corporations to the area. Interstate Island in Van Buren, at the intersection of Routes 690 and the Thruway, also presented an attractive site for manufacturing. Beyond these two locations the manufacturing that developed was largely local grown, manufacturing businesses started by one or two individuals that prospered or perhaps never expanded.

An attempt will be made to list these manufacturers and some information about them. Without question some manufacturers will be inadvertently overlooked.

An asterisk (*) indicates manufacturers still in business in the towns of Lysander and Van Buren in 2011.

Baldwinsville Fabrication Co., on Sixty Road, was listed in the *1957 Baldwinsville Directory*. It was owned by Elmer Whorral and did steel fabrication and made ornamental railings.

* **Brookfield Power** operates the hydroelectric generating plant, owned at one time by Niagara Mohawk, on the north side of the Seneca River adjacent to the dam in Baldwinsville. There are two generating units furnishing a total of 0.6 megawatts that is fed into the electric grid.

Carrington Tool & Die of 16 E. Oneida St. was operated from 1953 to 1980 by Ralph M. Carrington. The business continued under the operation of Robert Carrington until 1998. The business had from two to four employees and manufactured machinery parts.

The Indian Springs Manufacturing Co. is located at 2095 W. Genesee Road. The firm originated in the basement of Bubb's Hardware at 27 Oswego St. in 1948. The company produces emergency equipment for the control of toxic gases.

J.R. Clancy, Inc. is located at 7041 Interstate Island Road in Van Buren. The company manufactures and installs theatre equipment, worldwide.

Durkee Manufacturing Company at 2914 Belgium Rd. was a manufacturer of fine wire mesh screens beginning in the 1960s.

Eagle Comtronics was the brainchild of Alan Devendorf and originated in his home in West Phoenix in the early 1970s. It has been located on Henry Clay Boulevard for many years.

Harlon Hyler Machine Shop in West Phoenix patented and made coil winding machines and other pieces of equipment for GE and others. Circa 1950.

* **Indian Springs Manufacturing** located at 2095 W. Genesee Rd. was established in 1948. Initially production was located in the basement of Bubb's Hardware at 27 Oswego St. The company makes precision quality machined parts for a variety of users. It also produces emergency kits for the control of chlorine, sulfur dioxide and ammonia gases.

Jardine Bronze & Aluminum Foundry was purchased from Morris Machine Works by James Jardine in 1945. It was located at 80 E. Genesee St. and had approximately 60 employees. It produced bronze, copper, aluminum, cupro-nickel and Monel Castings.

* **J.R. Clancy, Inc.** at 7041 Interstate Island Road was founded in 1885 on N. Salina St. in Syracuse and moved to Interstate Island in 1976. The company is owned by Bob Theis, has 59 employees and manufactures and installs theatre equipment worldwide.

Henry E. Karkut, on Rt. 48 north of Lamson Road received a special use permit for manufacturing in 1965. He manufactured a variety of metal products and continued in business for a number of years.

* **Memphis Hardwood Lumber Co.** at 210 Church St. in Memphis owned by Paul Anthony manufactures kitchen cabinets and does millwork. The business was founded in 1974 and has four employees.

* **Metropolitan Signs** at 3760 Patchett Road has been in business for 38 years. It fabricates and installs signs of all sizes.

An aerial view of the main farm at Plainville Turkey Farm, located at 7830 Plainville Road, taken in the 1980s. The processing plant for the manufacture of turkey products is located in the left, center. The photograph was taken from the northwest looking southeast toward the Seneca River hidden among the trees in the background.

A few of the turkey products manufactured at Plainville Turkey Farm and marketed throughout the eastern US. The firm was sold in 2007 and Plainville Turkey products are now being manufactured in Pennsylvania and marketed throughout the US.

* **Neon Bright** at 7900 Hicks Road, owned by Tony Bedard, has manufactured neon signs since the 1990s.

* **NuTop Sales** started business on State Fair Boulevard in the early 1950s. It was owned by Gary Suddaby, who sold it to Joe Peta in the early 1990s. The business is now located at 3653 Hayes Road and does business as Coverall Manufacturing. Boat covers and convertible tops were the original items manufactured but in recent years golf cart covers and specialty production items for various manufacturing companies have been added to the business. There are six employees.

* **Oswego Hydro Partners**, a subsidiary of Algonquin Power Income Fund, owns a 3,500-kilowatt hydroelectric plant on the Oswego River in West Phoenix. The plant is operated by Algonquin Power Systems. The Oswego River has furnished waterpower at this location since a sawmill was constructed in 1829.

Parks & Aller Sawmill was located on the east side of Van Buren Road and slightly north of the present Van Buren town building. Charles Larman Parks and Bill Aller operated the business, which cut logs, sawed the logs and did millwork and planing. It was established in the late 1940s and closed at the time of the Van Buren Road improvements in the middle 1950s.

Plainville Turkey Farm, Inc., doing business as Plainville Farms, began as a family farm in 1835. Turkeys were added to the products grown in 1923, and the business entered further processing in the late 1950s under the leadership of Robert Bitz. The company had a record of steady expansion from a few thousand turkeys annually to over a million in the 21st century. Mark Bitz joined his father in the business in 1986, growing the turkeys without antibiotics, no animal by-products and with recognized animal friendly practices. The business operated a feed mill in Cayuga County, a cooking operation in the Town of Salina, a storage facility in the Town of Van Buren and growing farms in several towns. Restaurants were an associated business. A multitude of turkey products were marketed throughout the eastern United States. The number of employees surpassed 200 at the time it was purchased by the Hains Celestial Group, Inc. in 2007. Hains moved most of the operation to PA but is still operating the Salina cooking operation.

The NuTop Sales Co. is located at 3653 Hayes Rd. The business originated on State Fair Blvd. in the 1950s. It does business as Coverall Manufacturing.

Syracuse Heat Treating is located at 7055 Interstate Island Road in Van Buren. The company does commercial heat treating and brazing of manufactured components.

Quality Custom Converter Inc. located at 80 E. Genesee St. was listed in the 2003 *Harris Book of Manufacturers* and was in the building formerly occupied by Jardine Bronze Foundry. It manufactured motors and generators, had five employees and was there for only a few years.

Scusa Machine Shop, Circa 1910 to 1990, Lino Scusa and later his son Paul Scusa operated a machine shop for many years in West Phoenix. They produced machines for the local paper industry including patenting a machine that folded tissue handkerchiefs so that when one was pulled out the next one was ready for removal.

Seneca Metal Products at the corner of Canton and Ellsworth Roads, circa 1957, did general manufacturing.

Stachurski Brothers Sawmill was owned by Ed and Pete Stachurski and located on Route 370 a half mile west of Plainville. The sawmill cut logs and sawed them into lumber, primarily hardwoods for the furniture industry. The business operated from the 1950s to the 1990s.

Sullivan Manufacturing Co. at 73 E. Genesee St. manufactured paper products. John J. Sullivan, who previously had been president of the National Cellulose Co, owned the company. The business originated in the late 1930s and discontinued after Mr. Sullivan's death in 1953.

* **Syracuse Heat Treating** at 7055 Interstate Island Road was founded on Solar St. in Syracuse in 1932. It is owned by John MacAllister and does commercial heat treating and brazing of manufactured components. The company has 20 employees and its market area is the United States and Canada.

SYROCO, previously named Syracuse Ornamental Co. and located on State Fair Boulevard, was established in Syracuse in 1890 by Adolph E. Holstein. Initially the company produced hand

Tessy Plastics storage and distribution facility located in the former SYROCO plant at 7528 State Fair Blvd. Tessy Plastics headquarters is in neighboring Elbridge and anticipates using part of this facility for manufacturing in the future.

carved wood mantels and carved wood decorations. A molding process, using a wood compound and casting fluids, developed by the company to make decorative wall ornaments increased the success of the company. The company came to Van Buren in 1965 and at that time changed its name to SYROCO. In 1980, the Holstein family sold SYROCO to Dart Industries, a subsidiary of Home Interiors & Gifts, Inc. SYROCO expanded its business in 1996 with the production of resin casual furniture, tables and chairs. There was a major fire at the plant in 1990 but it was rebuilt with the aid of $10 million in tax-exempt bonds from the Onondaga County Development Agency. In 1995, it was sold to Marley PLC, a large British company. Two years later the company announced a million dollar investment in the manufacturing facility and the addition of 150 new jobs, making a total labor force close to 550.[1] An article in the June 18, 2007 *Post Standard* states that the SYROCO plant went out of business that day. It also stated that it was owned by Vassallo Industries of Puerto Rico, and the company ran out of money.

* **Tessy Plastics** purchased the 270,000 square foot building formerly owned by SYROCO at 7528 State Fair Blvd. in 2010. Currently the building is used as a distribution and warehousing center but will likely also be used for manufacturing some time in the future. Tessy Plastics was founded in 1973 and their headquarters is on Route 5 in the Town of Elbridge. The company supplies plastic components for the medical field, consumer products, business machines, electronics and packaging industries.

* **Wave Hydro LLC** purchased the hydropower plant on the south side of the dam in Baldwinsville at a county tax sale in 2004. The hydropower plant had been previously owned by Seneca Hydro.

White Signs, started by Ted White in 1946, was located at 13 E. Genesee St., on the second floor of a two-story building, later adding the first floor to the business. There was a fire in the building in the 50s and the business was temporarily moved to Syracuse St. A site was purchased at 7852 West River Road, southeast of the present Cold Springs-Belgium Fire Department, and a new steel building was erected. The company manufactured signs and erected the signs from Albany to Buffalo and from Binghamton to the Canadian border. In 1969 White Signs merged with a company in Binghamton and became known as the White Division of Arnold Meyer Signs. White Signs continued on West River Road until about 1985 when the entire company was sold.

Wiltech Products, Inc. at 7841 River Road, had 15 employees and manufactured light industrial machinery from 1991 to approximately 2007.

---

1 *The Baldwinsville Messenger* October 22, 1997

25

The Changing Face of Manufacturing

It is difficult to comprehend the tremendous changes that have occurred in manufacturing since the time when our forefathers settled in today's Baldwinsville area. Early settlers arrived by foot or by boat powered with a paddle in their hands. With effort, 20 miles could be covered in a day. Now, 200 years later, we can easily transverse thousands of miles of ocean, from here to Europe and back, in a single day. A settler of Baldwinsville in 1800 could correspond with his family in London and receive a reply in four or five months, whereas today, a response is instantaneous. New ideas and new technologies, developed into new products manufactured for mass consumption, become the formula for progress.

We accept change as part of our everyday life. Each new idea and product is based upon a multitude of earlier ideas, like a pyramid with its broad base gradually tapering to its apex. The manufacturers of Lysander and Van Buren were part of the base upon which the new inventions of today rest. Today's Internet and space travel will help form the base for the yet unknown inventions future generations will enjoy.

While many things change, there are some that do not. One of those is an innate desire in mankind to improve upon what already exists. Sometimes it is the desire for fame, other times for fortune, and other times it is a selfless goal to make life better for mankind. We will never know for certain but perhaps all of these reasons motivated Dr. Baldwin to respond positively to the 1807 petition from dozens of local residents to build a dam, sawmill and gristmill in Baldwinsville.

A review of the development of local dairy product manufacturing exemplifies a continual improvement in the quality of the product and the efficiency of production while even lowering the cost of the end product. Until after the middle of the 19th century, all butter and cheese was produced by the housewife on the farm. It was an inefficient process with the end product varying in quality. Cheese factories and, later, creameries, were constructed that produced higher quality products, with greater efficiency, at lower cost to the consumer. Everyone benefited: the farm family, the owner of the processing facility and the consumer.

The desire to improve products still exists today, although it less visible at the local level. We do not have nearly as many small manufacturers as we did in the early 1800s because major manufacturing has drifted to large cities and foreign countries. However, the entrepreneurial spirit still exists, dwelling in the hearts of the young men and women who graduate from our local schools and go off to distant points. The fruits of their minds and labor gradually drift back home through the innovations they help develop.

What percentage of the population of Lysander and Van Buren was directly involved in manufacturing in the early 1800s? It is impossible to determine with certainty, but if we added together the number of people working in each of the many manufacturing businesses at that time, the

Almost every family in the 19th century had a few apple trees. Cider, both sweet and hard, was an important end product. The crude wooden object shown here is an apple grinder. After grinding, the apples were placed in a huge wooden press to squeeze out every possible drop of juice. Photo at Old Sturbridge Village by the author

percentage of the population involved in manufacturing would likely exceed 50%. If we were to add to that number the farmers, who in reality were working with nature to manufacture food, and include the women, most of whom manufactured clothing for their family, we would be including the vast majority of the population.

The percentage of our population involved in manufacturing has gradually diminished since the early 1800s. In 1961, the six largest local manufacturers employed 924 workers. Adding another 200 that might have been employed with other manufacturing businesses, the figure drops to less than 10% of our population working in manufacturing at that time. Today there are approximately 1,200 people employed in manufacturing in Radisson, about 100 at Interstate Island and less than 100 at other locations in the towns of Lysander and Van Buren. With a population of over 30,000 in the two towns today, manufacturing employment represents less than 5% of the current population, even if farmers are included.

There has been a gradual increase in the productivity per worker since 1811, which is many times greater today. According to figures from the Federal Reserve and the United States Bureau of Labor Statistics, productivity has more than tripled in just the last 40 years. Imagine what the multiplier would be if we could compare the productivity of today with 1811. When we consider the decrease in the length of the workday from 12 hours to eight and the decrease in the workweek from six days to five and factor in the much smaller percentage of the population involved in manufacturing, we

The Changing Face of Manufacturing

An aerial view of Baldwinsville circa late 1930s. On the lower left is the National Cellulose Paper Mill and to its right the Mercer Milling Co. The electric power generating plant is just north of the dam, exactly where it is today. It appears that the Amos Mill, on the middle right, is in the process of being dismantled. The upper lock on the Baldwin Canal is clearly visible just above the power plant.

begin to obtain a feel of the dramatic improvement in productivity. The change in productivity is almost beyond belief.

The changes in manufacturing that Lysander and Van Buren have experienced are similar to thousands of other small communities throughout the United States. First, the cottage industries gradually disappeared giving way to larger industries that utilized the waterpower of the river and small streams. Next, manufacturing moved to large population centers in the United States and then overseas where an abundance of inexpensive labor, readily available supply of raw materials and convenient transportation facilities provided the lowest production costs. Only unusual circumstances can overcome the lowest cost manufacturing syndrome.

The manufacturing in Radisson is an example of unusual circumstances. Radisson, with the backing of the Urban Development Corporation, desirable Lake Ontario water, a partially developed infrastructure and central location, brought the brewery with its associated industries to Lysander. Interstate Island with its readily available utilities and its proximity to both Route 690 and the New York State Thruway brought manufacturing to Van Buren. Forces friendly to manufacturing, created by the State of New York, combined with cooperation from the two local towns, made these two industrial areas successful. Unless some yet unknown force appears, it is likely that Lysander and Van Buren will continue to evolve into bedroom communities with their residents commuting to work outside of their local communities. Meanwhile the percentage of manufacturing jobs in the two towns, in relation to the towns' population, will continue to decrease.

Since 1800, each generation in our community has enjoyed an improvement in its standard of living. The tremendous increase in manufacturing productivity throughout the world has made this possible. The Baldwinsville area community has played a part in the development of this manufacturing productivity and can justly take pride in its contributions.

Appendix

Table 1 New York 1835 Census of Manufacturing Enterprises in Lysander & Van Buren

Category	Number		Raw Material $		Finished Prod. $	
	Lys.	Van B.	Lys.	Van B.	Lys.	Van B.
Grist Mills	5	2	12,500	10,500	13,550	14,800
Saw Mills	17	6	22,375	6,375	49,400	14,400
Fulling Mills	0	1	0	600	0	1,200
Carding Machines	2	1	2,500	300	2,820	900
Iron Works	0	1	0	250	0	500
Asheries	4	2	895	846	1,585	1,500
Tanneries	3	2	1,500	2,300	3,000	3,600

Table 2 New York 1845 Census of Manufacturing Enterprises in Lysander & Van Buren

Category	Number		Raw Material $		Finished Prod. $	
	Lys.	V B	Lys.	V B	Lys	V B
Grist Mills	2	2	54,000	55,125	60,400	62,637
Saw Mills	13	6	30,380	4,400	61,910	7,900
Fulling Mills	0	1	0	1,140	0	2,640
Carding Machines	0	2	0	2,400	0	2,720
Woolen Factory	1	0	45,000	0	50,000*	0
Iron Works	0	1	0	1,500	0	3,000
Asheries	0	0				
Tanneries	5	1	4,920	250	8,600	500

*80,000 yards of finished material were produced

Table 3 New York 1855 Census of Manufacturing Enterprises in Lysander & Van Buren

Category	No. Firms		No. Employee		Raw Material $		Finished Prod. $	
	Lys.	V B	Lys.	V B	Lys.	V B	Lys.	V B
Heading Mills	3	0	—	0	—	0	660	0
Saw Mills	9	2	37	4	22,990	1,240	34,750	2,480
Turning Shops	1	0	3	0	500	1,500	0	0
Lime Mfg.	1	0	2	0	550	0	1,725	0
Plaster Mills	1	0	10	0	600	0	1,080	0
Potteries	0	1	0	9	0	600	0	3,000
Boot & Shoe Shops	8	0	21	0	5,677	0	12,228	0
Harness, Saddle & Trunks	2	0	4	0	2,550	0	2,300	0
Tanneries	5	0	16	0	8,213	0	44,750	0
Cabinet Shops	1	2	2	4	150	634	1,500	2,300
Tobacco & Cigar	0	1	0	3	0	400	0	1,500
Cradles & Scythes		1				264		2,620
Metal Manufacturers	4				1,082		4,600	
Furnaces	1				5,610		9,030	
Woolen cloth & yarn	1				600		775	
Coach & wagons	6				1,736		6,223	
Spoke mfgs.		1				230		1,750
Grist mills	1	1			2,700	115,000	5,100	118,000
Cooper shops	2	3			3,450	1,998	9,825	4,193

1865 New York Census of Manufacturers provides less information than the previous census periods. In Lysander it indicated that there were three boat building businesses, six making coaches and wagons, one harness firm, five producing boots and shoes and one producing plaster. In Van Buren, two firms produced coaches and wagons, one pottery and one cabinet ware. Very little information was provided concerning the sales of these businesses.

Lists of Manufacturing Businesses from Various Directories

The author took these names from the lists of businesses he was able to locate. Undoubtedly some manufacturers were overlooked when the Directories were first assembled. The author, in some instances, may have inadvertently included a business as a manufacturer when it actually was not.

Boyd's Onondaga County Directory 1859-60

Blacksmiths – Baldwinsville: Fink, J; Virginia, D: Little Utica: Palmer, Joel: Lysander: Lounds, David G.; Mason, Orren; Feck & Houser: Plainville: Schenck, James L.: Van Buren: Frazee, James: Houlahan, P.

Boot & Shoe Makers – Baldwinsville: Allen, R.E.; Bigelow, Otis; Bolton, John; Highriter, D.: Lamsons: Berry, Major: Lysander: Ells, Horace; Wooster, Dennis K.; Vedder, Elisha: Plainville: Elliott, James; Hubbard, Chauncy; Spaulding, Burns: Polkville: Cram, Daniel; Cram Jehiel; Hazard, Sewell: Van Buren Center: Betts, Stephen

Cabinet Makers – Baldwinsville: Brown, Seth; Dundore, J.G.; Mosely, Jerome, S.; Huntington, William E.

Carriage & Coach Makers – Baldwinsville: Lask, William; McCabe, Patrick; West, E.K.: Lysander: Berry, Clark; Peck & Avery; Winchell, William C.: Plainville: Van Horn, Barnet: Polkville: Fancher, Alanson: Van Buren: McCabe, P.; Higgins, William

Coopers – Lysander: Merrifield, Hastings; Merrifield, Norman

Distillers – Baldwinsville: Johnson, Cook & Co.

Edge Tool Manufacturers – Baldwinsville: Morris, H.D.; Sharps & Co.

Grist Mills – Baldwinsville: Flaherty, John; Johnson, Cook & Co.; Wilkins, William: Lysander: Kennedy, George W.

Harness, Saddles & Trunks: Baldwinsville: Dowdall, Michael; Seager, C.H.: Lysander; Irvine, John: Van Buren: Betts, Alanson

Iron Founders – Baldwinsville: Baldwin, I.M. & S.W.

Lime, Plaster & Cement – Lysander: Vedder, Albert, A

Flour Mills – Baldwinsville: Frazee & Williams

Sashes, Blinds & Doors – Baldwinsville: Peelor, Martin

Saw Mills – Baldwinsville: Frazee & Williams; Munroe, James; Jones & VanWie; Smith, Augustus: Van Buren: Smith, Maynard; Warner, Simeon

Scythes – Baldwinsville: Sharp & Co.

Tanners & Curriers – Baldwinsville: Cebory, J.; Starks, Henry P.: Lysander: Ballard, Leander & Co.: Plainville: Tillotson, Sanford: Polkville: Hazard, B.; Rice, D.P.

Boyd's Onondaga County Business Directory 1870-71

Rake Manufacturer – Lysander: Pardee, John

Blacksmiths & Wheelrights – Baldwinsville: Hilton & Eggleston: Little Utica: Dunham, Alanson: Lysander: Beard, A.W.; Hammond, Thomas; Lean & Tillotson; lown, David G.: Plainville: Allen, Ebenezer; Denna, David; Schenck, James L.

Boot & Shoe Makers & Dealers – Baldwinsville: Fitzgerald, Andrew; Kinney, Patrick; Marshall, Robert: Little Utica: Baker, Erastus; Wright, Atwell P.: Lysander: Barnes, Ira; Ells, Horace: Plainville: Elliott, James; Hubbard, Chauncy

Carriage Makers – Baldwinsville: Lusk, W.; Martin, C.: White & Perkins: Little Utica: Fancher, Alanson; Ferguson, Nathan; Soan & Filliston: Lysander: Berry, Clark; Loan & Tillotson: Plainville: Allen Ebenezer

Edge Tool Makers – Baldwinsville: Morris Axe & Tool Co.

Flour, Feed & Grain – Baldwinsville: Frazee, James & Co.; Jones, W.F.; Kenyon, G. & Co.; Wilkins, W.L.: Little Utica: Palmer, A.R.: Lysander: Halsted, Herman: Memphis: Mooney, W.W.

Cabinet Makers - Baldwinsville: Brown, Seth

Harness, Saddles & Trunks – Baldwinsville: Jessep, D.B.; Taggart, T.C.; Taylor, W.H.: Little Utica: Allen, Oscar: Lysander: Irvine, John

Iron Founders & Machinists – Baldwinsville: Heald, Sisco & Co.: Lysander: Peck & Brown

Marble Workers – Baldwinsville: Chase, G.T.

Paper Mills – Baldwinsville: Monroe, H.

Tanners & Curriers – Baldwinsville: Stark & Kaulback: Little Utica: Hazard, B.: Lysander: Smith & Sutphir

New York State Business Directory 1876

Blacksmiths – Baldwinsville: Billings, William on Canton St.; Hilton & Eggleston on Canal St.; Reed & Eaton on Water St.: Lysander: Briggs, Jeremiah; Seager, Sylvester: Plainville: Dennie, D: Polkville: Virginia, Joseph: Memphis: Nagley & Harris; Newport R.P.: Little Utica: Dunham, Alanson; Fisher, George: Lamson's: Stevens, Alanson

Brewers – Baldwinsville: Scoville, John M. at 54 Bridge

Millers – Baldwinsville: Jacob Amos & Sons on Bridge St.; Frazee, James on Canal St.; Hotaling, G.H. and A. on Canton St.; Wilkins, W.L. on n. Canal St.: Lysander: Halsted, Herman

Paper Mill – Baldwinsville: A.S. Schoonmaker & Co.

Shoemakers – Baldwinsville: Bolton, James on Seneca; Fitzgerald,A. at 31 Canal; Marshall, Robert on Bridge St.; Wickett, Joseph at 27 Bridge; Stockton, T. on Water St.: Lysander: Barnes, Ira; Ells, Horace: Polkville: Wright, A.P.: Plainville: Hubbard, Chauncey; Scott, J.R.: Memphis: Birch, Irving R.

Cabinet Maker – Baldwinsville: Brown, Seth on Canal

Carriage Makers – Baldwinsville: Buck & Wight on Canal St.; Fancher, R.J. at 34 Canal; William Lusk & Son on Syracuse St.: Lysander: Berry, Clark; Hand, Parley; Lone, James

Sawmills – Baldwinsville: Frazee, J.O. & W. L. below Canal: Lysander: Clute, Richard; Perine, Francis: Little Utica: Dunham, N.C.

Sash Doors & Blinds – Baldwinsville: Fuller, Bliss & Co. on Canal

Pumps – Baldwinsville: Heald, Sisco & Co. on Canal

Harness – Baldwinsville: Jessup, B.D. at 23 Bridge; Taggart & Woodford at 7 Canal St.: Lysander: Irvin, John: Memphis: Bliss, J.D.

Tobacconists – Baldwinsville: Tappen & Allen on Canal St.; Tucker & Crippen on Canal St.; Weller, Wm. At 40 Bridge St.: Plainville: McCall, Thomas; Ward, William C.; Wilson, William: Little Utica: Allen, W.A.

Cheese Factories – Lysander: Coppernall, John: Plainville: Cheese Factory Company: Memphis: Daboll, Henry

Bed Springs – Lysander: Decker, James, E.

Foundry – Lysander: Spratt, Mrs. Margarette

Wagons – Polkville: Fancher, A. & Son: Plainville: Allen, Ebenezer: Memphis: Weaver, L.A.

Tanner – Polkville: Hazard S.

Baskets – Plainville: Blakeman, John & A.; Bittel, Jacob

Furniture – Memphis: Holcomb, J.

Onondaga County Business Directory 1878 (Baldwinsville)

Blacksmiths – Hilton & Eggleston on Canal; James T. Lyndon on Syracuse; J. Russell on Canal near Bridge; Byron F. Veeder on Water north of Syracuse; Daniel Virginia on Syracuse

Boots & Shoes – Andrew Fitzgerald on Canal; Robert Marshall on Bridge; John M. Stearns on Bridge; Thomas A. Stockton on Mill near Water

Cabinets – Seth S. Brown on Canal north of Bridge

Carriages – Buck & Wright on Canal; R. I. Fancher on Syracuse; William L. Howe on Canal

Cigars – John & Wm McGuigan on Canal; John M. Scoville on Bridge

Coopers – Andrew P. Clary on Syracuse; David R. Delano on Water

Engines – White & Fox on Bridge

Flourmills – Jacob Amos & Sons on Bridge; James Frazee & Co. props. of Union Mills; G.H. & A.T. Hotaling props. stone mills at foot of Canton; D. & G. Morris

Harness – Wm H. Carpenter on Syracuse; P.D. Jessup on Bridge; John McGonegal on Bridge; Charles F. Woodford on Syracuse

Hosiery – Robert Miller, Jr.

Knit underwear – J.C. Miller & Co. on Bridge

Marble worker – James R. Blanchard on Syracuse

Pumps – Heald C. Morris on Canal; White, Clark & Co. on Bridge

Rakes – J.M. Young

Sash, doors & blinds – Fuller & Bliss on Canal

Sawmill – W.L. Frazee

Stoneware – J. Darrow & Son

Boyd's Directory of Onondaga County 1881

Agricultural Implements – Baldwinsville: Fairbanks & Co.: Lysander: Gaylord, James,

Blacksmithing & Wheelwrights – Baldwinsville: Hilton & Eggleston; Larmer, Joseph; Newport, Michael; Russell, Joseph; Veeder, Byron F.; Virginia, Daniel; Weaver, Charles A.: Jack's Reef: Cavenor, Thomas; Harrington, Thomas P.; Lysander: Biggs, Jerry; Seager, Sylvester: Little Utica: Dunham, Alanson; Fisher, George: Memphis: Nagley, Charles Mrs.: Plainville: Scott, John: Warners: Wellington, William

Boot & Shoe Makers & Dealers – Baldwinsville: Donovan, D.; Fitzgerald, Andrew; Marshall, Robert; Red, Edward; Stearns, J. M.; Stockton, Thomas A.: Lysander: Barnes, Ira; Ellis, Horace: Memphis: Birch, Irving: Plainville: Hubbard, Chauncey: Polkville: Wright, A.P.

Broom Manufacturer – Baldwinsville: Virginia, John

Carriage & Coach Manufacturers – Baldwinsville: Allen, Ebenezer; Buck & Wright; Fancher, R.I.; Larmer, Joseph; Martin, Ephraim; Walker, B.V.: Little Utica: Fancher & Son; Ferguson, Nathan: Lysander: Avery, F.P.; Berry, Clark; Van Derver, Leslie: Memphis: Weaver, L.A.: Polkville: Fancher, A. & Son: Warners: Weaver, L.A.

Cheese Factories – Lysander: Alexander, Mrs.: Memphis: Daboll, Henry

Cider & Vinegar Manufacturers – Baldwinsville: Snyder, Jerome: Polkville: Allen & Lewis

Cloth & Woolen Mills – Baldwinsville: Miller, J.C. & Co.

Coopers – Baldwinsville: Clary, Andrew; Delano, David R.

Engine Makers – Baldwinsville: Heald, Sisco & Co.

Flour Feed & Grain – Baldwinsville: Amos, Jacob & Son; Clark & Mercer; Frazee, James Union Mills; Red Mills, Clark, Mercer & Co.; Seneca Mills, W.H. Wilkins: Lysander: Halstead, Herman

Harness, Saddles & Trunks – Baldwinsville: Jesseps, J. Mrs.; McGonegal J.H.: Lysander: Irvine, John: Memphis: Bliss, J.D.

Iron Founders & Machinists – Baldwinsville: Heald, Sisco & Co.: Lysander: Spratt, Mariette Mrs.

Lime, Cement & Plaster – Lysander: Dietrich, Casper

Paper Mills & Dealers – Baldwinsville: Schoonmaker & Co.

Planing & Molding Mills – Plainville: Osborn & Ford

Pump Manufactures – Baldwinsville: Clark & Van Wie; Heald, Sisco & Co.: Lysander: House A.F.

Salt Manufactures – Fairbanks & Co.

Sash, Blinds & Doors – Baldwinsville: Fuller & Bliss

Saw Mills – Baldwinsville: Frazee, W.L.: Little Utica: Dunham & Bellinger

Stoves, Tin & Coppersmiths – Baldwinsville: Baker Bros.; Burtch C.M.; Dunbar, S.M.; Morley, George; Voorhees, J.L. & Son; Wilson, G.W. Jr.

Tanners & Curriers – Polkville; Hazard, B: Little Utica: Hazard, B.

Tobacco & Cigars – Baldwinsville: Allen, Wells A.; Buck H.M.; Tappan & Skinner (leaf); McGuigan, John; McGuigan, William; Reed, S.; Rosenwald, E. & Bros. (leaf);

Scoville, J.N.;Tucker E.W. (leaf): Plainville: McCall, Thomas; Wilson, William & Son

Businesses listed in Baldwinsville area Directories that were likely manufacturing firms and a Community Profile of 1961 showing employee numbers in six firms. Not all were listed for various reasons and a few may have come from other sources.

1895 – Carriages, wagons & sleighs - E.A. Woods, Corner of Syracuse & Water

Carriages - South Side Carriage Works (Parley L. Hand)

Flour & Feed - Empire State Mills (Jacob Amos)

Millers - Hotaling & Co.

Probable Manufacturers from the 1909 Baldwinsville Business Directory

Machine Knives - American Knife Works, Lock St.

Shoemakers – Baker, Archie, 2 Oswego St.; Piton, Albert, 19 Syracuse St.

Tin, Copper & Sheet Iron Ware – Baker Bros., 13 Oswego St.

Folding Boxes – Breroha Paper Box Co., 8 Syracuse St.

Cigars – Ellis, William, 12 Oswego; Scoville, J.M., 7 Oswego St.

Flour – Clark & Mercer, 6 Syracuse St.; Frazee Milling Co.

Soft Drinks – Darrow, E. S., 11 Oswego St.

Flexible Shafts – Fancher Machine Co., 47 Downer St.

Creamery – Garrett & Snell, 37 E. Genesee St.

Wagons – Haywood Wagon Co., 34 E. Genesee St.; Wm Sizeland, Water St.

Tissue Paper – Kenyon Paper Co.

Blacksmiths – Larmer, Joseph, 6 E. Genesee St.; Maroney, Martin, River St.; Neupert, George, 10 E. Genesee St., White & McDonald, 35 Water St.

Harness – McGonegal, J.H., 16 Oswego Street

Oar Locks – Montague, Stewart & Montague, 27 Syracuse St.

Centrifugal Pumps & Engines – Morris Machine Works, 31 E. Genesee St.

Carriage & Automobile Springs – Penn Spring Works, Lock St.

Electric Light & Power – Seneca River Power Co., 5 Oswego St.

Urico – Smith Drug Co., 28 Oswego St.

Boats & Boat Frames – Valley Boat Works, Canton St.

Baldwinsville Directory 1915

Blacksmiths – Knoblock, John, 62 E. Genesee; Moroney, M.J., 1 River; Neupert, George L., E. Genesee

Creameries – Baldwinsville Creamery, Garrett & Snell, E. Genesee; Seiler Bros., D.L. & W. station

Flour Milling – Frazee Milling Co., E. Genesee; Mercer Milling Co., Syracuse St.

Harness Makers – Kenfield, E.B., 25 Oswego; McGonegal, John H., 16 Oswego

Machine Knives – American Knife Works, Lock St.

Tissue & Waxed Paper - Hoffman Paper Mill, Water Street

Centrifugal Pumps – Morris Machine Works, E. Genesee St.

Vehicle Springs – Penn Spring Works, Lock St.

Bluings & Ammonias – So-jer Mfg. Co., 4 Syracuse

Tobacco & Cigars – Beebe, Edward L., Oswego St.; Sheldon, L.R., Oswego St.; Shoens, T.H., 25 Water St.

Natural Gas – Baldwinsville Light & Heat Co., 8 W. Genesee

Electricity – Seneca River Power Co., Oswego St.

1917 – From the *Farm Journal Rural Directory of Onondaga County*

Seneca River Iron Works

Appendix

1936 – From the *Baldwinsville Directory*
Syracuse Lighting Co., Inc. (Baldwinsville Light & Heat Co.)

Baldwinsville Bottling Works

Mercer Milling Co. – Flour & Feeds

Letterman – Batteries

Wyker-McGann Feed Co.

Orlando Houghtaling – Ice, cider, custom sawing

American Knife Co. – Manufacturers of woodworking machine knives

1950 – From the *Baldwinsville Directory*
Suddaby Sales & Service, RD1, Convertible car tops

Indian Springs Manufacturing, 2095 West Genesee

Parks & Aller Sawmill, Van Buren Rd. - Lumber, planing & millwork

International Milling Co., Eastern semolina mill division

White "Neon Signs", 13 E. Genesee St.

Morris Centrifugal Pumps, Morris Machine Works

Baldwinsville Bottling Works, Corner Mechanic & Elizabeth Streets

1957 – From the *Baldwinsville Directory*
Mercer Milling Co. – flour & feeds

Seneca Metal Products Co., Canton & Ellsworth Roads – general manufacturing

International Milling Co., 81 E. Genesee St

Bville Fabrication Co., Sixty Road – Ornamental railings

Parks & Aller Sawmill, Van Buren Rd.

White "Neon Signs" of Baldwinsville

1961 – From the *Baldwinsville Directory*
(Community profile of Baldwinsville that lists six large employers and the number of their employees)

Five firms employ 924 workers

Morris Machine Works, pumps 280

Jardine Bronze and Aluminum Foundry 60

International Milling, semolina, 69

Syracuse Ornamental, ornaments 500

Mercer Milling, flour 15

1983 – From the *Baldwinsville Directory*
Anheuser-Busch

Mercer Mill

1991 – From *Greater Baldwinsville Chamber of Commerce Directory*
Anheuser-Busch, 2265 Belgium Road

Carrington Tool & Die, Inc., 16 E. Oneida St., Robert Carrington

Goetz Dolls, Inc., 8257 Loop Rd. Radisson

Gould Pumps, 31 East Genesee St.

Indian Springs Mfg. Co. Inc., 2095 West Genesee St.

Lambert Fabricators Inc., 8265 Loop Road

Plainville Turkey Farm, Inc., 7830 Plainville Road

Syroco, Inc., State Fair Blvd.

Birchier-Sheehan, Inc.

Hydroqual Corp.

Kummert Tools for Industry

Mercer Milling

Syracuse Heat Treating

Ty-Pac, Inc.

Wiltech Products, Inc.

1994 – From *Greater Baldwinsville Chamber of Commerce Membership Directory*
Harland Simon Control Systems, Inc., 8255 Willett Parkway

Anheuser-Busch Inc.

DEG Enterprises, Inc.

Goetz Dolls, Inc.

Hydroqual Corporation

Indian Springs Mfg. Co.

Mercer Milling

Ty-Pac, Inc.

Wiltech Products, Inc.

Plainville Turkey Farm, Inc.

Partial Guide to Manufacturing Locations in Baldwinsville
during the 19th and 20th Centuries

This guide gives the approximate location of some of the Baldwinsville manufacturing business locations using the street names of today. During much of the 1800s, the downtown portion of Syracuse and Oswego streets was known as Bridge St. and East Genesee St. was known as Canal St.

Syracuse St. west including Paper Mill Point
Sawmill, James Johnson, 1825

Sawmill, Stephen & Harvey Baldwin and other later owners, 1826-1856

Flourmill, Sanford C. Parker (made of stone) 1836-1861, Johnson, Cook & Co., Hotaling Mill, Johnson, Cook & Co. later became Wetherby, Cook & Co. distillery 1856-1866

Paper mill, Kenyon & Co. and several later owners, 1867-1956

McHarrie, gristmill, 1830, next Stephen Baldwin mill, next Red Mill, next Farmer's Mill of Van Buren, next Clark & Mercer Mill, next Clark, Mercer & Co., next Mercer Milling Co. 1912-2002

Woolen mill

New Process Rawhide Gear Factory

Blanchard & Frazee Novelty Mill

Water St.
Mack-Miller Candle Co., 1898-1907

Baldwinsville Canning & Preserving Co., 1898-1912

James Stewart & Co., Barges, 1918

E. Allen Wagon Shop

Allen & Crum Planing Mill

W. Lusk & Son Carriage Shop

Oswego St. west (between river and Baldwin Canal)
Carding & cloth dressing mill, later converted to veneering

Fork & hoe factory

Red mill, 1833-1841

Dr. Baldwin's sawmill 1819, Kellogg & Farr woolen mill 1841

Darrow Pottery, 1845-1848, Niagara-Mohawk Power Co.

Morris axe & edge tool factory, 1850

Sash & blind factory

Harvey & Stephen Baldwin, sawmill, 1819-20

J.C. Miller & J.C. Miller Knitting Mill, 1876-1902, Edison Illuminating Co. 1886-1902, Syracuse Lighting Co. 1925, later Niagara-Mohawk, then Orion, then Reliant and now Brookfield Power

Clark Woolen Mill

Young & Frazee Tool Co.

I.M. & S.W. Baldwin Machinists & Founders

Oswego St. east (between river and Baldwin Canal as far as Tannery Creek (Palmer Lane) at Lock St.)
Gristmill, Dr. Baldwin, circa 1809, later woolen mill which burned in 1841 and was rebuilt burning again in 1851

Log boring company

Sawmill

Otsego Fork Factory

Share & Co. Scythe Factory

Frazee Mill, 1859, also Frazee cooper shop and Frazee plaster mill

Old Red Mill, Amos Flour Mill, 1868, also cooper shop on riverbank later on

Foot of North St. on river
Brown's Boat Works (two locations)

Appendix

East Genesee St. north
Dr. Baldwin, sawmill, west of Tannery Creek, 1808

Heald & Sisco, 1864, later Heald & Morris, later Morris Machine Works, later Morris Pumps until 1981, and then Morris Pumps, A division of Gould Pumps

East Genesee St. south
Sawmill

Sash & blind factory, 1866-1902, Haywood Wagon works, 1903-1914

Tannery Creek east
Tannery

Lock St. south
Wilkins gristmill, 1854-1874, American Knife Factory, 1901-1950

Fairbanks & Taggart Sawmill, 1839-1890s

Hart gristmill

Brown's Boat Works (two locations)

Lock St. north and south
Penn Spring Works, 1880-1934

Partial Information of the Dun Reports from the 1850s to the 1880s

Baker Library at Harvard University

These reports were handwritten and the author may have misread some names and dates. There was some hesitancy in deciding to enter these notes into the Appendix. The fact that these businesses were visited by a Dun representative in specific years indicates that these firms were in business at that time. Not all manufacturing businesses in the community were visited and those that were visited were not every year. There were additional comments regarding the businesses that the author felt should be considered confidential and these comments are not included.

Name of Business	Items Manufactured	Comments & Year of Visit	Location
A.S. Schoonmaker & Co.	Paper mill	1875	Baldwinsville
Clark & Mercer	Miller	1879	Baldwinsville
G.W. Morley	Stoves	1875	Baldwinsville
J. Miriam	Miller	1879	Memphis
E. Martin	Wagons	1879	Baldwinsville
Joseph Virginia	Blacksmith	1872	Polkville
Thayer, Cornell & Co.	Pumps	1870	Baldwinsville
White & Clark & Co.	Pumps	1870	Baldwinsville
F. Whitbeck	Blacksmith	1882	Polkville
Hand & Avery	Carriages	1875	Lysander
Oscar Allen	Harness	1873	Little Utica
Joseph Russell	Blacksmith	1878 & 1880	Baldwinsville
Charles G. Kenyon	Miller	1869	Baldwinsville
David Dennie	Blacksmith	1871	Plainville
Chauncey Hubbard	Boots & Shoes	1871 been here 25 years	Plainville
Jacob Lamb	Blacksmith	1876	Plainville
H. Hilliard	Miller	1874	Memphis
Ebenezer Allen	Wagonmaker	1870 been here several years	Plainville
James L. Schenck	Blacksmith	1876	Plainville
James Elliott	Shoemaker	1869	Plainville
Thomas Cavenor	Blacksmith	1874	Jacks Reef
Ira Barnes	Shoemaker	1874	Lysander

Name of Business	Items Manufactured	Comments & Year of Visit	Location
D.C. Harrington	Shoemaker	1874	Warners
James Smythe	Gristmill	10/11/71 been here 4 or 5 years	Little Utica
F.S. Baldwin & Co.	Carriages	1866	Baldwinsville
Wilson & Warren	Tinware	1855	Baldwinsville
H.P. Sharp & Co.	Edge tools	1855-1862	Baldwinsville
Isaac U. & Stephen W. Baldwin	Machinists	1859-63	Baldwinsville
Johnson, Cook & Co.	Distillery	1861 dissolved in 1868 and became below	Baldwinsville
Charles G. Kenyon & Co.	Paper mill	1868	Baldwinsville
Seth Brown	Cabinets	1859	Baldwinsville
David H. Highriter	Shoes	1861	Baldwinsville
Morris Axe & Tool Co.	Axes	1868	Baldwinsville
Morris Axe Edge Tool Co.	Tools	1872	Baldwinsville
John Bollow	Blacksmith	1862	Baldwinsville
William L. Wilkins	Miller	1869 been in business here 20 years	Baldwinsville
Jeremiah Fink	Blacksmith	1861	Baldwinsville
Chase & Blanchard	Marble	1872	Baldwinsville
White & Lankin	Foundry	Became Warren White in 1868	Baldwinsville
L.E. Warner	Cabinets	1868	Baldwinsville
J.M. Scoville	Cigar Mfg.	1879	Baldwinsville
Downer & Voorhees	Woolen factory	1868	Baldwinsville
Smith & Sutfon	Tanners	1868	Lysander
Loan & Tillotson	Carriage Mfgs.	1869	Lysander
Horace Ells	Shoemaker	1869 been here 25 years	Lysander
Ira Barnes	Shoemaker	1869	Lysander
Peck & Brown	Foundry	1869 been in business 8 years	Lysander
Thomas Hammond	Blacksmith	1869	Lysander
John Irvine	Harness & blacksmith	1869	Lysander

Name of Business	Items Manufactured	Comments & Year of Visit	Location
Mrs. Ann Alexander	Cheese Mfg.	1869	Lysander
John Coppernoll	Succeeded Ann Alexander in 1870	1870	Lysander
Clark Perry	Carriage Mfg.	1869	Lysander
David G. Lown	Blacksmith	1869	Lysander
Andrew W. Baird	Blacksmith	1869	Lysander
Herman Halsted	Miller	1869 been here long time	Lysander
John Pardee	Rakes	1869	Lysander
George Fisher	Blacksmith	1871	Little Utica
Plainville Cheese Mfg. Co.	Cheese factory	1872–1877 1877 factory burned	Plainville
Fuller & Bliss	Sash, doors & blinds	1869	Baldwinsville
Jacob Amos	Pearl barley mills	1870	Baldwinsville
Alanson Dunham	Blacksmith	1869	Little Utica
Alanson Fancher	Wagon Mfg	1869	Polkville
Atwell P. Wright	Shoemaker	1869	Little Utica
J. S. Kenyon	Paper mill	1872	Baldwinsville
Wellington Brothers	Blacksmiths & wagons	1874	Warners
C.S. Sand	Harness Mfg	1870	VB Centre
J.P. Smith	Harness Mfg	1870	Memphis
W.P. Taylor	Harness	1873	Baldwinsville
Hilton & Eggleston	Blacksmiths	1869 notes to 1882	Baldwinsville
Charles Martin	Wagons	1869	Baldwinsville
Darrow & Son	Stoneware	1870 to out of business 1879	Baldwinsville
William Miller	Cigar Mfg.	1875	Baldwinsville
H. Monroe	Paper	1869	Baldwinsville
John & A. Blakeman	Baskets	1875	Plainville
W. Wilson	Tobacco	1875	Plainville
John Bratt	Blacksmith & wagonmaker	1879	Plainville
Lefever & Palen	Paper	1873 suceeded Kenyon	Baldwinsville

Appendix

Name of Business	Items Manufactured	Comments & Year of Visit	Location
J.A. & W. L. Frazee	Sawmill	1874	Baldwinsville
B.Y. Veeder	Blacksmith	1878	Baldwinsville
R.P. Newport	Blacksmith	1876	Memphis
Joseph M. Fugett	Blacksmith	1879	Baldwinsville
Seager & Vinal	Blacksmith	1870	Lysander
Joseph Larmer	Blacksmith	1875	Baldwinsville
D. & A. Stone	Mill	1877	Plainville
Otsego Fork Co.	Forks	1869	Baldwinsville
William L. Wilkins	Miller	1871	Baldwinsville
Stark & Kaulback	Hides & leather	1868 to out of business 1871	Baldwinsville
Heald & Sisco	Machinists	1865 to 1875	Baldwinsville
James Frazee & Co.	Millers	1866	Baldwinsville
Baldwinsville Woolen Mfg. Co. James Frazee		1867	Baldwinsville
Irvin R. Burch	Shoemaker	1871	Memphis
Charles Bratt	Blacksmith	1882	Plainville
Horace Ells	Shoemaker	1883	Lysander
John Bratt & Son	Blacksmith	1883	Plainville
Allen & Chubb	Mfg of tobacco & cigar cases	1883	Baldwinsville
James M. Fugett	Blacksmith	1883	Baldwinsville
Schoonmaker & Co.	Paper mill	1879	Baldwinsville
Heald, Sisco & Co.	Pumps	1880 &1881 changed to Heald & Morris	Baldwinsville
Heald & Fancher	Mfg pat plugs ?	1884	Baldwinsville
William Wilson & Son	Cigars	1880	Plainville
E.R. & B.C. Brown	Cabinets	1881	Baldwinsville
Clark & Van Wie	Centrifugal pumps	1880 suceeded White, Clark & Co.	Baldwinsville
Buck & Wight	Carriages	1881	Baldwinsville
Clark & Mercer	Millers	1881	Baldwinsville
E. Martin	Wagonmaker	1881	Baldwinsville
James Russell	Blacksmith	1881	Baldwinsville

Name of Business	Items Manufactured	Comments & Year of Visit	Location
Michael Neupert	Blacksmith	1882	Baldwinsville
James Stearns	Shoemaker	1881	Baldwinsville
William Wellington	Blacksmith & wagonmaker	1881	Warners
Robert Marshall	Shoemaker	1881	Baldwinsville
Peck & Gaylord	Wagons	1881	Lysander
Mrs. M. Pratt	Foundry	1882	Lysander
Sylvester Seager	Blacksmith	1882	Lysander
L.A. Weaver	Wagonmaker	1882	Memphis
Dixon & Kenyon	Paper	1882	Baldwinsville
Hilton & Eggleston	Blacksmith	1883	Baldwinsville
Young & Frazee Tool Co.	Tools	1883	Baldwinsville
Andrew Fitzgerald	Shoemaker	1883	Baldwinsville
Nathan Fergeson	Wagons	1870	Little Utica
Mrs. Charles Nagley	Blacksmith	1875	Memphis
Durant & Co.	Flour	1871	Baldwinsville
S. Fox	Paper	1871	Baldwinsville
Leigh McKiernan	Harness	1871	Polkville
Charles Higley	Blacksmith	1873	Memphis
G.H. & A.J. Hotaling	Miller	1872	Baldwinsville
McGuigan Bros.	Cigars	1876	Baldwinsville
E. Martin	Wagons	1879	Baldwinsville
L.A. Weaver	Wagons	1875	Memphis
Clarke Woolen Co.		1871 to 1881	Baldwinsville
A. F. House	Pumps	1871 to 1881	Lysander
James Frazee	Miller	1871 to 1879	Baldwinsville
Harris, Baldwin & Co.	Axe heading machines	1872	Baldwinsville
Blanchard & Frazee	Marble	1875 to 1881	Baldwinsville
Allen & Adsit	Lumber	1874	Baldwinsville
A. Meartin	Wagons	1873	Lysander

Appendix

Name of Business	Items Manufactured	Comments & Year of Visit	Location
Osborn & Ford	Planing mill	1880 to 1882	Plainville
D. Delane	Cooper	1882	Baldwinsville
G.P. Harrington	Wagons	1881	Memphis
R.J. Fancher	Wagons	1874 to 1885	Baldwinsville
John M. Scoville	Cigars	1878	Baldwinsville
L.A. Groves & Co.	Woolen mill	1874	Successor to Clark Woolen Mills Baldwinsville
Bidwell Schermerhorn	Foundry	1876 to 1883	Lysander
Andrew Clary	Cooper	1877 to 1883	Baldwinsville
Morris Bros.	Millers	1878	Baldwinsville
Franklin P. Avery	Carriages	1877 to 1882	Lysander
John Scott	Blacksmith	1877 to 1881	Plainville
Ebenezer Allen	Wagons	1877 to 1883	Baldwinsville
Ovid Brown	Cheese Factory	1880 to 1883	Lysander
J.G. Miller & Co.	Woolen mill	1877 to 1883	Baldwinsville
Beeder & Hoolihan	Blacksmith	1877 to 1878	Baldwinsville
C.N. Sizeland	Carriages	1881 to 1884	Plainville
Edward Fay	Blacksmith	1879	Plainville
William Wilkins	Miller	1879	Baldwinsville
William Wilson	Cigars	1879 to 1881	Plainville
James Frazee & Co.	Millers	1871 to 1881	Baldwinsville
Henry Daboll	Cheese factory	1881 to 1883	Memphis
Winchell or Tillitson	Foundry	1881 to 1884	Lysander
Young & Frazee	Forks	1881 & 1882	Baldwinsville
Fuller & Bliss	Sash & doors	1882	Baldwinsville
Clark & Mercer	Millers	1881 to 1883	Baldwinsville
John Scott	Blacksmith	1882	Plainville
Maryett Spratt	Foundry	1883	Lysander
Norris Hazzard	Wagons	1883	Lysander
Knapp & Williams	Cigars	1883 & 1884	Memphis

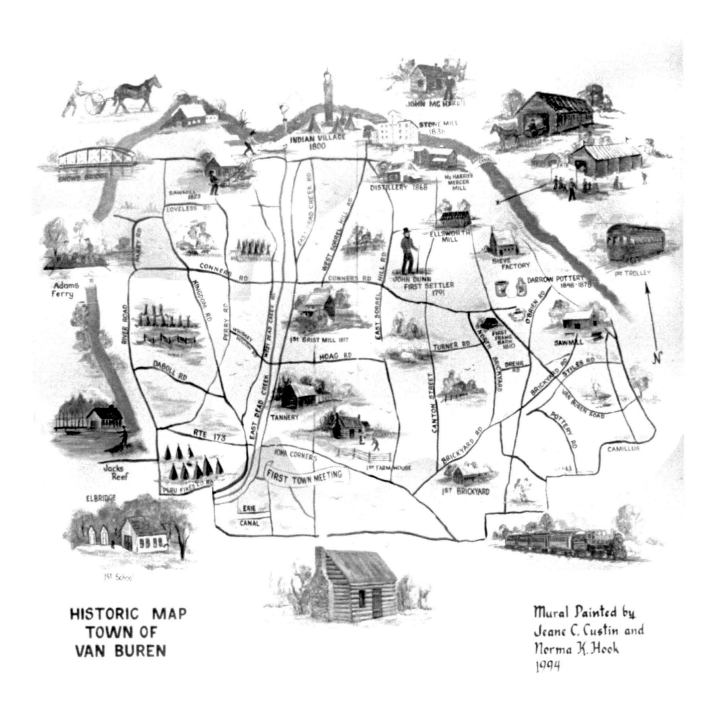

An historic map of the Town of Van Buren painted by Jeane Custin and Norma Hook in 1994.

Bibliography

Adams, Sampson and Co., *New York State Business Directory* (New York: John F. Trow, 1859-).

Arbor, Marilyn, *Tools and Trades of America's Past: The Mercer Collection* (Bucks County Historical Society, 1994).

Baker, C. Alan, "New York Ordnance Works", *The Baldwinsville Messenger*, 1961, 1981.

Baldwinsville Messenger, (Baldwinsville, NY).

Beauchamp, William M., *Past and Present of Syracuse and Onondaga County, New York, from prehistoric times to the beginning of 1908* (New York: S.J. Clarke Publishing Co., 1908).

Boyd Andrew, comp. *Boyd's Directory of Onondaga, Cayuga, Oswego, Madison and Cortland Counties, with a map* (Syracuse, NY: Central City Publishing House).

Bruce, Dwight H., *Onondaga's Centennial: Gleanings of a Century* (Boston, MA: The Boston History Company, 1896).

Chard, Jack, *Making Iron & Steel: the Historic Processes: 1700-1900* (Bogota, NJ).

Christopher, Anthony J., "Sketches of Yesterday" *The Messenger*, 1965-1970.

Chrysler Corporation, *The Gear Box* (Vol. 14, No. 6, June 1973).

Clark, Joshua, *Onondaga; or, Reminiscences of earlier and later times; being a series of historical sketches relative to Onondaga; with notes on the several towns in the county, and Oswego* (Syracuse, NY: Stoddard & Babcock, 1849).

Clayton, Professor W.W., *History of Onondaga County, New York with illustrations and biographical sketches of some of its prominent men and pioneers* (Syracuse, NY: D. Mason, 1878).

Community Directory...: Town of Van Buren/Lysander, (Syracuse, NY: Scotsman Press, Inc.).

Connell, Ruth M., *A Pure Gold Enterprise* (Baldwinsville, NY: Beauchamp Club, 1986).

Connell, Ruth M., *Baldwin Canal Water Power* (Baldwinsville, NY: Beauchamp Club, 1984).

Directory of Baldwinsville, 1936, (Clyde, NY: Goodell Print Shop).

Directory of Baldwinsville, New York: 1950-1951, (Syracuse, NY: Trinity Advertising Company, 1950).

Directory of the Village of Baldwinsville, (Baldwinsville, NY: Directory Publishing Co., 1885-1936).

Dun Reports – accessed at Baker Library Harvard University.

Farm Journal Illustrated Rural Directory of Onondaga County, New York 1917-1922 (Philadelphia: Wilmer Atkinson Company, 1917).

Gazette and Farmer's Journal Newspaper (Baldwinsville, NY).

"Grip's" Historical Review of Phoenix, 1902, (Grip, Syracuse, NY)

Hall, Edith, *The History of Baldwinsville* (Baldwinsville, N.Y.: McHarrie's Legacy, 1981, 1936).

Harris InfoSource, Harris Manufacturers Directory of New York (1980-2011, assessed at Cornell University Library).

How Dairy Products are Made, *Butter and Cheese*.

Hutchinson, Peter, *A Publisher's History of American Magazines*.

International Dairy Foods Assoc., *History of Cheese*. (Society for Industrial Archaeology, 1986).

Kisselstein, Bonnie P., "*Early Industries of Baldwinsville*" (Power Point Program, 2008).

Kleber, John E., *The Kentucky Encyclopedia* (Lexington, Ky.: University Press of Kentucky, 1992).

Liverpool–Baldwinsville Directory, 1957 (North Syracuse, NY: Lighthouse Directories, 1957).

Mann, Dorothy E., *Darrow Pottery* (Baldwinsville, NY: Beauchamp Historical Club, 1982).

McManus, Sue Ellen, *Greater Baldwinsville* (Charleston: S.C.: Arcadia Publishing Co., 2010).

Membership Directory/Greater Baldwinsville Chamber of Commerce, (Baldwinsville, NY: The Chamber, 1980-).

New York Business Directory, 1876.

Nostrant, Robert F., *Chronology of Paper Mill Island*.

Nostrant, Robert F., *The Erie Canal and Cement*

Onondaga County Business Directory. 1876.

Palmer, L. Pearl, *Historical Review of the Town of Lysander/* by Miss L. Pearl Palmer; with additional name and subject indexes compiled by Robert F. Nostrant and Jane H. Kinsley, Margaret C. Bye (Baldwinsville NY: Town of Lysander, 1997, 1947).

Post Standard. (Syracuse, NY).

Sauers, Evelyn L., *The Story of Schroeppel (Oswego County, NY)* (Phoenix Press May 1974).

Scisco, Louis Dow, *Early History of the Town of Van Buren, Onondaga County, N.Y.* (Baldwinsville, N.Y.: W.F. Morris Publishing Co., 1895).

Shapiro, Missy Eileen, *Time Past: People, Life and Landscape in Northern Lysander, New York, during the Nineteenth Century* (PhD diss. Syracuse University, 1977).

Smith, Elmer L., *Grist Mills of Early America and Today: with recipes using their products, notes and illustrations of other early mills* (Lebanon Pa.: Applied Arts Publishing, 1979).

Stockham, Peter, *Old-Time Crafts and Trades* (New York: Dover Publications, 1992, 1807).

Sweet's New Atlas of Onondaga Co. New York: from recent and actual surveys and records under the superintendence of Homer D.L. Sweet (N.Y.: Walker Bros. & Co.,1874).

Tremblay, Victor J. and Carol Horton, *Industry and Firm Studies* (Armonk, New York: M.E. Sharpe, 2007).

Van Wagenen, Jared, *Golden Age of Homespun* (Cornell University Press, 1953).

Wexler, Sanford, *From Soap Suds to Beer Suds.*

Historical Collections at the Baldwinsville Public Library and The Museum at the Shacksboro Schoolhouse and Town of Lysander Historians Files (Baldwinsville, NY).

Index

1820 Census of Manufacturers 60

A

Abbott, Warren J. 85
ABB/SSAC 150, 152
agricultural implements 17, 129
Alexander, Mrs. Ann 96, 127
Algonquin Power Income Fund 156
Algonquin Power Systems 122, 123, 156
Allen & Chubb 90, 92, 177
Allen, Ebenezer 103, 174, 179
Allen, Oscar 65
Allen, R. E. 65
Allen, W.A. 91
Aller, Bill 156
Ambler, Thomas 51
American Gas Motor Company 135, 136
American Knife Co. 132, 133, 171
ammonia 130, 155
ammonium picrate 141, 142, 143, 144
Amos, Jacob 49, 50, 168, 169, 170, 176
Amos Milling Company 121
Anheuser-Busch 145, 146, 147, 148, 149, 171
Anheuser-Busch InBev 148
Anheuser, Eberhard 146
Anthony, Paul 155
anvil 35, 36
Armstrong, John 85
Arnold Meyer Signs 159
ashery 3, 17, 31, 32, 72
ashes 31, 32, 72
Astor, William Waldorf 144
Avery & Northrup Furniture Factory 135
Avery's Cabinet Works 131
axes 129, 175

B

Babcock, George 69
Baird, Andrew W. 36, 37, 176
Baird's Corners 3, 15, 17, 32, 36, 44, 51, 56, 62, 64
Baker, Archie 64
Baker Brothers 139

Baker, C. Alan 109, 144
Baker Library v, 37, 174, 181
Baldwin Brothers 41
Baldwin Canal 6, 7, 8, 9, 13, 34, 36, 40, 42, 45, 50, 51, 57, 70, 85, 93, 114, 124, 130, 133, 137, 139, 163, 172, 181
Baldwin & Co. 132
Baldwin, Dr. Jonas 5, 6, 40, 45
Baldwin, Harvey 41, 172
Baldwin, Horace 136
Baldwin, Isaac U. & Stephen 136
Baldwin's Bridge 3
Baldwinsville i, v-vii, ix, 2, 3, 5, 7-11, 13, 21, 23, 27, 32-34, 36, 37, 39-46, 49-53, 55-57, 59-62, 64, 65, 67-72, 75-79, 81, 84-87, 89-94, 96-99, 101, 103-105, 107-112, 114, 115, 117-127, 129-141, 143-149, 151, 153, 159, 161, 163, 164, 167-172, 174-179, 181, 182
Baldwinsville Bottling Works 137, 171
Baldwinsville Canning & Preserving Company 139
Baldwinsville Cheese Factory 96
Baldwinsville Creamery 96, 97, 98, 170
Baldwinsville Fabrication Co. 153
Baldwinsville Light and Heat Company 123, 124
Baldwinsville Messenger v, 7, 21, 33, 41, 43, 60, 86, 92, 103, 109, 144, 145, 146, 153, 159, 181
Baldwinsville Novelty Works 77
Baldwinsville Stoneware 71
Ball Plastic Container Corporation 149
Bangall 3, 24, 26, 42, 44, 51, 52, 60, 85, 99, 139
Barge Canal 7, 8, 12, 34, 68, 117, 119, 122, 129, 131, 132, 134
barges 68, 129
Barnes Dairy 99
Barnes, Ira 43
barrel 21, 39, 49, 50, 53, 55, 56, 57, 59, 60, 72, 73, 145
basket maker 15
baskets 130, 168, 176
batteries 130, 171
Beach, Moses 139
Beach, Richard M. 41

Beaver Lake 17, 19, 39, 40, 42, 43, 52, 136
bedspring 17
Beebe, Edward L. 92
Beebe Mills, Inc. 118
beer 56, 60, 145, 146, 148
Belding Resseguie 42
Belgium 3, 21, 34, 68, 97, 99, 103, 148, 149, 155, 159, 171
bellows 35, 75, 80
Bentley & Son 73
Berry, Clark 103
Betts, Chauncey 15, 32, 59, 72
Betts Corners 3, 15, 18
Betts, Daniel 62
Bigelow 49, 60, 167
Biggs, William C. 62
Birge, Jonathan 139
Bitz, Mark vii, 156
Bitz, Robert vii, 156
black salts 31, 32
blacksmith 3, 15, 17, 21, 26, 30, 33, 34, 35, 36, 37, 45, 75, 76, 101, 102, 103, 104, 129, 175
Blakeman, John & A. 130, 176
Blanchard & Frazee 136, 172, 178
Bliss, C.N. 136
Bliss & Suydam 104, 136, 137
boat 8, 21, 29, 35, 50, 72, 93, 97, 101, 129, 130, 161, 166
boat works 21, 97, 130
Boley, John 107, 112, 135
Bolles, Tompkins 139
bolter 48
boots 61, 63, 64, 166
boring machines 130
Bostwick, Alvin 137
Bowen & Smith 42
Bowman, Miss Laura 126
boxes 55, 85, 94, 134
Boyd's 17, 42, 52, 56, 57, 65, 72, 73, 103, 126, 167, 169, 181
Breed, Dudley 68
Breroha Paper Box Co. 134, 170
brewery 145, 146, 147, 148, 149, 163
brick 21, 26, 32, 67, 68, 69, 75, 115, 118
brickyard 21, 68, 69
bridge 3, 19, 21, 41, 42, 65, 68, 77, 92, 97, 112, 126, 133, 168, 169, 172

183

Bridge Street 41, 42, 65, 77, 92, 133
Brookfield Power 122, 153, 172
Brooks, Elmer E. 92
brooms 131
Brown, E.R. & E.C. 131
Brown, Eva 127
Brown, Joseph P. 64
Brown, M.P. 130
Brown, Ovid 96
Brown, Seth 131, 175
Buck, Mrs. Harriet 126
bungs 55, 129
Burgess, Warren A. 103
Burtch, C.M. 139
Busch, Adolphus 146
butter 95, 96, 97, 98, 99, 126, 161
Byrne Dairy 99

C

cabinets 131, 168, 175, 177
Camillus 1, 5, 24, 40, 45, 64, 83
Campbell, Thomas P. 41
canal 3, 6-9, 12, 13, 21, 24-26, 28, 29, 34, 36, 37, 40-42, 45, 48-51, 56, 57, 68, 70, 72, 73, 78, 85, 92, 93, 107, 108, 111, 114, 117, 119, 122, 124, 126, 129-137, 139, 163, 168, 169, 172, 181, 182
Canal Street 42, 92, 111, 135, 136
Candee, Asa 57
candles 132
Canton 3, 25, 26, 32, 42, 60, 123, 127, 130, 133, 135, 158, 168, 169, 170, 171
Cardell, Mrs. E. 126
carding 83, 84, 85, 86, 136, 139
Carpenter, A. 64
Carpenter, Abram 118
carriage maker 15, 101, 103
carriages 41, 101, 102, 103, 105, 131, 137, 138
Carrington & Magee 37
Carrington, Ralph M. 153
Carrington, Robert 153, 171
Carrington Tool & Die 153, 171
caustic lye 31
Cayuga Lake 6, 7
C.C. Nagley & Son 30, 129
cement 21, 72, 73
Central City Knife Co. 132
Central Industrial Packaging Supply Inc. 149
C.G. Kenyon and Co. 117
Chapman, Paul 125
Chase & Blanchard 136, 175

cheese 15, 17, 18, 19, 20, 21, 44, 95, 96, 97, 98, 99, 126, 161
cheese factory 15, 17, 18, 19, 20, 21, 44, 95, 96, 97, 99
chime 55
Christopher, A. J. 21, 33, 41, 60, 103, 118
Church, Fred and Charles 97
churn 17, 132
cider 17, 20, 26, 43, 56, 132, 162, 169, 171
cider and jelly mill 17
cigar maker 17, 91
cigar manufacturers 15
cigars 89, 90, 91, 92, 93, 94
C.J. Hay 34
Clancy, Andrew 57
Clark, Aaron P. 133
Clark and Mercer 53
Clark & Co. 112
Clark, Joshua V. H. 67, 72
Clark & VanWie 112
Clark Woolen Mills 85, 179
Clary, Andrew 57, 179
Clay Post Office 21
Clute, Richard 44
coal 35
cobbler 63, 64
Colitre, W.B. 132
Columbia 3, 6, 7
Commodity Specialists Co. 149
ConAgra 54
Cook & Co. 60, 117
Cook's Distillery 60
Cook's Mill 43
cooper 17, 26, 55, 56, 57
Cooper Street 21, 57, 71
Coppernoll, John 96, 176
Costello, Miss S.T. 126
Coverall Manufacturing 156, 157
cradles 112, 135
Crawford, Walter 68
creamery 15, 17, 27, 62, 96, 97, 98, 99
Cronkite & Reese 37
Crooked Brook 42, 132, 135
Cunningham, John 2
curd 95

D

Daboll, Henry 96, 179
Dam ix, 5, 7, 9, 11, 13, 60
Darrow, E.S. 137
Darrow, John 70, 71
Dart & Goble 65

Dart Industries 159
David Hunt Canning Company 139
Dayton, Amon 62
Decker, James E. 130
Delane, D. 57, 179
Del Nero Homes 144
Detroit Steel Products Co. 138
Dettbarn, Isaac Lynn 57
Devendorf, Alan 155
Dietrich, Casper 72
distiller's grains 60
distillery 3, 11, 17, 27, 42, 51, 57, 59, 60, 117, 172
Dixie Cloth 86
Dixie Knit Products Corporation 86
Dixon, Isaac 118
Dixon & Kenyon 118, 178
D. L. & W. Railroad 134
Dowdall, Michael 65
Downer & Voorhees 85, 175
dressmaker 126
Dunbar, S.M. 139
Dun & Bradstreet 37
Dun & Co. v, 37, 85, 92, 96, 118
Dundore, J.G. 131
Dunham & Baker 42
Dunham & Bellinger 42, 169
Dunham, N.C. 42
Dunham & Son 103
Durkee Manufacturing Company 155
Dutton, G.C. 132

E

Eagle Comtronics 155
Eason, H.J. 73
Edison Electric Company 121
Edison Illuminating Company 85, 121
E. Genesee St. 7, 12, 13, 32, 34, 37, 49, 50, 62, 78, 86, 90, 93, 96, 99, 103, 104, 108, 111, 113, 114, 126, 132, 133, 136, 155, 158, 159, 170, 171
Ellison, George 137
Ellison Road 17, 44
Ells, Horace 64, 175, 177
E.L. Montague & Son 93
Elsworth 42, 76
Elsworth, Levi 76
emery 133
Empire Blacksmith Shop 37
Empire Portland Cement Co. 73
engines 133, 168, 170

Erie Canal 3, 7, 21, 24, 25, 26, 28, 29, 40, 48, 56, 57, 73, 182
excise tax 59

F

Fairbanks and Taggart 42
Fairbanks & Co. 129, 137, 169
Fancher, Alanson 103, 176
Fancher Machine Co. 133, 170
Fancher, R.I. 133
Fancher & Son 20, 103, 169
Farmers' Mill 49, 50
Ferguson, Enoch 43
fertilizer 11, 31, 72, 73
Fink, Jeremiah 37, 175
Fisher, Elmer E. 96, 98
flax 47, 65, 83, 126
Fluid Power Sales, Inc. 149
flume 41, 45, 49, 137
Ford, William 52
forge 35, 37, 76, 80, 102, 107
fork 134
Forssell, Alfred G. 109
Fosham Realty Corporation 144
L.B. Foster Co. 143
foundry 17, 21, 26, 75, 76, 77, 78, 104, 109, 127
Fox, Lewis A. 118
Fox, S. 118, 178
Frazee & Decker 41
Frazee Milling Co. 13, 53, 54, 170
Frazee Plaster Mill 72
Frazee, W.L. 42, 169
Fugette & Burgess 34, 104
Fugette, Joseph M. 34
Fugett, J.W. 103
Fuller & Bliss 136, 137, 169, 176, 179
Fuller, William L. 136
fulling 83, 84, 85
furniture 17, 19, 21, 39, 44, 66, 131, 132, 134, 135, 158, 159

G

gaiters 63
Garrett, Ovid 96, 98
Garrett & Snell 96, 97, 98, 170
Gates Road 15, 42
Gayetty, John 77
Gayetty & Randall 21, 136, 138
Gaylord, James 129
General Sullivan 1
Genesee Trail 2
Gifford, Lawerence 93

Gilley, Mrs. Louisa M. 126
Goble, Milton 136
Goetz Dolls 149, 171
Gould Pump Company 110
government project 141
gristmill 3, 5, 17, 26, 44, 45, 46, 49, 50, 51, 52, 59, 60, 67, 85, 98, 161, 172, 173

H

Haendle, Martin 57
Haines, Theodore 118
Hains Celestial Group 156
Hall, Charles A. 68
Hall, Edith 60, 68, 77, 85, 90, 103, 139
Halsted, Herman 51, 176
Hamilton Co. 143
Hammond, George 73
Hand, Parley 34
Handy, Timothy J. 85
Hardscrabble 3, 21, 23
Harland Simon Control Systems, Inc. 151, 171
Harlon Hyler Machine Shop 155
harness maker 17, 26, 64, 65
Harris 132
Harris, Baldwin & Co. 132, 178
Hax, John 68
Hay, C.J. 34
Haywood Wagon Co. 104, 170
Hazard, B. 62
Heald 78
Heald & Morris 107, 111, 173, 177
Heald & Sisco 107, 108, 136, 173, 177
Heald, Sisco & Co. 78, 108, 111, 133, 168, 169, 177
Herrick, O.B. 21, 139
Herrick's Corners 21, 136, 138, 139
Hickok, Elisha 62
Hill, Isaac 32
Hitchcock, Abner 36
Hitchcock, R. 62
Hoffman, E.H. 118
Hoffman, Richard S. 118
Hoffman, Youmans Paper Co. 118
Holcomb, J. 134
Home Interiors & Gifts, Inc. 159
Hopkins, Joseph 42
Hotaling flourmill 65
Hotaling, Gary 109
Houghtaling, Orlando 132
House, A.F. 77, 112
Howard and Cool 41

Hubbard, Chauncey 64, 174
Hubbard, Cornelius 32
Hubbard, Isaac 57
Hudson, Abijah 32
Hudson River 23, 26, 31
Hull, Mrs. Spratt 56
Humphrey, John 77, 78
Huntington, William E. 131
hydraulic 73, 149
hydroelectric 21, 121, 122, 153, 156

I

InBev 148
Indian Springs Manufacturing 154, 155, 171
Ingoldsby, Warren 43
Inland Lock Navigation Co. 6
International Milling Company 54
Interstate Island 153, 154, 155, 157, 158, 162, 163
Ionia 3, 24, 26, 42, 62, 135
Ira Barnes 43, 174, 175
iron 21, 31, 32, 33, 34, 35, 36, 37, 40, 55, 66, 75, 76, 77, 78, 79, 80, 81, 102, 103, 135, 165, 167, 168, 169, 170, 181
Irvine, John 65

J

Jacksonville 3, 17, 20, 62, 64, 91, 103, 132, 136
Jack's Reef 3, 27, 99, 169
Jacques, Joseph 133
James Frazee & Co. 50, 85, 169, 177, 179
James Stewart Co. 129
Jardine Bronze & Aluminum Foundry 155
Jardine Bronze Foundry 78, 158
Jardine, James 78, 109, 155
Jaycox, A.R. 96
J. Ballard & Co. 17
J.C. & J.C. Miller Knitting Co. 85
J. Darrow & Son 70, 169
Jerome, Aaron 62
J.M. Young's Fork Company 121
Johnson, Albert 123
Johnson, Cook & Co. 11, 50, 60, 167, 172, 175
Johnson, Howard 44
Johnson, James 41, 42, 172
J.R. Clancy, Inc. 154, 155

185

K

Karkut, Henry E. 155
Kellogg & Farr 46, 85, 172
Kennedy, George W. 51
Kenyon, Charles A. 117
Kenyon & Dixon 118
Kenyon, Jacob 65, 134
Kenyon, Jacob C. 118
Kenyon, John S. 117, 118
Kenyon Manufacturing Co. 130
Kenyon Paper Mill 118, 139
kettles 136
Kingsley, Mrs. Celia 93
Kinney, Delos 57
Kisselstein, Bonnie v, 52
Knapp & Williams 92, 179

L

Lager, Carl 109
Lamson 3, 18, 19, 21, 44, 155, 168
Lane Bradley Company 139
Larkin, Albion J. 51, 85
Lawrence Warehousing Co. 143
L.B. Foster Co. 143
Leander Ballard & Co. 62
Lefever & Palen 118, 176
Leopold, Gustav 122
Letterman, William 130
lime manufacturers 17, 72
Lindon, Mrs. Lizzie 126
Lipe, Adam 36
Little Falls 5, 129
Little Utica 3, 17, 19, 21, 37, 42, 44, 52, 65, 91, 96, 167, 168, 169, 174, 175, 176, 178
Lock St. 8, 13, 50, 124, 130, 136, 170, 172, 173
Loveless, Edward 123
lye 31, 32, 62
Lysander i, iv, v, vii, ix, 1, 2, 3, 5, 15-19, 21, 23, 25, 27, 29, 32, 33, 36, 37, 40, 42, 44, 50-52, 54-56, 59-62, 64-67, 72, 73, 76, 77, 83-85, 89-91, 95, 96, 98, 99, 103, 104, 111, 112, 121, 124, 126, 127, 129, 130, 132, 136, 141, 145, 148, 153, 161-169, 174-179, 181, 182
Lysander Cheese Manufacturing Co. 96

M

MacAllister, John 158
Mack-Miller Candle Company 131, 132
Macksville 1, 3, 7
Mahoney, F. L. 132
Mann, Dorothy E. 70
Maple Road 21, 57, 71, 77
marble 96, 136, 168, 169, 175, 178
Marcellus 75, 83, 89, 124
Mardon, Lawson 151
Marshall, James 85, 139
Marvin, Thomas 69
Marvin, W.F. 132
Mary E. Wormuth 126
Mawhinney, Fred L. 68
Mawhinney, John 68
McCall, Thomas 91
McGonegal, John 65, 169
McGuigan Bros. 92
McHarrie, John 3, 42, 45, 49
McHarrie's Rifts 2, 3, 5, 7
Meachem, Thomas W. 65
Memphis 3, 15, 24, 25, 26, 28, 29, 30, 36, 37, 43, 76, 92, 96, 103, 126, 129, 132, 134, 155, 167, 168, 169, 174, 176, 177, 178, 179
Memphis Hardwood Lumber Co. 155
Mercer's Mill 49, 53
Merrifield, Hastings 56
Merrifield, Norman 56
Metropolitan Signs 155
Meyers, John C. 109
Military Tract 1
miller 21, 45, 47, 48, 52
Miller, James C. 85
Miller, J.C. 49, 84, 85, 107, 121, 169, 172
Miller, John Charles 85
Miller, Robert 85, 169
Miller, Jr., Robert 85, 169
Miller, William 92, 176
milliner 125, 126
millinery 87, 125
millstone 33, 45, 47
Minnoe, Mrs. Bi 93
Mohawk Valley 31
molding 15, 136, 159
Molumby, Michael 57
Monarch & Eureka Co. 135
Monroe, H. 118, 176
Montague 136
E.L. Montague & Son 93
Montague, Stewart & Montague 136, 170
Montezuma 26
Morley, G.W. 138
Morris Axe Co. 129
Morris Axe Factory 36, 107
Morris, Ezekial 107, 129
Morris, H.D. and W.F. 129
Morris Machine Works 8, 13, 53, 78, 85, 104, 107, 108, 109, 110, 111, 114, 121, 126, 130, 155, 170, 171, 173
Morris, William F. 107, 108, 109, 110
Mosely, Jerome S. 131
Moyer, H.A. 68
Moyer, Harvey A. 104
Mud Lake 43, 44, 96
Mumford, Peter 117
Munro, Squire 68
Myneer, Frank 57

N

Nagley, Charles 37, 129, 178
National Aniline Defense Corporation 141
National Cellulose Corp. 118
National Grid 121
Neon Bright 156
Neupert, Michael 34, 37, 178
New Bridge 21, 68, 97
New Process Rawhide Co. 62, 139
New York Central & Hudson River Railroad 23, 26
New York Ordnance Plant 141
New York State Urban Development Corporation 144, 145
Niagara-Mohawk Power Company 121
Nichols, Tibbits 65
Northern Graphics 151
North St. 130, 172
Northup, Reynolds & Sweet 19, 21
Norton, L.H. 96
Nostrand, James 132
Nostrant, Robert v, 57
NuTop Sales 156, 157

Index

O

oar locks 136
Oneida River 6
Onondaga County iv, v, 1, 34, 36, 40, 42, 43, 49, 51, 52, 56, 57, 59, 60, 61, 62, 65, 72, 73, 76, 83, 85, 89, 91, 103, 126, 145, 146, 152, 159, 167, 168, 169, 170, 181, 182
Onondaga Gazette Business Directory 37, 65, 85
Onondaga Hill 5, 21
The Ordnance Works ix, 141, 143
Orlando Houghtaling 132, 171
Osborn & Ford 136, 169, 179
Oscar Allen 65, 174
Oswego Canal 7, 21, 40, 48
Oswego county 21
Oswego Hydro Partners 156
Oswego St. 36, 49, 50, 65, 71, 118, 121, 126, 134, 137, 139, 154, 155, 170, 172
Otsego Fork Co. 134, 177
Ovid 5, 65, 96, 98, 179
Ovid Brown 96, 179
Ox Creek 17, 96
oxen 3, 31, 33, 61, 65, 68, 69, 101

P

Paddock, James 51, 60
Paddock, Solomon 42
Palmer, A. R. 52
Palmer, Behm 36
Palmer, Jessie 131
Palmer, Jonathan 1, 2, 17, 45
Palmer, Pearl v, 55, 56, 60, 62, 72, 85, 91, 182
Palmertown 3, 17, 20
paper 5, 13, 17, 21, 32, 41, 42, 65, 66, 70, 72, 73, 91, 103, 109, 111, 117, 118, 119, 120, 131, 132, 134, 135, 144, 149, 151, 158
Papermill Island 11, 62, 134
Paper Mill Point 60, 118, 172
Pardee, John 136, 176
Parker, Sandford C. 49
Parks & Aller 44, 156, 171
Parks, Charles Larman 156
Patient Portal Technologies 151
Paynesville 3, 17, 19
pearl ash 31, 32
Peck & Brown 76, 168, 175
Peelor, Martin 136
Pelton, Richard 93

Penn Spring Works 137, 138, 170, 173
Perine, Francis 44
Perry & Boley 112
Perry, Eli 112
Perry & Kasso 37
Phillips & Bentley 62
Phoenix Toilet and Paper Manufacturing Co. 119
Phosphate Alley 72, 73
Pickard, Fred 33, 36, 37
pickets 136
Picketville 17, 44
Pierce, Miss Ada 126
pig iron 75, 78, 80
pitman 39
Piton, Albert 64
Plainville vii, 3, 15, 20, 21, 33, 36, 37, 39, 42, 44, 52, 62, 64, 91, 92, 96, 99, 103, 121, 122, 130, 136, 155, 156, 158, 167, 168, 169, 170, 171, 174, 176, 177, 179
Plainville Cheese Mfg. Co. 96, 176
Plainville Turkey Farm, Inc. 156, 171
planing 15, 136, 156, 169, 171, 172, 179
plaster 72, 73, 166, 172
plows 136
Polkville 3, 17, 20, 37, 167, 168, 169, 174, 176, 178
Portland cement 73
Post Standard 149, 159, 182
potash 3, 31, 32, 72
pottery 69, 70, 71, 166
"the project" 141, 142, 143, 144
Prouty, Stephen 36
Pulver, George M. 85
Pulver, George W. 121
pump logs 136
pump manufacturer 17, 77

Q

Quality Custom Converter Inc. 158
quarry 45, 49, 67

R

Radisson ix, 60, 142, 144, 145, 146, 147, 148, 149, 151, 152, 153, 162, 163, 171
rake manufacturer 17
rakes 136, 169, 176
Red Mill 49, 50, 52, 53, 54, 67, 172
Red Mill Inn 49, 50, 52, 53, 54, 67

Resseguie, Belding 42
Rice, D.P. 62
Richards, Samuel 62
Ridall, Charles 73
Riddle, Thompson 62
Ringe, Charles 137
River Paper Mill 119
Riverside Brick Co. 69
River Valley Paper Co. 120
R. J. Dun & Co. 37
Robinson, E. M. 65
Rogers, Alexander 77
Rogers, Robert 129
roller mills 48, 53
Rome 1, 26, 63, 97
Root, Mrs. Charles 126
Russell, Henry 34

S

S.A. Groves & Co. 85
Sand Springs 3, 24, 26
sash 39, 104, 136, 137
sawmill 3, 6, 12, 15, 17, 19, 21, 26, 31, 39, 40, 41, 42, 43, 44, 45, 51, 52, 55, 60, 67, 101, 123, 132, 156, 158, 161, 172, 173
sawyer 39
Schermerhorn, Bidwell 76
Schlitz Brewing Co. 145
Schoonmaker, A.S. 118, 168, 174
Schoonmaker & Co 118, 119, 168, 169, 174, 177
Scisco, Louis Dow 21, 42
Scoville 42, 92, 93, 126, 132, 168, 170, 175, 179
Scoville, J.M. 92, 93, 175
Scoville, John 92
Scoville, Mrs. J. M. 126
screens 139, 155
Scusa Machine Shop 158
scythes 137, 166, 167
Seager, Miss Emma 126
Seaver, Luthur 32
Segar., C.H. 65
Seifert, T.S. 132
Seiler Brothers Creamery 99
Seneca Metal Products 158, 171
Seneca River 2, 3, 5, 6, 7, 9, 11, 12, 13, 21, 27, 34, 40, 41, 42, 45, 48, 49, 50, 69, 84, 85, 101, 108, 117, 121, 122, 124, 133, 135, 136, 137, 139, 153, 155, 170
Seneca River Brick Co. 69
Seneca River Iron Works 135, 170

Seneca River Power Company 85, 121
Seneca Turnpike 2
Seneca Woolen Factory 85
shafts 133
Shants, Harry 52
Sharp & Co. 132, 137, 167, 175
Sheldon, L.R. 92
shoemakers ix, 3, 17, 21, 61, 63, 64, 65, 66, 168, 170
Shoens, T.H. 92
Shumway, J.P. 117
sieves 46, 139
Simmons, A. 131
Sisco & Co. 78
Sixty Road 145, 146, 147, 148, 151, 153, 171
Skeels, Nathan 42
Slab City 3, 24, 26
sleighs 33, 39, 102, 103, 170
Smith Drug Co. 139, 170
Smith, Judson 131
Smith & Sutfin 62
Smyth, James 43
Snell, John 96, 98
Snyder, Jerome 132
Sodus Bay 26
So-jer Manufacturing Co 130
Specialized Packaging 151
Spector, Sol 144
speculators 2, 31
Spratt, Mrs. Maryiette 76, 127
springs 42, 102, 122, 130, 137, 138
SSAC 152
Stachurski Brothers 44, 158
Stachurski Brothers Sawmill 158
Stark & Kaulback 62, 168, 177
Start & Mott 40
staves 55, 56
steam power 17, 76
Stewart & Montague 136
Stilwell, H. 62
stone 42, 50, 52, 67, 177
stoneware 70, 71
stoves 138, 169, 174
straw 65, 117, 118, 119
Suddaby, Gary 156
Sullivan & Bogardus 52
Sullivan, General 1
Sullivan Manufacturing Co 158
Sweet, A. Wayne 135
Sweet's Maps 21
Symansky, Frank 133
Syracuse and Oswego Railroad 21, 136

Syracuse Bamboo Furniture Co. 134
Syracuse Heat Treating 157, 158, 171
Syracuse Lighting Company 121, 122
Syracuse Ornamental Co. 158
Syracuse, Rochester & Eastern trolley 26
Syracuse St. 13, 37, 47, 50, 53, 67, 103, 126, 130, 136, 159, 168, 170, 172
Syracuse University 143, 182
SYROCO 158, 159

T

Tanneries ix, 61, 62, 63, 65, 165, 166
tannery 3, 15, 17, 18, 61, 62
Tannery Creek 5, 6, 8, 12, 40, 62, 96, 98, 172, 173
tannin 61, 62
Tappan & Allen 92
Tappan Mills 86
Tappan, W.H. 133
Tappen, Gabriel 42
Technical Fabricators 145, 152
Tessy Plastics 158, 159
"the project" 141
Thomas Millen & Sons 73
Three Rivers Game Management Area 143
Tillotson, C.H. 73
Tillotson, David 62
Tillotson, Harlo 62
Tincker, Stephen 85
tobacco 11, 15, 30, 55, 60, 89, 90, 91, 92, 93, 115, 118, 129, 177
Tobin, Michael 91
Tooley, Addison 132
Town of Camillus 1, 64, 83
trip hammer 36
Tucker & Crippen 92, 168
Tucker, E.W. 91
Turner, Elias 44
Turner, Nettie J. 126

U

Upson, J.W. 91

V

Valley Boat Works 130, 170
VanAllen, M. 77
Van Buren i, iv, v, ix, 1-3, 5, 7, 15, 17, 19, 21-27, 29, 32, 36, 37, 40, 42-44, 50, 51, 53, 54, 59-62, 64, 66, 68-73, 76, 77, 83-85, 89, 90, 93, 95, 99, 103, 118, 121, 122, 126, 127, 135-139, 145, 148, 153, 154, 156, 157, 159, 161-167, 171, 172, 180-182
Van Buren Center 3, 21, 23, 167
Van Doran, J.I. 132
Van Velzar, L. 64
VanWagner, Rome 97
Vassallo Industries 159
Vedder, Albert A. 72
Velvetknit 86
Velvet Tissue Co. 120
Veneer 139
Virginia, John 131
Voorhees, James L. 21, 39, 136
Voorhees & Son 139

W

wagon maker 17, 21, 101, 103
wagon repair 21
wagons 33, 39, 93, 101, 102, 103, 104, 105, 135, 138, 166, 170, 176
Wall, John 42
Ward, Nathan 62
Ward, William C. 91
Warner, Jonathan 43
Warner, Mrs. L. 127
Warner, L.E. 131, 175
Warners 3, 21, 23, 26, 27, 29, 32, 34, 36, 37, 42, 57, 62, 68, 69, 72, 73, 99, 103, 122, 135, 169, 175, 176, 178
Warner, Simon 43
Warners Portland Cement Company 73
Washington, General George 1
waterpower 3, 6, 17, 21, 26, 27, 36, 39, 40, 41, 42, 53, 75, 83, 84, 85, 119, 121, 127, 133, 137, 156, 163
Water St. 7, 134, 139, 168, 170, 172
Wave Hydro LLC 122, 159
Weller, Wm 92
Wells, George S. 131
West Brothers 85, 86
West Cicero 21

West Phoenix 3, 17, 19, 21, 119, 120, 122, 123, 131, 132, 135, 155, 156, 158
West Shore 26
Wetherby 117
Wetherby, Cook & Co 60, 117, 172
Wetherby, Herber 60
wheel-stone 33
wheelwright 101, 102
whey 95
whiskey 46, 47, 56, 59, 60
Whiskey Hollow 3, 60
White 112
White and Lankin 77
White, Clark & Co. 112, 169, 177
White & Fox 133, 168
White Mill 49
White Signs 110, 159
White, Ted 110, 159
White, Warren 77, 175
Whorral, Elmer 153
Williamson Brothers 62
Wilson, Mrs. Lucy 127
Wilson's Corners 3, 15
Wilson & Warren 139, 175
Wilson Jr., G.W. 139
Wilson, William 91, 177, 179
Wiltech Products, Inc. 159, 171
wing dam 5, 6, 40
Wooden Jacket Can Co. 149
Wood, George 43
Woodford, Mrs. Charles 126
Woods Paper Co. 120
woodworking 21
Woolen Mill Company 85
Wooster, Mrs. E.H. 126
Worden, Ambrose S. 62
Wormuth, Mary E. 126
Wright, W.A. 132

Y

Yeomans Chicago Corporation 110, 113
Youmans Paper Co. 118
Young & Frazee 132, 134, 172, 178, 179
Young & Frazee Tool Co. 132, 172, 178
Young, J.M. 121, 136, 169
Young, John M. 134

CPSIA information can be obtained at www.ICGtesting.com
Printed in the USA
BVOW060138150911

271297BV00002B/281-376/P